THE ORIGIN AND

DEVELOPMENT OF

SCHOLARLY HISTORICAL

PERIODICALS

MARGARET F. STIEG ❦ THE
ORIGIN AND DEVELOPMENT
OF SCHOLARLY HISTORICAL
PERIODICALS ❦ THE
UNIVERSITY OF ALABAMA
PRESS

Library of Congress Cataloging in Publication Data

Stieg, Margaret F.

The origin and development of scholarly historical
periodicals.

Bibliography: p.
Includes index.
1. History—Periodicals—History. 2. Oral history—
Periodicals—History. I. Title.
D13.S835   1986   907'.2   85-1048
ISBN 0-8173-0273-5

Publication of this book was made possible, in part, by financial assistance from the
Andrew W. Mellon Foundation and the American Council of Learned Societies.

FOR PRESTY

who was always there

❦ CONTENTS

ACKNOWLEDGMENTS

Like most published research, this book has had a long gestation period. Over the years, many debts have been incurred that it is now a pleasure to acknowledge. The idea itself I owe to Professor Abraham Bookstein, of the Graduate Library School, University of Chicago. I have known him and his wife, Marguerite, since our graduate student days at Berkeley. One evening the three of us were discussing research possibilities in librarianship and how to combine advanced work in a subject discipline with a career in library education. Abe suggested that I might look into scholarly communication among historians. I did, found it interesting, and this book is the result.

The broad scope of the research took me to archives throughout Western Europe and the United States. I benefited from the careful collecting, organizing, and describing of generations of archivists; without their efforts it would have been impossible to complete this study. Several cheerfully went to considerable trouble to facilitate my access to their collections. In Tübingen, the director of the J. C. B. Mohr (Paul Siebeck) firm, Georg Siebeck, kindly opened to me its records, a truly impressive collection, and provided me with working space and support.

The cooperation of a number of people who are associated with the different scholarly historical periodicals that are presently being published made it possible to make this account reasonably current. I am very grateful to those who were willing to take the time to speak with me. Their friendliness and cordiality were welcome during the solitary round of research. Martha Vicinus graciously extended to me the hospitality of her home while I was in Bloomington.

I would also like to thank those who wrote to me or made available records in their possession. Professor Eric Hobsbawm, of the University of London, wrote a particularly informative letter about the early days of *Past and Present*. Professor Edwin Davis, of Louisiana State University, made available his collection of materials on the *Journal of Southern History*. The papers of R. W. Seton-Watson were indispensable to the chapter on interdisciplinary periodicals. They are in the possession of his sons, Professor G. H. N. Seton-Watson and Dr.

Christopher Seton-Watson, who made me welcome in their homes and shared these papers and their own recollections with me.

Several research assistants made important contributions. Dawn Fuller and David Lowe, at the University of Alabama, were involved in the early stages. At Columbia, Allen Asaf helped with translating and summarizing the voluminous material on the *Historische Zeitschrift*. Pamela Skinner rendered even more aid with the complex Russian sources.

As always, my father has been helpful throughout. His numerous editorial suggestions greatly improved the presentation, and his willingness to help type the last draft made the final preparation much easier.

I am grateful to the two organizations that awarded me grants to help with the costs associated with the research: the Council on Library Resources and the Spencer Foundation. Their generosity considerably facilitated my work.

Finally, I would like to express my gratitude to several people at the University of Alabama and the University of Alabama Press. My dean, James D. Ramer, provided invaluable encouragement and practical help. It has been a pleasure to work with the director of the press, Malcolm MacDonald, and members of his staff. The anxious process of review and acceptance was smoothed by their courtesy and efficiency. The anonymous readers were unbelievably prompt. As one friend, who is familiar with the vicissitudes of scholarly publishing, remarked after hearing my account, "You have been treated like royalty."

ABBREVIATIONS

AHA American Historical Association

AHR American Historical Review

CHR Catholic Historical Review

DZG Deutsche Zeitschrift für Geschichtswissenschaft

EHR English Historical Review

EPHE École Pratique des Hautes Études

HV Historische Vierteljahresschrift

HZ Historische Zeitschrift

IBZ Internationale Bibliographie der Zeitschriften Literatur

IM Istorik-Marksist

JAH Journal of American History

JHI Journal of the History of Ideas

JNH Journal of Negro History

JSH Journal of Southern History

JTH Journal of Transport History

LSU Louisiana State University

MGH Monumenta Germaniae Historica

MVHA Mississippi Valley Historical Association

MVHR Mississippi Valley Historical Review

RH Revue historique

RQH Revue des questions historiques

SEER Slavonic and East European Review

SSCI Social Sciences Citation Index

VI Voprosy istorii

VI KPSS Voprosy istorii KPSS

VS Victorian Studies

VSWG Vierteljahresschrift für Sozial- und Wirtschaftsgeschichte

ZSWG Zeitschrift für Sozial- und Wirtschaftsgeschichte

THE ORIGIN AND

DEVELOPMENT OF

SCHOLARLY HISTORICAL

PERIODICALS

ONE ❦ INTRODUCTION

As a discipline or profession matures, it takes more interest in its own history, in the record of its evolution and growth. Because of its essential nature, history has from its beginnings been concerned with its own history. Recent technological advances in communications, among other reasons, have focused attention in history and in many other disciplines on the structure and institutionalization of their communication systems. This study attempts to elucidate the role in history's communication system of the scholarly historical periodical, its structure, its institutionalization, and its interaction with the profession.

An effective network of communication adapted to its peculiar needs is crucial in every professional field. Students of professionalization usually identify a theoretical knowledge base as the fundamental characteristic of every profession. Other professional attributes are in varying degrees related to it and consequently to the communication system. Responsibility for expansion of that knowledge base requires publication of the results of research, which by its very nature generates further research. Autonomy of the profession within its field and recognition by society of its right to that autonomy find expression in peer evaluation of the knowledge base and of its application to the problems of society. Many of the topics investigated in history, the ways in which the results of research are presented, and the need for a continuing mechanism for peer evaluation make the scholarly historical periodical indispensable in its communication system.

The first publications to use the periodical format were neither scholarly nor historical. Newsletters, printed in centers of political activity like London and Paris, were published for the information of residents of the provinces. In 1667 the earliest scholarly periodical, the *Journal des Sçavans,* began publication, closely followed by the *Proceedings* of the Royal Society. Both were founded to disseminate the results of scientific experiments, by members of the French Académie in the *Journal* and of the Royal Society in the *Proceedings.* Historical journals began to appear in the eighteenth century, not as publications of scholars but of groups with a part-time interest in history, usually local. The first scholarly historical periodicals were established in nineteenth-century Germany in conjunction with the development of the professional approach to the study of history, then usually termed "scientific history."

In 1859 the *Historische Zeitschrift* (*HZ*) appeared, the first scholarly historical periodical to survive to the present. In form and character, it was an idea whose time had come, and contemporary scholars hailed it as the fulfillment of long-cherished hopes. It quickly acquired and has maintained an outstanding position and influence in the professional historical world.

The *HZ* profited from the experience of earlier attempts at scholarly historical periodicals. At least two important journals preceded it, one founded in the 1830s by Leopold von Ranke, dean of German historical scholarship, another in the 1840s by Adolf Schmidt, one of his early students. Various factors contributed to the demise of these journals, but not before Ranke and Schmidt had demonstrated the contribution that a scholarly journal could make to the community of professional historians.

That community in Germany by 1859 was large enough and sufficiently cohesive to support a scholarly historical periodical. Although statistical verification is impossible, enough professional historians existed to submit to such a journal an adequate number of articles for publication and to read what it published. They shared enough common aims and convictions to ensure that it would be a common enterprise. Professional historians possessed a rudimentary organization and had an institutional base in the academic world. Many of them shared the conviction of the *HZ*'s founding editor, Heinrich von Sybel, that no journal existed where scholarly articles could appropriately be published. In part, the *HZ* was a response to that conviction.

Another contributing factor when the *HZ* was founded was the assumption, shared by most German historians, that history is not a remote subject, unrelated to daily life, but a discipline that has highly relevant things to say to Germans. In terms of the sociological paradigm of a profession, they believed that their knowledge base could and should be applied to the problems of society, in their case primarily in the social and political realm. They considered it appropriate, even necessary, to use their knowledge to contribute to the solution of the burning question of German national unity. The *HZ*'s explicit commitment to this cause gave its early existence an urgency it would otherwise have lacked.

The original conception of the *HZ* encompassed a dedication to two purposes: academic, or the expansion and evaluation of history's knowledge base; and political, or its application to the problems of society. German historians of the nineteenth century found nothing inconsistent in combining the two in one journal, for they were inextricably interwoven in their thinking. The relationship of these two elements is a continuing theme in the later development of the *HZ* as it was in German historical thinking. The evolution of the *HZ* is part of the evolution of German historiography.

A different perception of the nature and purpose of history distinguished the *HZ* from other journals in which articles by historians appeared. Professional historians might have political convictions and interests, but they also subscribed to a set of standards and to a methodology that did not permit them consciously to adapt their findings to suit their political views. They might select subjects to investigate for immediate political purposes, but, once selected, each topic had to be treated in its own terms by the professionally accepted methodology. Articles might not differ much in style from those published in political journals, but they differed significantly in their dedication to scholarly standards.

The *HZ* also differed from other journals in its complete commitment to history. Other journals, such as the comprehensive publications of a university or an academy, might publish scholarly articles by professional historians, but they did not give history pride of place. A scholarly journal devoted exclusively to history is a statement that the discipline has reached a new level of maturity. It is also a statement of self-consciousness.

Related to the scholarly historical periodical's complete commitment to history was a new approach to the coverage of historical literature that would provide systematic and continuing information on professional historical literature within its scope. Such a journal included, in effect, a mechanism for peer evaluation of the professional historian's work and in that area was governed by the same professional criteria of standards and methodology that were applied to the articles. The development of the most efficient and satisfactory format and method for this coverage was a slow process requiring experimentation and adaptation, but it was an integral part of the *HZ*'s concept from its beginning.

The *HZ* helped to shape the discipline of history as a whole in a way that no other periodical has since been able to do. Several fortunate circumstances contributed, at least in part, to its success. It was the first scholarly historical periodical to survive; it was German in a day when German historical scholarship set the pace in the world; and it benefited from the organizational structure of German universities. It established a model structural pattern for the scholarly historical periodical and demonstrated the value of its institutionalization; it contributed to important scholarly discussions; it exercised great power in making and breaking careers.

The *HZ* may have been a product of the particular circumstances of German historical scholarship in the mid-nineteenth century, but the form it created for the scholarly historical periodical has proved to be extraordinarily adaptable. It was soon followed by French, English, Italian, and American equivalents. The environments in which these later journals emerged and the historical establishments of their respective countries were quite different from the German, but the journals have far more similarities than differences. The establishment of each of these journals was a major milestone in the evolution of its country's historical scholarship, but it was a different milestone in each country.

In France, the *Revue historique* (*RH*) was founded by Gabriel Monod, a young scholar who had been trained in Germany and was an outsider among French historians. The *RH* was one of the methods he used in his effort to reform French historical scholarship. He hoped it would create a community of scholars who followed German standards of historical scholarship. Until such a community existed, the *RH* would lack a strong institutional base. Like the *HZ*, the *RH* had political aims. Monod believed that German historians and specifically the *HZ* had contributed greatly to German unification. He hoped that the *RH* would also contribute to a political objective: the revitalization of the French national spirit in the aftermath of 1870.

The *English Historical Review* (*EHR*) was founded not by a single, strong personality but by a small group of scholars, who like Monod admired German historical scholarship and were not part of the dominant tradition of historical scholarship in their own country. When it was founded, the *EHR* lacked any close academic affiliation, but, when an academically centered historical profession later evolved in England, the *EHR* was the obvious publishing institution for its scholarship. The *EHR* differed from both the *HZ* and the *RH* in its explicit disavowal of political aims.

The last of the major scholarly historical periodicals to be founded, the *American Historical Review* (*AHR*), was also a cooperative enterprise. A group of historians, all professors at leading American universities, united to establish a scholarly historical periodical. Because professional history in the United States was at the time firmly institutionalized academically, the *AHR* could be, like the *HZ* rather than the *RH* or the *EHR*, a unifying agent instead of a mechanism to redirect historians' approach to their subject. Like the *EHR*, the *AHR* at the outset defined its apolitical status.

All the new journals shared a common purpose that overshadowed any differences among them. Their purpose was the advancement of professional historical scholarship defined primarily in methodological terms and inextricably associated with an academic setting. Two quite different patterns for the process of establishing a major scholarly historical periodical are apparent. A single, dedicated scholar, competent, aggressive, and lucky, could, like Sybel or Monod, succeed in founding a major scholarly historical periodical that survived. The other pattern, exemplified in the English and American experience, depends upon the cooperation of a group of scholars who share similar aims and convictions with respect to professional history. The first pattern can be related, at least to some degree, to the then strongly hierarchical structure of the academic world in Germany and to the somewhat less strongly hierarchical structure in France. In contrast, England and the United States, which used the cooperative pattern, had a strong democratic tradition. In either case, the essential institutional infrastructure, a community of academic professional historians, existed or was soon developed. And in every case the structure of the scholarly historical periodical pioneered by the *HZ* determined the format of the new periodicals and the professional character of the material they published.

Each periodical influenced significantly the direction of the evolution of historical scholarship in its country. Influence was direct through what the journals published and indirect through example, the standards they set for later periodicals. Ability to accommodate change was common to all. The *HZ* and *RH* were depoliticized, the *EHR* came to concentrate on English history, and an association acquired the publication rights and therefore the management of the *AHR*. All these changes and others responded to trends within the professional historical establishments of the respective countries.

The first scholarly historical periodical in each country was invariably general, but specialization characterized its successors. They defined it in various ways, usually geographical, topical, or chronological. The specialization of periodicals is intimately associated with the specialization of historical studies that has occurred in most countries, although it has not followed the same pattern in each. Specialization in professional history is inherent in the discipline, a characteristic it shares with other professional disciplines, which tend to concentrate intensive study on increasingly smaller segments of the subject. The specialized journal supports the growth of specialized subfields by providing a medium for publication and by helping to establish their identity through the definition of boundaries.

Reaction to specialization quickly followed its increased emphasis and spread and contributed to the continuing search for synthesis. The reaction usually took the form either of an interest in a redefined concept of universal history or of an interdisciplinary approach to historical problems. The trend toward interdisciplinarity in history and the periodicals that exemplified this point of view appeared first in France. Such journals, though not as numerous as specialized periodicals, are now common. The underlying rationale discourages multiplication of periodicals just as that of specialization encourages their increase.

The broad outlines of these intellectual currents are apparent, but precise dating is impossible. In some ways, the journals devoted to specialization and interdisciplinarity are the best guides to those trends. Because they are an integral part of their existence, successes and failures are measures of strengths and weaknesses of the trends. The symbiotic nature of the relationship between scholarly historical periodicals and the historical establishment provides in the journals themselves primary sources for the study of each.

This study concentrates on the scholarly historical periodical and its interaction with professional history, but it cannot ignore completely two other types of historical periodical, the local history journal and the popular historical periodical. All three have evolved for the most part independently of each other, but occasionally professional history has to a limited extent influenced or has been affected by the two other categories of journals.

Local history periodicals are usually published by groups of amateurs interested in the history of the group, its locality, ethnic origin, or religion. Different factors have contributed to the foundation and growth of these journals, but most of them were influenced by romanticism of the past, the rise of local patriotism, and the interest of the middle class in organizations for self-help and improvement. Most of their articles express the romantic view of history and are nonprofessional descriptions of the unique, the picturesque, and the charming. The journals thus find their institutional home in antiquarianism instead of in professional history.

During the early years of the nineteenth century, before the distinction between amateur and professional historian was clear-cut and complete, professional historians as they were then defined did interest themselves in local history periodicals. At the other end of the evolutionary process, a marked revival of interest has occurred during the last two decades among professional historians as they are now defined. They have increasingly published in local history journals and a few have even founded new periodicals of this type. This revival can be related in part to the increased pressure to publish and the necessity to consider acceptable substitutes for the traditional scholarly periodical. In part, it may also be related to the ever-expanding specialization of historical study, reflecting, for example, the trend in the "new" social history toward more and more study of particular communities. Greater interest among professional historians has not altered the fact that local history journals are still a separate and distinct group. Almost all still have different goals, different standards, and a very different view of history from that of the scholarly historical periodical.

Popular historical periodicals are still further removed from the scholarly. Their only goals are to disseminate as widely as possible what is already known and to attract and hold the interest of that vaguely defined individual, the "general reader," or educated layman. Without large numbers of adequately educated individuals interested in their subject, sufficiently affluent to afford them, and with leisure to read them, the popular periodicals could not exist or survive. They belong to the journalistic world of commercial publishing, from which their own professionalism, quite different from that of scholarly historical periodicals, derives.

Popular periodicals are a comparatively recent phenomenon. They are few in number and are to be found in the highly developed Western nations: France, Germany, England, the United States, Italy, and Spain. Professional historians, who are still interested in reaching the general reader, have in several cases been instrumental in founding them. Many historians contribute to them, but the style of their contributions, whose content is based on professional scholarship, resembles that of the journalist and would not be appropriate for the scholarly historical periodical.

Because of their diversification and heterogeneity, a detailed classification of scholarly historical periodicals into precisely defined subgroups was impractical for this study. The terminology of the broad classes into which the scholarly historical periodicals were grouped is to a degree self-explanatory. All the groups except the interdisciplinary periodicals share a primary or exclusive commitment to history in one or more of its many ramifications. The scope of the interdisciplinary journals that were studied includes a prominent role for the discipline of history.

The identification of the universe of scholarly historical periodicals is difficult as well as onerous and reliable statistical data about them are not readily obtainable. No dependable bibliographies of them are available and the few that do exist provide only retrospective information. The frequent failure of the bibliographies to define their scope further limits their usefulness. The best and most comprehensive current inventory is included in *Ulrich's International Periodicals Directory*,[1] but its listings for history are selective and cover scholarly, local history and popular titles.

In an attempt to obtain more data, especially quantitative data, a questionnaire was sent to 391 periodicals listed in *Ulrich's* under "History" or under other disciplines if the title indicated its scope as historical. Excluded were archival publications, newsletters, and journals of less than a thousand circulation unless they were known to be of special importance. The sample's bias is that of *Ulrich's*. The emphasis is on the United States and Western Europe; representation of Latin American titles is sparse. Of the 391 periodicals, 163 were classified as scholarly, but it is impossible to estimate the proportion they represent of the total universe of scholarly historical periodicals. Of the 163, 61 percent, or 99, responded, but in a number of cases responses were incomplete. The return from Communist countries was slight. The results are summarized in table 1.

The majority of scholarly historical periodicals are published by an association. Some associations exist solely to publish a journal, and the only purpose of some journals seems to be justification of their associations. Other publishers include commercial firms, universities, and the journal itself. No organization in the historical world of the West is comparable to the American Institute of Physics, which publishes sixty-seven journals in physics; this confirms in yet another way the loosely organized character of Western historical scholarship.

Circulation figures for the scholarly historical periodicals range from three hundred to approximately twenty thousand, but 90 percent number four thousand or less.[2] Journals with high circulation figures tend to be those with greater prestige and influence. Approximately half of the journals indicate that libraries and institutions are 40 percent or less of their subscriptions. One foreign periodical, a startling exception, reports that its entire circulation is to libraries and institutions. Journals with lower circulation figures tend to have a higher percentage of individual subscribers. North American and foreign periodicals differ markedly in their dependence upon a foreign market. Of the North American journals, almost all (93 percent) have 40 percent or fewer foreign subscribers. The comparable figure for foreign periodicals is 61 percent.

Inflation and other current economic problems exacerbate the ever-present financial problems of scholarly publishing. Half of the periodicals, for example, report an increase since 1970 in the proportion of their budgets devoted to printing. They have usually responded to financial difficulties by raising subscription rates; a majority report a rise of 100 percent or more since 1970. The foreign journals have most frequently resorted to the extreme in this strategy.

Other financial considerations include dependence upon subsidies and unpaid contributions. Foreign journals are an exception to the tradition of nonpayment for contributions like articles and book reviews. Subsidies come from many sources, but the pattern in North America differs considerably from that abroad. The private benefactor, although no longer common, does on occasion still survive. Subsidy by a university is much more frequent in North America; governmental support, abroad.

Editorial practices reveal both policy and problems. The title "managing editor" that is often used indicates the twofold function of that individual. Editorial boards are common, but foreign periodicals are

Table 1.
*Scholarly Historical Periodicals: Statistical Data**
(99 Respondents)

	North American**	Foreign	Total
Publisher			
Association	19	41	60
Other	12	27	39
CIRCULATION			
Number of subscriptions			
To 1,000	7	23	30
1,001–2,000	11	23	34
2,001–4,000	8	11	19
4,001–6,000	—	1	1
6,001–9,000	3	1	4
9,001–13,000	1	—	1
Over 13,000	1	2	3
Decrease in circulation since 1970	9	9	18
Library and institutional subscriptions (percent)			
1–10%	1	13	14
11–20%	4	7	11
21–40%	7	13	20
41–60%	12	7	19
61–80%	5	7	12
81–90%	2	4	6
Over 90%	1	1	2
Foreign subscriptions (percent)			
0–10%	15	14	29
11–20%	7	8	15
21–40%	7	12	19
41–60%	2	12	14
61–80%	—	7	7
81–90%	—	2	2
Over 90%	—	—	—

Table 1. (*Continued*)

	North American	Foreign	Total
FINANCIAL DATA			
Number subsidized by			
University	16	7	23
Individual	5	2	7
Foundation	5	6	11
Government	1	15	16
Other	2	9	11
Total subsidized	29	39	68
Number carrying advertising	29	29	58
Subscription rate—1970***			
Under $10	22		
$11–15	6		
$16–20	2		
$21–25	—		
$26 and over	—		
Subscription rate—1980			
Under $10	7		
$11–15	6		
$16–20	6		
$21–25	3		
$26 and over	3		
Price increase to institutions (percent)			
None	3	5	8
1–30%	3	4	7
31–50%	3	6	9
51–75%	2	1	3
76–99%	1	1	2
100% or more	4	38	42
Percent of budget for printing			
to 50%	8	7	15
51–75%	11	14	25
76–99%	7	15	22
100%	1	6	7

(*continued*)

Table 1.   (*Continued*)

	North American	Foreign	Total
Increase since 1970 in percent of budget for printing (number)	16	28	44
Payment to authors			
For articles	1	15	16
For book reviews	2	11	13
For other contributions	—	10	10
EDITORIAL POLICY AND MANAGEMENT			
Principal evaluation by			
Editor	19	47	66
Member of editorial board	7	11	18
Outside referee	12	8	20
Percent of articles rejected			
to 25%	4	16	20
26–50%	4	22	26
51–75%	13	10	23
76–90%	5	2	7
91% and over	4	3	7
No limit set for length of articles	9	15	24
Time between acceptance and publication			
To 3 months	1	1	2
4–6 months	6	6	12
7–12 months	6	34	40
13–18 months	15	11	26
19 months and over	3	10	13
Editorial board			
Number with board	27	49	76
Number without board	3	19	22
Board advises on policy only	10	12	22

Table 1.   (*Continued*)

	North American	Foreign	Total
Board participates in decisions	23	27	50

*Totals in each category are not necessarily consistent because some returns were incomplete.
**United States and Canadian.
***All subscription rates are the institutional rates when they vary from those to individual subscribers.

much more likely than those in North America to operate without them. They usually participate in both policymaking and management decisions. Editors are invariably central in the evaluation of content; for two-thirds of the periodicals, they are responsible for the principal decision on acceptance of articles. The editorial board or an outside referee makes this decision for less than half the journals, but foreign periodicals use the outside referee much less often than the North American. For a few journals, all three share responsibility for the decision in the evaluation process.

More than half of the periodicals accept half or more of the articles submitted to them, and 17 percent reject three-fourths or more. The journals with the highest rejection rates have larger circulations and greater prestige. The lapse of time between the acceptance of an article and its publication is a matter of serious concern to many authors, who believe it is far too long.[3] The editors report comparatively short delays, though their perspective on this matter is probably different from that of a junior faculty member. More than half of the periodicals publish articles within a year or less, and 86 percent report publication within eighteen months or less. Only four journals, all of them foreign, indicate a delay of two to three years.

The differences among scholarly historical periodicals thus extend beyond subject emphasis, orientation, and purpose to the ways in which they are produced and managed. They operate in comparative isolation from one another, and any relationships are informal and accidental, often resulting from personal connections between editors. The periodicals vary in prestige and influence, but no one of them has achieved the eminence and dominating position nationally or internationally of the *HZ* during its early years.

The number of new scholarly historical periodicals grew at a continuously accelerating rate from the end of World War II to the mid-1970s. The survival of many to the present demonstrates their success and suggests that they perform a useful function. That success has brought a new set of economic and professional problems. The most serious is both economic and professional: the inability of existing information systems and the bibliographical apparatus for the identification and retrieval of their content to accommodate the growing volume. The trend is not unique to history and has occurred in many other disciplines. By the 1970s the conviction was growing that the publication of scholarly periodicals was facing a crisis.

This conviction stimulated research and study of scholarly publishing through conferences on various aspects of it, national inquiries into scholarly communication, general studies of periodicals, and investigations of the communication network in specific disciplines. Most attention has been concentrated on the sciences, where the problem is especially acute. The growth rate of scientific periodicals has been exponential, for scientists are particularly dependent upon current information of the kind that periodicals can provide. Financial support from a variety of sources, including the government, is available for research on the information systems of scientific disciplines. History has not been so fortunate, but it too depends upon the periodical to perform certain functions in its communication system, although their character and methods are somewhat different from those of the sciences. One objective of this study is to expand discussion and study in the area of the achievements and problems of periodicals in historical communication.

Only a few scholars, most of them psychologists, have suggested such drastic action as the elimination of periodicals.[4] Substitutes have been suggested, often involving more utilization of computers. One proposal for a substitute in the social sciences, including history, suggested separately published articles in the format of the technical report so frequently used in the sciences and technology.[5] Also recommended was the retention of two distinctive features of the scholarly periodical: editorial supervision and the refereeing process. The majority of scholars in all fields recognize that the periodical in its present form performs functions that are essential to modern scholarship. If it is to be abolished, a more acceptable substitute than any yet proposed must be found.

A periodical must possess certain distinguishing characteristics to fit the American Library Association's definition: a distinctive title, appearance at regular intervals for an indefinite time, and articles by several contributors in each number or part. It then becomes an identifiable, continuing, cooperative effort.[6] Its form may impose restrictions, but it also offers distinctive possibilities, some of them unique. What the periodical is profoundly influences what it does. Conversely, what it has sought to do has influenced the evolution into its present form.

The scholarly periodical's most important contribution is the provision of a mechanism for communication among those scholars interested in its subject. It enables them to keep informed on current research and to a certain extent on research in progress. The article is the most suitable format for the scope of some research projects and in some instances the only form in which they will appear. In other instances, the article may anticipate various aspects of research on a more comprehensive scale and will later contribute to a synthesis for presentation in book form. Book reviews and other types of bibliographical information enable scholars to discover what is being published in their fields. The "Letters to the Editor" section of many periodicals offers an opportunity for response and two-way communication.

The professional contribution of the scholarly periodical is twofold: it expands the corpus of knowledge in the field, and it facilitates evaluation of that corpus by its book reviews and by the selection of the articles it publishes. The possibility of publication is in itself a stimulus to research and writing, to a contribution to the discipline's intellectual base. The selection process to determine what will be published is part of peer evaluation. It usually involves preliminary screening by the editor, referral to a referee, and, if the article is accepted, may require revision in response to criticisms. Acceptance of an article is in effect recognition of a certain level of quality.

Scholarly periodicals have acquired as a by-product of their professional contribution an important role in establishing professional status. Competition to publish them is not keen because they present so many problems, but some universities view them as one measure of their commitment to research and the expansion of knowledge. For the individual, publication in scholarly journals provides objective evidence for the peer evaluation of colleagues that is an essential element in the academic personnel process. Membership on an editorial board, particularly those of the more prestigious journals, is another form of professional recognition.

Scholarly historical periodicals possess distinctive characteristics in addition to those they share with scholarly periodicals in general. Their content, like that of most periodicals in the social sciences and humanities, almost invariably consists of articles, news notes, and book reviews. Document sections were at one time a special feature, but these have now disappeared. The publication of documents has evolved a specialized pattern of its own, concentrating on finite publications of large collections in the tradition of the *Monumenta Germaniae Historica* or incorporating them in archival serial publications. When a scholarly historical publication does not follow the format common to the discipline, it reveals a concept of its purpose and task that is different, even on occasion unique.

The format of scholarly historical periodicals differs from that of scientific periodicals, which are composed almost exclusively of articles and sections of letters to the editor. The format can be related to the nature of the discipline. Monographs and therefore book reviews are a major method of disseminating and evaluating historical research. By comparison, book publication in the sciences is relatively infrequent. In 1970 in the United States, 1,995 books on history were published; in all the pure sciences, the eight or nine disciplines classified under the number 500 in the Dewey Decimal Classification accounted for 2,358.[7] Letters to the editor are significant in the sciences because of their tradition of correcting or challenging research as soon as possible.

Scholarly periodicals are important in disciplinary history, which Brinton classifies as a subfield of intellectual history,[8] whose first step is to collect the "facts," including those about the form in which the discipline's ideas are transmitted. These facts about the periodical form of publication are significant for historians, sociologists, editors as well as publishers, and librarians. For the librarian, they are relevant to his or her interest in the organization of knowledge and scholarship; for the editor and publisher, they have practical implications; for the sociologist, they provide information on the process of professionalization; for the historian, they can contribute to an understanding of the nature and evolution of the discipline.

This study began with the collection of facts about the scholarly historical periodical. It is not a citation study anatomizing authors' sources, nor is it primarily concerned with the history of the ideas that appear in the periodicals. Its emphasis is on structure, and it is a contribution to historiography to the extent that it is a study of the institutional form of periodicals. Its organization by general, specialized, and interdisciplinary periodicals approximates their chronology and minimizes repetition, but retains the identity of each periodical. Most importantly, the organization emphasizes the purpose of the study: to identify and describe what different scholarly periodicals, regardless of their nationality or focus, have in common.

For each type of periodical and each individual periodical, certain characteristics were studied. The circumstances of their founding reveal perhaps the most information for the fundamental purpose of the study. Other topics were editors and editorial policies, management, financing, format and content, and audience. Information on content for the titles studied in depth was obtained by analysis of every tenth year. Not all information was available for each periodical, nor is each fact about a periodical necessarily determined by its type.

The methodology of the study is based on an approach common in intellectual and political history. The leaders who established the patterns are studied in detail, but sufficient attention is given to the followers to understand how the models were adopted and modified. The emphasis is upon Western European and North American periodicals, the result not of cultural chauvinism but of the pattern in the growth of historical scholarship.

This study is of necessity a pioneering venture. Existing studies of the historical discipline have addressed themselves to quite different kinds of questions, and studies of the periodical form as a means of scholarly communication have almost exclusively been devoted to other disciplines. The periodical's role in historical scholarship deserves more attention.[9]

TWO ❧ THE HISTORISCHE ZEITSCHRIFT

Although the *Historische Zeitschrift* cannot be called the first scholarly historical periodical without extensive qualification, it was the first in ways that count. The first to realize fully the modern concept of the scholarly historical periodical, it represented a quantum leap forward over its predecessors and exerted enormous impact on those that followed it. Its first fifty years, during which it defined its role in the profession and thus to some extent defined the role for all subsequent scholarly historical periodicals, were crucial to the discipline of history. Since then, the *HZ* has remained a leading scholarly historical journal, but by inspiring the creation of others that have also achieved success it has lost its unique commanding position.

In 1859, when the first issue of the *HZ* appeared, history lacked only a means of communication to be a mature profession. Perhaps most basic, a core of professionally trained individuals existed to provide the periodical's intellectual base, contribute to it, and be its audience. Several generations of students had studied history, and many were now productive scholars.

In Germany, history was by 1859 a recognized academic study. A student could obtain professional instruction in any one of several universities. Ranke had been at the University of Berlin for more than twenty years and had trained many scholars in his seminar. His former students, men like Georg Waitz, Gustav Droysen, and Heinrich von Sybel, were now professors at various German universities and were training students in the mold of the professional historian.

Important to the advancement of historical scholarship, but outside the university system, was the *Monumenta Germaniae Historica* (*MGH*). It had been founded in 1819 by Freiherr vom Stein, the Prussian leader during the period of the Wars of Liberation, who hoped it would contribute to German nationalism. The *MGH* was an enormous collecting and editing project that published medieval manuscripts of the kind essential as sources for professionally trained historians. It was a valuable supplementary training ground and a source of employment for many young historians who served an apprenticeship with it and obtained practical experience in historical research of a high standard.[1]

By 1859 history possessed intellectual traditions of its own and a significant degree of self-consciousness. Building on earlier work by Barthold Niebuhr and other historians and philologists, Ranke had described a distinctive historical methodology in the famous appendix to his "Histories of the Romance and Teutonic Peoples."[2] Only by closely examining original sources could the historian hope to know "how it really happened," in Ranke's oft-quoted phrase. Ranke's views were accepted in most quarters; as Georg Iggers explains, "The critical method became the common property of honest historical scholars everywhere."[3]

German historians had also developed a mature world view and theoretical convictions on the nature of history as well as its proper role that by and large gave them a clear sense of purpose. Variations existed within the dominant tradition, usually called historicism or by its German name, *Historismus.* Some historians did not subscribe to its basic tenets. It was, however, the faith of the most important and most numerous group of German historians, and its main outlines survived until the German catastrophe of 1945.[4]

The fundamental principle of historicism is that history is the only guide to the understanding of human affairs. It rejected the previously dominant doctrine of natural law, which maintained that, although events in nature can recur following laws, no such laws apply in the human sphere. History had previously looked to political philosophy for its theoretical guidance, now other fields must look to history. Not coincidentally, the development of the historicist position was an integral part of the German national revival, which rejected France and everything French. German intellectuals shared a conviction that natural-law doctrines had contributed to the outbreak of the French Revolution, whose subsequent excesses and perversions horrified them.

Iggers has identified three sets of ideas that are central to the German historicist position. It conceived the state as an end in itself, not, as in French or British thinking, existing to maximize the welfare of its citizens. Closely related to this view of the state, freedom for the individual was defined in terms of individual spiritual growth rather

than in terms of political participation.[5] Secondly, the German historicist position espoused a theory of value that was highly relativistic.
No historical phenomenon can be judged by standards external to the
situation in which it arose, but only by its own values. As corollaries,
all values are culture-bound and all culture a manifestation of the
divine will. The task of the state thus becomes to provide the most
favorable environment to encourage its innate tendencies, a task it
can only fulfill if it is strong and independent. Finally, the historicist
position rejected conceptualized thinking. Because historical phenomena are unique, each must be treated on its own terms.

The practical, present-oriented character of the historicist position
distinguishes it from many intellectual theories. It derives this quality
from its roots in the spirit of the Wars of Liberation, the period when
its fundamental precepts were first articulated. As Ranke wrote to
Bismarck, the value of history is the light it sheds on the course of
world events.[6] Its study is not merely an academic exercise; the historian has a vital contribution to make to contemporary political discussion. A number of historians were members of the Frankfurt Parliament of 1848.

These principles impelled historians to participate directly in pol-
itics and encouraged them to apply their knowledge in other ways.
Often this meant popular or semipopular journalism. Sybel wrote
extensively for the *Kölnische Zeitung* and contributed as well to the
Neue Hessische Zeitung and the *Frankfurther Ober-Postamts Zeitung*.[7]
Gervinus founded the *Deutsche Zeitung* in 1847, with the assistance of
Dahlmann, Droysen, and Hausser among others, to work for con-
stitutional government and German unity.[8]

Two journals that historians founded anticipated the *HZ*: the *Historisch-Politische Zeitschrift* (1832–34), and the *Zeitschrift für Geschichtswissenschaft* (1844–48). Leopold von Ranke founded and edited the *Historisch-Politische Zeitschrift*, sponsored by Count von Bernstorff, foreign
minister of Prussia. Bernstorff's motives were unquestionably political: to provide an organ to defend the policies of the Prussian bureau-
cracy and to distinguish the positions of the government from those
of the reactionary right.[9] Ranke's, expressed in the introduction, are
somewhat less strongly political. He argued that politics could only
be understood against a historical background. He hoped his readers
would discern and keep in mind the unchangeable, true principles, as
he spoke to the needs of the times.[10]

Although Ranke obviously hoped to make the *Historisch-Politische Zeitschrift* a scholarly historical journal, its political quality is the more apparent. The articles treat contemporary problems almost exclusively; one, for example, discusses the map of Europe in 1830, another French pamphlets of the last months of 1831. The format, typical of popular rather than scholarly journals, is restricted to articles except for a section entitled "Reflexionen." Ranke wrote almost all the articles; among the few exceptions are two by Savigny.

The *Historisch-Politische Zeitschrift*, like German historical scholarship, was inherently dichotomous. Despite its inescapably political character, it published some material valuable to the historian. In its pages, Ranke addressed major historiographical issues, almost the only place he did so in print. Srbik has described some of these pieces as "jewels."[11]

The second significant precursor of the *HZ* was the *Zeitschrift für Geschichtswissenschaft* (later the *Allgemeine Zeitschrift für Geschichte*), founded by Adolf Schmidt in 1844. More scholarly in content than Ranke's *Historisch-Politische Zeitschrift*, it too involved itself with contemporary politics, albeit to a more limited extent. Its articles do not deal so frequently with current affairs. It even reports on historical literature through that relatively common nineteenth-century form, essays, as well as through book reviews. Schmidt was fortunate to obtain the cooperation of the most important scholars of the Ranke school, which meant in effect the most important historians. Articles by Giesebrecht, Sybel, Jaffé, and Ranke appear in its pages. Ranke and Pertz are listed on the title page as assistants, along with Boeckh, a well-known classical scholar, and J. W. Grimm, the distinguished linguist. The *Zeitschrift für Geschichtswissenschaft* was indeed, as Srbik describes it, "notable,"[12] and anticipated the *HZ* in many ways.

Eleven years after the demise of the *Zeitschrift für Geschichtswissenschaft*, the first issue of the *HZ* appeared. Heinrich von Sybel, its founder, had been, like Schmidt, a student under Ranke at the University of Berlin; Gooch considers him Ranke's most brilliant student.[13] By 1859 he had plainly become one of the leading German historians and was well placed to undertake such a venture. He came of an old Westphalian Protestant family. He was born in 1817 in Düsseldorf, where his father held prominent positions in the public service under both the French and the Prussians. In 1831 his father was raised to the hereditary nobility, and the family home was one of the centers of literary and artistic life for which Düsseldorf was at the time renowned. After the local gymnasium, young Sybel studied at the University of Berlin from 1834 to 1838 under Ranke and Savigny. He then held positions at the universities of Bonn and Marburg, after which King Maximilian invited him to become a professor at Munich in 1856. During this period, he was active in politics and served as a moderate Liberal in the Parliament of Erfurt in 1850. At Munich, in addition to his professorial duties, he founded and was active in the Historical Seminar and served as secretary to the new Historische Kommission.[14]

The appearance of the *HZ* was the culmination of a long campaign. In 1853 Sybel had written to Droysen inquiring rather plaintively if a journal for historical scholarship was not necessary. He made clear that he saw the journal as Protestant, with strong Prussian influence.[15] Four years later, in June 1857, when he approached the Catholic King Maximilian, he emphasized instead that a journal was necessary if Munich was to become the center of historical scholarship of which the king dreamed. A journal would make the king's concern for history and his munificence visible in distant circles. The time was, moreover, ripe for such an enterprise. On all sides, German historians felt the need for such a journal. In fact, a Dr. Lanz of Stuttgart was planning to start one. Although Lanz was an able scholar, Sybel felt he would be unable to handle all aspects of the task, and the existence of his journal would make a second one of the same kind impossible.[16]

Sybel's formal proposal to the king must have been preceded by less formal discussions because, in a letter to Waitz that antedates this proposal by a month, he is quite definite in discussing his plans. He is talking about the *HZ*, not about a historical journal. It would be founded in Munich, appear quarterly, and address itself to a broad but not exclusively scholarly audience. It would fight both dilettantism and the Ultramontane Catholic historians, both of which Sybel charged with "Unwissenschaftlichkeit." The goal was a journal that would engender a strong consciousness of the true methods of historical scholarship, which would turn historians from false ways.[17]

The first public announcement of the *HZ* is in the *Börsenblatt*, number 11 of July 21, 1858. The I. G. Cotta'sche Buchhandlung reported that a contract had been signed between the firm and Professor von Sybel, who was to edit a "Historische Zeitschrift." Details of the contract were given: such historians as Droysen, Hausser,

Mommsen, Ranke, and Waitz were to contribute; proof sheets were to number sixty per year, for each of which the editor would receive thirty-three florins, from which he would pay editorial costs and contributors.[18]

Without Maximilian's interest and generous support, the *HZ* would probably never have reached this stage. His background and interests were unusual for a monarch. He had studied with Ranke at Göttingen and Berlin and had been heard to say that, had he not been born a prince, he would have chosen to be a professor. He tried to make Munich a center of historical learning by founding the Historische Kommission and strengthening the university's historical faculty. As crown prince, he gathered around himself artists and men of learning, a practice he continued after he became king of Bavaria in 1848. Although the events of 1848 had changed his liberal politics, he invited scholars to Munich without regard to their religious or political views and supported them, often in the face of bitter criticism from his absolutist governments and a strong Ultramontanist clerical party. Sybel was a case in point.[19]

When Sybel proposed his scholarly historical journal, Maximilian, after consulting Ranke, responded favorably. He offered a direct subvention, although whether or not he actually provided any money is doubtful. A listing of the king's donations to scholarship from his private means includes 2,000 florins for the founding of a historical journal.[20] Schieder, on the other hand, claims that all editorial costs from the beginning were borne by the publisher.[21] Certainly the contract with I. G. Cotta mentions no royal donations. Any grants that might have been made must have lasted only a few years. When he first approached the royal treasury, Sybel emphasized that any grant would be temporary. Once the journal had come into existence, it would need to maintain itself. If it could not, it did not deserve to survive. Sybel recognized that financial independence was inseparable from editorial independence. That the journal did survive and flourish vindicates his conviction that the profession needed it.

Maximilian's role should not be underestimated. He was willing to do for the historical journal what foundations and government agencies do for some scholarly projects: provide seed money. His encouragement turned Sybel's dream into reality. In the social context of nineteenth-century Germany, royal support was a guarantee of a successful inaugural.

Also important in the founding and early years of the *HZ* was

Rudolf Oldenbourg, a highly successful businessman and entrepreneur who had intellectual interests. In 1858 he was a partner in the I. G. Cotta'sche Buchhandlung, responsible for its Munich operations. His contribution was persuading the company to undertake publication of the proposed journal. When Cotta disposed of its Munich branch in 1868, Oldenbourg took over its journals, including the *HZ*, and those operations not returned to the main office in Stuttgart. The Rudolf Oldenbourg Verlag continues to publish the *HZ* today.[22]

Sybel's plans, as published in a foreword to the first issue of the *HZ*, correspond closely with what he had written earlier to Droysen and Waitz. The king had made several suggestions, among them that nothing on ancient history be included unless it was already part of the general education,[23] but Sybel apparently did not accept them. The journal was to be "eine historische Zeitschrift," "nicht eine antiquarische und nicht eine politische."[24] Sybel then proceeded to declare war on feudalism, radicalism, and Ultramontanism, the forces that, hardly coincidentally, were the enemies of moderate liberalism. The *HZ* was obviously intended to be "historical" in the historicist sense of the word, though Sybel had given a new *Kleindeutsch* orientation to historicist assumptions.[25]

Sybel's plans were general rather than specific, a guide, not a map. Much remained to be decided. The volumes during the thirty-six years of his editorship reveal experiments with different approaches to fundamental questions. The result served as a model to the entire historical profession, influencing its members far beyond the borders of Germany.

In the pages of the *HZ*, the scholarly historical article achieved its preeminence as the core of the scholarly historical periodical. Written on a single topic, the result of scholarly investigation that is documented and not tied to any other publication, the article is a distinct literary form. The first volume of the *HZ* contained several pieces that were clearly articles, such as Zeller's on the Platonic state and Theodor Mommsen's on the Roman law of hospitality. Other pieces were just as clearly not articles. Ludwig Hausser wrote an essay on Macaulay's "Frederick the Great"; Sybel, on Joseph de Maistre. Both are the kind of review essay found in the general reviews of the day, like the *Edinburgh Review* or the *Deutsche Rundschau*.

This mixture resulted from Sybel's desire to meet the needs of professional historians, to whom the articles were primarily addressed, and to influence a larger public politically, the purpose of the essays. Ultimately these intentions proved incompatible, and during the early years of the *HZ* the essay gradually disappeared from its pages. Mommsen told Sybel that the desire to reach a nonscholarly public acted as a major deterrent to scholarly contributions.[26] The *HZ*'s relinquishing of popularly focused articles did not mean that German historicists relinquished their political involvement or interests. Men like Sybel and Treitschke continued to take a major part in shaping German intellectual discourse on power, the state, and political morality in the Second Empire to such an extent that they have been blamed for the strident, jingoistic German nationalism that played such a big part in bringing about the First World War.[27] What the *HZ*'s abandonment of popularly oriented articles did mean was that historians wrote either for newspapers and popular journals, influencing the public directly, or for scholarly media, influencing it indirectly. Different periodicals met different needs.

The subjects of the articles during Sybel's editorship were typical of the historicist school. They dealt overwhelmingly with German history and political history; even diplomatic history, that staple of traditional history, had only a small share. As time passed, greater attention was paid to more recent times, although in the first year a disproportionate number of articles were published on relatively recent history. The six articles on the eighteenth century in the volume for 1879 and again in the volume for 1889 represent another deviation from the pattern. It may be coincidence, but during those years Max Lehmann was Sybel's assistant editor, and that is the century in which he was the most interested.

In spite of its concentration on a relatively small area of the historiographical universe, the *HZ* rapidly achieved a central position in the world of German historians, a position it maintains today. No historian could safely ignore it; it was quoted even in the publications of historians who did not accept the historicist assumptions. One measure of its significance is that almost all the major disagreements in German history have received an airing in its pages; the only significant exception was Sybel's differences of opinion with the Catholic historian Julius Ficker over the nature of the medieval empire. Sybel may well have decided to avoid controversy until the *HZ* was firmly established.

The *HZ* did play a prominent role in the question of the origins of the Seven Years' War and Frederick the Great's "guilt." From 1864[28] this question was discussed almost continuously, regularly receiving new impetus from the appearance of works like Arneth's biography of Maria Theresa and especially from the publication of Ranke's studies of the war's origins. During this period, the task of vindicating Frederick's conduct in 1756 became a patriotic duty for Prussian historians, and after the mid-1870s the Prussian point of view increasingly dominated the *HZ*. As the debate progressed, two prominent historians, Max Lehmann and Hans Delbrück, renounced the Prussian view, and Lehmann's apostasy was a major contributory factor in his later break with Sybel. Only after 1896 did the *HZ* break with the Prussian point of view. The controversy was particularly important for its contribution to the doctrine of realpolitik and as an illustration of Sybel's position that history can be both scientific and prejudiced.

The characteristics of contributors were quickly established and have seldom under any editor deviated from the pattern. Almost all have held the doctorate. Almost invariably they have been university faculty, although in the late nineteenth century a number of them were secondary school teachers and archivists. Most have been professors, and the average age at the time of the contribution has risen steadily. The articles for the *HZ* have increasingly been written by mature scholars. The few foreign contributors have usually been Austrian or Swiss.

These general characteristics do not highlight the fact that during the years of Sybel's editorship a number of prominent historians did not write for the *HZ*. Sybel deliberately excluded several groups, of which the most important was the Catholic historians, unless they were of the old Catholic persuasion. The Catholic historians eventually created their own publication outlet in the *Historisches Jahrbuch* of the Görres Gesellschaft.

A group, usually called dilettantes, whose tradition was literary rather than scientific history, did not often appear in the *HZ*. Sybel's intended emphasis on scientific history would seem to have barred them from the *HZ*'s pages, but in fact he tried to recruit articles from them. Men like Ferdinand Gregorovius, Alfred von Reumont, and Karl Hillebrand were widely read by the middle-class reading public, and Sybel hoped through them to reach a wider audience. His efforts were largely unsuccessful; the journals already open to them were more attractive from their point of view.

Sybel's failure had serious structural implications for the *HZ*. The unwillingness of the belletristic historians to write for it reinforced its limitation to scholarship. They were asserting what Sybel himself had earlier recognized: their brand of history was essentially different. No comfortable blend of scientific and literary was possible. Professional historians did not relinquish their desire to influence literary culture, a desire that persists today,[29] but they have yet to discover a successful method to achieve it. Their involvement with popular historical periodicals is an attempt that has met with only slight success.

More serious than the exclusion of the Catholic historians or the indifference of literary historians was the absence from the *HZ* during its early years of leading scientific historians. Sybel had counted on their cooperation. Droysen, Hausser, Mommsen, Ranke, and Waitz had all been named in the Cotta contract as intended contributors. Mommsen contributed one article in the first volume; he did not appear again until volume 38, eighteen years later. Ranke is represented by a few minor pieces, chiefly unpublished speeches for the Historische Kommission. Waitz, Droysen, and Hausser do have several each, usually essays rather than articles, hardly enough to fulfill the role Sybel had in mind for them. Other contemporaries of Sybel conspicuously absent included Treitschke, whose only contribution was made after he himself became editor.

Sybel believed that these and other leading historians supported him but did not appear in the *HZ* because they had better things to do than write articles.[30] It is quite true that for that generation and for historians since then the monograph has been the form of publication that mattered, but Sybel was mistaken in his belief that they did not write articles. These prominent historians contributed so little to the *HZ* because they had already established themselves. They did write articles,[31] but they published them in journals in related fields, in undifferentiated scholarly publications, or in the few specifically scholarly journals that existed. During the first decade of the *HZ*'s existence, Mommsen wrote many article-length studies, which appeared in journals like the *Archaeologische Zeitung*, the *Zeitschrift für Rechtsgeschichte*, the *Bulletino* of the Instituto di Diritto Romano and the *Annali* of the Instituto di Corrispondenza Archeologica. Waitz preferred to be published in the *Nachrichten und Abhandlungen* of the Göttingen Gesellschaft, and most of Treitschke's articles appeared in the *Preussische Jahrbücher*, of which he was editor.

The absence of these scholars is not in itself significant, but that the *HZ* managed to survive and flourish without them is noteworthy. It suggests that, although the *HZ* was not fulfilling the need for a place to publish articles, hypothesized with these historians in mind, it was fulfilling a different need. The wide range of publications in which their scholarly articles were published could not provide adequate communication within the historical profession. The *HZ*, by its existence, affirmed the presence of a historical profession possessing some degree of unity. It was a central organizing point to which all historians could refer. It also provided the essential service of facilitating bibliographical access.

The nature of historical scholarship is such that its practitioners depend to a greater degree than scholars in most other fields on published books, articles, newspapers, and collections of documents. Such published materials can either serve as primary sources or influence the interpretation of evidence. To discover what has been published, systematic bibliographies are needed. Sybel seems originally to have intended the *HZ* to provide complete bibliographical coverage; the historian would need to consult no other bibliographical source.

The many changes in the way the *HZ* has handled this function indicate that the task is much more complex than it might at first appear. The first volume contained, in addition to articles, a section labelled "Übersicht," which was intended to cover the literature of the field. The "Übersichten" of the first volume were a mixture of brief, noncritical reviews and simple listings of those works not singled out as the focal point of essays. In 1866 a combination of concise reports on the literature, mentioning only the most important books on their respective themes, and a separate section for reviews replaced that system. Sybel was forced to give up his efforts at completeness. In 1866 he foresaw a time when the size of the bibliography would allow room for nothing else if it continued to grow at its present rate. Oldenbourg reinforced his doubts by pointing out the financial difficulties caused by the bibliographical section.[32]

In 1893 the *HZ* introduced a new section that, though it would pass through many changes, retained its basic goal of informing historians of the primarily nonmonographic publications in their field. Its changing manifestations give a sense of groping for improvement. In 1893, as "Notizen und Nachrichten," it presented news, principally concerning the publications of the national and provincial academies, the *Monumenta Germaniae Historica,* and learned groups like the Görres Gesellschaft. In 1969, as "Aus Zeitschriften und Sammel-bänden," a straight bibliographical listing replaced the narrative form, and the section became a current contents list similar to those in many scholarly journals. Ten years later, it became "Historische Literatur," a bibliographical essay on topics like German liberalism between the revolution and the founding of the Reich.

The variability of this section contrasts markedly with the stability of the book review section as it was organized in 1866. Book reviews serve a radically different purpose from bibliographical listings; they provide the evaluation of new knowledge that is indispensable to any profession. Historians could more easily agree on this goal and on the appropriateness of book reviews to meet it than they could on the purposes and scope of bibliographical listing. Book reviews are essen-tial in almost any journal that has scholarly pretensions, general or disciplinary. Generations of reviewers and editors have established the criteria for good book reviews. To some extent, a book review section also fulfills a secondary purpose; in a limited and un-systematic way, it informs scholars of what has been published and thus becomes part of the apparatus for bibliographical access.

The *HZ* book reviews cover primarily secondary monographic liter-ature. Over the years, less and less attention has been given to origi-nal sources. In 1869 and 1879, 17 and 22 percent of the items reviewed can be classified as original source material; in 1959 and 1969 the figures are 7.5 and 10 percent, respectively. As historical studies have matured in different countries, the scope of the book reviews has reflected it. In 1959 and 1969, for example, approximately a quarter of the titles reviewed in the *HZ* were in English, compared to 2 out of 104 in 1869 and 6 of 214 in 1879. Reviews of books written in German and of those written about German history have predominated. The numerical preponderance of books in the national language and about the nation's history is not only consonant with the focus of the historicist school, but is true of most of the scholarly journals that take all history as their scope. Some geographical areas, such as Western Europe, Eastern Europe, and the Mediterranean, have received a dis-proportionate share of attention in the *HZ*. Others, like the United States, Latin America, Africa, and the Middle East have been slighted. To some extent, this means only that few German historians worked in these areas, but the *HZ* also seems to have lacked real interest in them, as it did in such topical areas as social and economic history.

The ways in which the *HZ* approached the problem of bibliographical coverage were closely related to the development of bibliographical methods. Sybel was able to settle for less than complete coverage because German bibliography, compared to that in other countries, was sophisticated and reliable. In 1859 good retrospective national bibliographies existed, and the *Halbjahrs-Katalog* was an outstanding current national trade bibliography. It enabled the user to find out, within approximately six months of publication, what books had been published. Author or main entry access and a rudimentary subject approach were provided. The *Halbjahrs-Katalog* was such a successful solution to one aspect of the bibliographical problem that it survived into the twentieth century, when it was taken over by the German publishers' association and became the basis of the present *Deutsche Bibliographie*.[33]

In addition to these general bibliographies, German historians could use the Dahlmann-Waitz bibliography, an early subject bibliography that has served as a model for others. The first edition, prepared by Friedrich Christoph Dahlmann, appeared in 1830, and a second improved edition in 1838. After Dahlmann's death, Georg Waitz prepared the third (1869), fourth (1875), and fifth (1883) editions. In 1981 it was in its tenth edition. It listed monographs, collections of source materials, and periodical articles. Its limitation to German history was not serious for German historians, whose primary interest was in that area. Dahlmann-Waitz, together with the *Halbjahrs-Katalog*, met many of their bibliographical needs. The *HZ* could adjust its bibliographical activities to take advantage of what they were already doing.

The attempt to provide bibliographical access to historical literature, even though of necessity limited in scope, is one indication that Sybel hoped to make the *HZ* not just a historical journal, but *the* historical journal. Srbik has described mid-nineteenth century historical journals as places to collect the activity of individuals who thought alike, "Sammelplätze der Tätigkeit der Gleichgesinnten."[34] Sybel's stated intentions indicate that he shared this view of periodicals, but his actions suggest larger ambitions as well. The attempts at bibliographical control were one such indicator. Another was his response to other periodicals.

Sybel strongly opposed the founding of the *Preussische Jahrbücher* in 1858,[35] undoubtedly because he saw it as a threat to his own journal. The plans for it were similar in many ways to his for the *HZ*. The founders of the *Preussische Jahrbücher* were, like him, committed to scientific history and were members of the historicist school. Their goal was a periodical that would appeal to the intelligent general reader as well as to the scholar and would also exert political influence. Rudolf Haym, the founder and first editor, and his successor as editor, Heinrich von Treitschke, were moderate liberals and favored the *Kleindeutsch* solution.

The German historical profession proved to be firmly enough established to support both journals, but the *Preussische Jahrbücher* clearly influenced the evolution of the *HZ*. The two periodicals pragmatically arrived at something approaching a division of labor; the *Preussische Jahrbücher* emphasized popular, political aims, and the *HZ* quickly became a journal addressed primarily to the scholar. Schieder has called them twin sisters; if they were, they were nonidentical twins who exhibited a strong sense of sibling rivalry.[36]

Sybel was equally hostile toward later journals, although by that time his own was well established. In 1889 he tried without success to persuade the founder of the *Forschungen für Brandenburgische und Preussische Geschichte*, Gustav Schmoller, to publish it as a supplement to the *HZ*. Sybel particularly feared the *Forschungen* because he felt it challenged the *HZ* in its own field,[37] although he was also cool toward another journal begun in 1889, the *Deutsche Zeitschrift für Geschichtswissenschaft*, a journal with quite different traditions from those of the *HZ*.

Friedrich Meinecke, who became editor of the *HZ* in 1896, shared this sensitivity to potential competition. When the *Archiv für Kulturgeschichte*, a journal that planned to emphasize areas of history the *HZ* had always ignored, was founded in 1903, the *HZ* responded by expanding its editorial board to include historians who were associated with cultural history. Although Karl Lamprecht, the principal advocate of social-cultural history and the principal challenger of the historicist assumptions, was not invited to join it, a close colleague of his, Erich Marcks, was, along with a major opponent of Lamprecht, Georg von Below. Meinecke reacted in much the same way to proposals during the 1920s to found a journal of German medieval history. When Albert Brackmann, a leader in this field, indicated that he would renounce his proposed periodical if the *HZ* would give more attention to the Middle Ages, Meinecke agreed, suspecting that a large group of medieval historians backed the new periodical. Brackmann became a coeditor of the *HZ* responsible for medieval history.[38]

Hostility toward rivals is a perfectly natural reaction, but the unvarying opposition of the *HZ* to other periodicals, regardless of the editor, goes considerably beyond the normal. Its roots lie in a vision of an ideal communication system in which one scholarly journal would serve all historians. Such a system would work against the fractionation of both discipline and profession. It is quite different from the system that has evolved in the United States.

This vision was not as self-serving as it seems; at least some other members of the scholarly community shared it. In his letter opening his campaign for the editorship of the *HZ* after the death of Sybel, Karl Lamprecht offered to merge the *Deutsche Zeitschrift für Geschichtswissenschaft*, which he was certain of being able to control, with the *HZ*. He stated explicitly that one major historical journal was sufficient for the discipline.[39] The tone of his letter implies that the *DZG* was a mere gadfly, its purpose in life to irritate the *HZ*. Oldenbourg, the publisher of the *HZ*, found Lamprecht's letter both correct and pleasing, but did not like being in a position to bring about the sacrifice of a rival.[40] When Lamprecht did not become editor of the *HZ*, the idea died.

Whether defending the *HZ* against imagined dangers represented by new scholarly historical periodicals, negotiating for support in its founding, or overseeing its operation, Heinrich von Sybel was the individual who was most responsible for what it became. It truly deserves to be called, as it was popularly known, "Sybel's Zeitschrift."[41]

Sybel had not intended to undertake the editing, but Ranke persuaded him to do so. He did not, in any case, do much of the routine work, for he was busy with academic tasks and was appointed director of the Prussian archives in 1875. The assistant editors did much of the work. The most important of these was Max Lehmann, who held the position from 1875 to 1893. A vigorous, able historian, Lehmann speeded up coverage of the literature and waged historiographical war. Sybel gave his assistant editors wide latitude. His willingness to delegate responsibility is clearly apparent in his letter breaking with Lehmann and in the memoirs of Friedrich Meinecke, Lehmann's successor.[42] Sybel retained only final decisions on policy.

Sybel's death in 1895 created a crisis in the affairs of the periodical. There was even some question, at least in the mind of Meinecke, the assistant editor, whether it would continue.[43] In spite of the almost complete identification of the *HZ* with Sybel, the publisher, Rudolf Oldenbourg, had no such doubts. His problem was to find an appropriate editor. Lehmann was to have been Sybel's successor, but his falling out with Sybel in 1893 had eliminated him as a candidate. Meinecke, who had become assistant editor only two years before, was simply too young and untried.

Into this breach stepped Karl Lamprecht, professor at the University of Leipzig and the foremost critic of the Rankean and Prussian historiographical traditions. Aided by Friedrich Ratzel, a friend of Oldenbourg, Lamprecht suggested himself to the publisher as editor. The terms of his proposal were at once indirect, Machiavellian, and completely unmistakable. Lamprecht offered to amalgamate the *HZ* with the *Deutsche Zeitschrift für Geschichtswissenschaft* and the *Historische Jahresberichte,* with both of which at that time he was also negotiating for the editorship.[44]

A decisive factor in defeating Lamprecht's bid was Meinecke's opposition. As soon as he heard of it, he wrote to Oldenbourg in unmistakable terms. He described Lamprecht's proposal as a great act of impiety against Sybel and against the former direction of the *HZ*.[45] Sybel had held a poor opinion of Lamprecht, whom he viewed as a "damaged soul," a "faltige Seele." Sybel had been personally responsible for Below's devastating review of Lamprecht's *Deutsche Geschichte,* printed two years earlier in the *HZ*. Meinecke also argued that, if Lamprecht became editor, most of the staff and contributors would leave, and another journal, probably under Max Lehmann's direction, would be established. The *HZ* would acquire to its disadvantage a pronounced party orientation.

Oldenbourg had his own doubts about Lamprecht, and his initial response was an attempt at delay.[46] At that time, he was uncertain of his right to choose the new editor, although eventually he did make the final choice. By contract, Sybel had the right to name his successor, and whether or not he had named anyone in his will was still unknown. Oldenbourg was also uncertain whether the right to name a successor had passed to Sybel's sons on his death. That he could even contemplate such a possibility is an indication of how strongly a journal was then regarded as the editor's personal property.

Eventually, Oldenbourg chose Heinrich von Treitschke, the only man who could be considered Sybel's equal. His selection was an unmistakable indication of Oldenbourg's agreement with Meinecke that the traditions of the *HZ* as established by Sybel must be perpetuated. Meinecke's appeal to the ghost of Sybel had succeeded, and some discreet lobbying with Sybel's sons had helped. There had been other possibilities. Meinecke had suggested Reinhold Koser, of Bonn, Conrad Varrentrapp, a former assistant editor, and von Bezold, a Bavarian historian. Alternative administrative arrangements had been studied,[47] but Oldenbourg finally chose to continue the existing editorial organization. The *HZ*, after all, had been a successful journal for thirty-six years under Sybel's direction.

Treitschke had recently broken with Delbrück and the *Preussische Jahrbücher* and after some persuasion by Meinecke he agreed to accept the appointment.[48] Meinecke combined the pathetic, that the *HZ* had been orphaned by Sybel's death, with flattery, that it would be an honor for the *HZ* if Treitschke became editor. Treitschke declared his intention to carry on in Sybel's footsteps: "I am of the same opinion as H. v. Sybel as to the purpose (Zweck) and interpretation (Sinn) of historical scholarship."[49] Unfortunately, the appointment proved to be more of a symbol to the historiographical traditions established by Sybel than a solution to the problem of a new editor. Treitschke died within a year of assuming the position.

This time no hesitation occurred; Oldenbourg chose Meinecke to replace Treitschke, although he recognized the risk. To compensate for Meinecke's inexperience, he suggested that an editorial board of experienced historians be created. He also recognized that no one else could become editor without altering the direction of the journal completely.

Although neither Oldenbourg nor Meinecke intended it, Meinecke's appointment in 1895 marked the beginning of a new era. He was still in his thirties, a member of a new generation. During his four decades as editor, his professional views underwent considerable change and modification, changes that were reflected in the *HZ*'s editorial policies. It is somewhat ironical that, although he remained within the historicist tradition, he criticised many of its most fundamental assumptions.[50] It is also ironical that, although the *HZ* under his direction published the most important criticism of Lamprecht,[51] it eventually accepted many of his conclusions, if not his premises. Meinecke, for example, opened the *HZ* to articles on intellectual history and other forms of cultural history, areas Sybel had excluded. In later years, Meinecke would be accused of giving too much attention to these new areas.[52]

Meinecke's style as editor was somewhat different from that of Sybel. For example, he participated more actively in the daily routine. He did continue Sybel's policy of writing frequently for the *HZ*. Such direct contributions helped to give the journal a clear direction. Later editors have continued the practice.

The transfer of power to Meinecke was significant beyond the inevitable replacement of one generation by the next. It was a part of the larger question of change. A scholarly historical periodical is a living entity; it cannot remain fixed and unaltered without the risk of obsolescence or irrelevance. The problem is particularly acute for a journal that aspires to remain the leading scholarly historical periodical in its country. Some parts of the scholarly environment may remain stable, but the totality that the journal aspires to lead does not. The *HZ* has nevertheless managed in many respects to change little. It remains, except for its philosophy, by and large the journal Sybel created.

When Heinrich von Sybel died on August 1, 1895, the *HZ* was, as Meinecke called it, the "Hauptorgan" of the profession, enjoying power and prestige.[53] It was at the center of historical scholarship, despite, or perhaps because of, its historicist tradition. By trial and error, it had established a format so successful that almost all later scholarly historical periodicals adopted it: articles, book reviews, a news section, and some form of bibliographical listing.

Since 1895 the world of German historical scholarship, to which the *HZ* is so intimately related, has changed considerably, primarily in its philosophical positions. The historicist school was first challenged, then discarded during World War II. The profession, in the aftermath of 1945, went through an agonizing process, first of self-examination, then of the regeneration of a consciousness of continuity in German history on a new basis.[54] Historians have discovered new areas of interest, such as social and economic history. Specialization has spread. Periodicals have multiplied.

Through all these vicissitudes, the *HZ* has succeeded in maintaining its position as the leading German scholarly historical periodical. It has made relatively minor adjustments, such as appointing advocates of newer ideas to its editorial board. It has broadened its focus by giving newer forms of history publication space. Indicative of its success, it has continued to contribute to almost every major historiographical controversy; one example is the Bismarck dispute of the 1950s. Many things did not need alteration. German history has remained its principal interest, although no longer quite so all-absorbing, for German history remains the primary interest of the country's historians. The years since Sybel's death are in a sense a postscript to the history of the *HZ*, despite its continuing vitality. Any changes have been in directions that brought it and kept it closer to Sybel's original conception: a journal that could serve the whole German historical profession.

Heinrich von Sybel's accomplishments were truly momentous. Under his direction, the *HZ* established what a scholarly historical journal should be. It made difficult decisions although no model was available. It created a tradition that was strong enough to withstand attack from powerful forces. Perhaps the best measure of its success is the large number of imitators it produced; later journals often explicitly and consciously borrowed from the *HZ*. Whether or not the debt is acknowledged, all scholarly historical periodicals owe something to the pioneer, the *Historische Zeitschrift*.

THREE ❦ THE SPREAD OF
SCHOLARLY HISTORICAL
PERIODICALS ❦ FRANCE,
GREAT BRITAIN, AND THE
UNITED STATES

The Founding of the *Revue Historique*, the *English Historical Review*, and the *American Historical Review*

The *HZ* did not long remain splendidly alone, but was soon joined by scholarly historical periodicals in other countries, most of which bore a strong family resemblance to it. It provided encouragement to the founders of these newcomers by its success and furnished them with a model. The diffusion of scholarly historical periodicals was a critical step in the growth of historical scholarship.

The first of these post-*HZ* journals appeared in France when Gabriel Monod founded the *Revue historique* (*RH*) in 1876. A medium for the publication of what he called "scientific history" and a source of information about the progress of historical scholarship in France and other countries,[1] the *RH* also had a political purpose. Monod hoped it would help to "provide our country with the moral unity and vigor it needs, enabling it both to become familiar with its historical traditions and to comprehend the transformations it has undergone."[2] Historical study was important to the nation, and the *RH* would be the means to promote it. This agenda limited the scope of the journal to European history and in particular to France.

The introduction to the *English Historical Review* (*EHR*), begun in 1886, does not state its plans so clearly. It does, by implication, say that the *EHR* was being founded to advance the common objectives of English historians. Nowhere are these defined, a reflection of the failure of English historians to articulate clearly their philosophy of history. The introduction does recognize a limited communications role for the journal, which hoped to "become the organ through which those who desire to make known the progress of their researches will address their fellow-labourers."[3]

The *American Historical Review* (*AHR*) had no proper introduction. W. M. Sloane, one of the group who cooperated to organize it in 1895, instead contributed a lengthy preface to the first issue on the role and methods of historical scholarship. He traced the creation of the *AHR* to the absence of a "check" on the expanding volume of historical writing, to the number of historical writers, and to the growing reading public. These circumstances created a need for coordination and intelligent criticism, presumably to be supplied by the *AHR*. His essay, significantly entitled "History and Democracy," hints at a role for the new journal in political education.[4] The prospectus sent out by the founders while they were organizing the journal supplements Sloane's statement and sets forth their purposes somewhat more lucidly. They intended that the *AHR* would be devoted to history and "establish a medium to which they [historical scholars and writers] may communicate to each other the results of their own work and bring American scholarship into relationships with that of other countries."[5]

In their broad outlines, these three statements sound much alike, but the similarity is deceptive. The journals were fulfilling different structural roles. For all their many likenesses, their scholarly environments differed from each other in significant ways, which they reflected. French, British, and American historians, however similar their outlook, did not share the same needs.

When the first issue of the *RH* appeared in 1876, French historical scholarship lacked much of the formal organization of a profession. The *RH* was thus part of the profession's foundation rather than, as the *HZ* had been, a consolidating force. In 1876 history had yet to become an academic discipline and scholarly endeavor in the French university. Because of the Sorbonne's system of lectures, historical instruction meant history popularized for the tastes of the public at large who attended those lectures. Such instruction in historical scholarship as there was took place either at the École des Chartes, where it was highly specialized, designed to prepare archivists and librarians who were specialists in the medieval period, or at the recently founded École Pratique des Hautes Études (EPHE), where Monod held a post.[6]

Within a few years, the program of educational reform in history, of which Monod was one of the leaders, produced major changes. By 1900 the reformers, in 1876 still outside the establishment, had captured the Sorbonne. Succeeding in changing both the examination system and instructional methods, they deemphasized the public lecture and introduced the seminar. As early as 1882, the visiting Belgian scholar Paul Frédéricq, who had come to Paris with the most dismal expectations, was expressing his admiration for French historical instruction.[7] By the end of the century, France had replaced Germany as the preferred place for young Americans to study abroad, a significant shift.[8]

Before the *RH*, French historians had been served by two journals. In 1866 the Marquis de Beaucourt founded the *Revue des questions historiques* (*RQH*) to rewrite history using the new methods of critical scholarship. Through its bibliographical sections, it made an effort to cover historical literature, but certain limitations prevented its becoming the leading French scholarly historical periodical of its day. Its outlook was Catholic, secondarily Royalist; its chief aim was to defend Catholic doctrines; and its chief focus was Christian history, although French history was also emphasized. The *RQH*'s contributors explain its failure to achieve leadership. They were predominantly nonprofessional Catholic gentlemen, many of them noble, and they included a sprinkling of archivists and some clergymen. Academic reformers were conspicuously absent.[9] The *RQH* succeeded in becoming a scholarly historical periodical; it failed to become a professional journal.

The second French periodical was the *Revue critique d'histoire et de la littérature*, also founded in 1866 and yet another journal inspired by the *HZ*. It printed no articles, but did publish reviews, prepared by specialists, of scholarly historical works. Charles Morel's review in 1866 of *Cité antique*, the popular book on ancient history by Fustel de Coulanges, was both an application of the new critical methods in historical research and a manifesto on their behalf. Unfortunately for the historians, the *Revue critique* suspended publication during the Franco-Prussian War and did not resume until 1876, and then in a considerably altered form.[10]

In 1876 the French historical profession lacked not only the necessary institutional infrastructure but also a philosophy. The leading historians who were trying to professionalize history, Monod and

Ernest Lavisse, had a program but nothing approaching a philosophy of history. Their program was practical in its aims: no less than the regeneration of France. They were primarily educational reformers and textbook writers rather than abstract thinkers. For a philosophy, they substituted a faith in the methods of German historical scholarship, which emphasized documentary research. Only when the somewhat younger Charles Seignobos began in 1896 to teach a course in historiography at the Sorbonne and to write on the subject did French historians begin to raise questions about their theoretical assumptions.

Professional historical scholarship in England, like that in France, was relatively unorganized, or, perhaps more accurately, haphazardly organized. Often older forms were adapted to serve new purposes. Both Oxford and Cambridge had Regius Professors of Modern History from 1724, but few if any of the incumbents had any real interest in history. One at Cambridge, for example, was the poet Thomas Gray. The appointment in 1841 of Thomas Arnold to the Oxford Regius Professorship began the process of change. He died only a year later, but he succeeded in arousing an interest in history by his well-prepared lectures on historical topics. In 1850 Oxford instituted the School of Law and Modern History to provide for those "who, not being candidates for distinctions which require greater powers of intellect as well as application, might nevertheless be most usefully employed on subjects within their reach, and yet in every respect well calculated to instruct and improve their minds."[11] In 1871 Modern History was separated from Law and awarded a degree in its own right. Yet, organization was left to chance; no Board of Studies was created until 1872 and no Board of Faculty until 1882. Most important, the Regius Professor was given no control over examinations or teaching; these were left to the colleges. Had he been given this power, Oxford might well have emerged with a system similar to the German professorial system. Instead, the preparation of undergraduates was the responsibility of the tutors, who organized the intercollegiate system of lectures, which was separate and rival to that of the professors.

At Cambridge, improvement of instruction in history moved more slowly. Beginning in 1870 Cambridge had examinations in history on the Oxford model, but it had fewer professors and tutors and fewer students in history. Only when Lord Rosebery appointed Lord Acton as Regius Professor of Modern History at Cambridge in 1895 did the discipline begin to achieve a status comparable to that at Oxford.[12]

Neither university offered seminar instruction in the techniques of historical research. Students themselves attempted to fill the gap, and under the leadership of an American, one Brearley, who had been to Germany, they organized a Historical Seminary at Oxford. It emphasized "practical" instruction like that offered in the seminars at German universities and in Monod's courses at Paris.

For historians, the great intellectual reviews dominated English periodical publishing in the nineteenth century. One general periodical was devoted exclusively to history, the *Transactions* of the Royal Historical Society, but it did not serve professional needs. Its most serious drawback was its essentially amateur approach. Nor did it make any attempt either to review or to list historical publications. Instead of writing for the *Transactions*, professional historians usually chose one of the national quarterlies. Periodicals like the *Edinburgh Review* and the *Quarterly Review* influenced opinion in Parliament, and writing for them established literary reputations. From the individual historian's point of view, they offered the further advantage of paying handsomely.[13]

From the profession's standpoint, the national reviews could not substitute for a scholarly historical periodical. Their content depended upon the editors' perceptions of their readers' interests, and clearly the editors did not detect any burning interest in history on the part of the general public. Such articles as the historians did write for them could not be scholarly in professional terms. Articles in reviews, for example, practically never carried footnotes, a *sine qua non* of scholarship. The largest contribution of the national reviews to the historians was the publication of reviews of many English historical works and even of the more significant foreign works.[14]

One exception for a brief period among the national reviews was the *North British Review*. A group of Catholics led by Lord Acton purchased it in 1869, primarily to replace the defunct *Rambler,* which had expressed the Catholic viewpoint. Thanks to Acton, it also published a number of worthwhile articles on history, beginning with his own classic on the Massacre of St. Bartholomew, and added an extensive review section.[15] Regrettably for the historian, the *North British Review* did not long survive in this guise.

Theoretical thinking by British historians was limited. To the extent they addressed such issues, they tended to concern themselves with theories of history rather than those dealing with historical knowledge. The Whig theory of history, known for its concomitant assumption of "progress," for example, antedated the establishment of the *EHR*. The founders of the *EHR* substituted for a common philosophy of history a commitment to documentary research, a desire to professionalize history, and shared Liberal politics.

Historical scholarship was considerably more institutionalized in the United States when the *AHR* was founded than it was in either France or England when the *RH* and the *EHR* were established. The *AHR* consequently could serve to coordinate rather than to initiate. Its structural role, therefore, was more analogous to that of the *HZ* than to that of either of the two more recent European journals.

The academic context of history in the United States resembles the German more than either the French or the English situation.[16] American historians had, in fact, consciously adopted the German pattern, and many had studied in that country. In 1895 no one center of historical study existed, but many universities maintained history departments. Several offered graduate instruction, usually including seminars, and awarded Ph.D.'s in history. The process of internal differentiation had begun: several universities not only had professors of history, but professors of American history as well.

American historians had in addition something no other country had: a national organization directed by a professional historian devoted to the advancement of history. Founded in 1884, the American Historical Association (AHA) was one of a number of professional societies that were begun in the late nineteenth century in the United States. Its energetic secretary, Herbert Baxter Adams, professor of history at Johns Hopkins, made it the focal point of American historical activities. In it, historians developed the habit of working together.

Before the *AHR*, the American publishing environment offered several alternatives to historians. The professional historians who founded it had contributed scholarly articles to the general reviews published by universities or other institutions of higher education. George Burton Adams, for example, had written on the feudal system in the *Andover Review*[17] and on Petrarch in the *Yale Review.*[18] Some historians had also contributed to the scholarly periodicals of other disciplines, such as Harry Pratt Judson in the *American Journal of Sociology*[19] and Albert Bushnell Hart in the *Quarterly Journal of Economics.*[20] Most frequently, their articles appeared in the more popular magazines and reviews like the *Nation* and the *North American Review.*[21]

Two periodicals that published their articles fit none of these categories. One was the *Chautauquan,* the periodical of the Chautauqua Literary and Scientific Circle, a notable cultural force in late-nineteenth-century America. A uniquely American institution, the Chautauqua, as it was familiarly known, provided rural America with both entertainment and education through its traveling lectures and shows. It also organized self-study programs that upon completion awarded diplomas. Most of the articles in the *Chautauquan* by the founders of the *AHR* were primarily educational and written for the section "Required Reading." The second periodical was the *Magazine of American History,* designed primarily for the amateur, but which nonetheless carried several articles by *AHR* founders. Jameson, for instance, contributed two fine, scholarly articles: one on the land system of Long Island, the other on municipal government in New York City.[22]

Analyzing the pre-*AHR* articles of its founders reveals why they were so convinced of the need for a new journal. The articles in the popular magazines and reviews were on "relevant" topics because they needed to appeal to a mass audience and usually lacked footnotes. Often they were superficial because they covered such large themes. Those in the scholarly journals of other disciplines or in the university reviews could be the kind of article the historian wanted to write, but they would rarely reach the reader for whom they were written. No one periodical among those that existed served to any appreciable extent the professional historians' needs; they were left with no alternative but to start their own.

Their well-established circumstances placed them in a relatively strong position to do so, and their strength was buttressed by a vigorous sense of purpose. Professional American historians were noticeably uninterested in theory. In their handbooks on historical methodology, they did not include the theoretical sections common in the European counterparts.[23] The professional historians of the generation who founded the *AHR* had ceased to search like their positivistic predecessors for the laws of history.[24] Instead, they tended to a rigid factualism that emphasized the criticism of documents and accumulation of facts.[25]

In place of a theory that could inspire and coordinate their work in the way historicism did for the German historians of the *HZ,* they shared a belief in their role. They believed that historical scholarship could vitally contribute to the consolidation of American culture as well as the establishment of authority in American intellectual life. The advancement of professional history was part of the movement, but by the end of the century professional historians were reaching beyond the boundaries of their own immediate concerns. Through the AHA, they attempted to provide leadership to the amateur historical groups. They concerned themselves with the teaching of history in secondary schools. More directly in their own interests, they brought pressure on the government to care for its vast archival treasures. The AHA was part of this general activity. It was a concrete solution to a perceived problem in the best pragmatic American tradition.[26]

The Founders of the New Journals

The founders of the *RH*, *EHR*, and *AHR* show many strong similarities when considered collectively. Invariably, they were historians whose professional outlook set them apart from most of their colleagues. They accepted the critical methods of historical scholarship, usually combining it with a concern to improve the quality of education in the field. Most were middle class; history was providing them with a living as well as an interest.

Although Gustave Fagniez collaborated in establishing the *RH* and was coeditor during its early years, the journal really had only one founder, Gabriel Monod. By all accounts, it was he who provided the leadership and determined its character. When Fagniez departed, no perceptible change occurred in the journal's outlook or form. Monod was very much the new model historian. He had received part of his training in Germany, where he had studied under Jaffé at Berlin and under Waitz at Göttingen. His family background was cosmopolitan; his grandfather Monod had served as minister of the French church in Copenhagen, and his wife was Olga Herzen, daughter of the Russian revolutionary Alexander Herzen. He was a Protestant and during his student days had lived with Edmond de Pressensé, a leader of French liberal Protestantism. Fagniez, on the other hand, was a paleographer who had been trained at the École des Chartes and was a Catholic.[27]

Although the *RH* was clearly Monod's, he had taken the precaution before its first issue to obtain a promise of assistance from most of the leading intellectuals who were interested in history. These included twenty-four professors of higher education, twelve archivists, and seven librarians. Among them were Victor Duruy, Fustel de Coulanges, Robert, Comte de Lasteyrie, Ernest Lavisse, Gaston Paris, Henri Taine, and P. Vidal de Lablache—an impressive group constituting most of the French historical establishment.[28] Its comprehensiveness is striking. Monod included not only Duruy, Lavisse, and Paris, his allies in educational reform, but also leading exponents of the nonprofessional, literary tradition, Fustel de Coulanges and Taine.

The founders of the *EHR* were a somewhat more cohesive group. The immediate event that led to the founding was a dinner party given by James Bryce in July 1885. On July 8 he sent an invitation to Lord Acton: "It is proposed to hold a small gathering of friends of the proposed Historical Review to talk over plans and the ways and means thereto, at 35 Bryanston Square next Wednesday at 7:45. Will you come and dine with me then? Creighton, York Powell, and four or five others will I hope appear and I greatly hope you may be able."[29] Bryce, Mandell Creighton, who became the *EHR*'s first editor, and Lord Acton were the principal organizers of this 1885 effort, but they received either active help or benevolent approval from most of the other contemporary English historians, like Freeman, Dean Church, A. W. Ward, and York Powell.

Of the three sets of founders, the English group is the least professionalized. No clear distinction between amateurs and professionals existed in England comparable to the obvious difference that is apparent in France, Germany, and the United States. In those three countries, the scholarly historical periodical founders were always professional historians. The amateur tradition in scholarship retained its strength longer in Britain than in other leading industrial nations, and the historians who founded the *EHR* remained a part of that tradition. Most lacked advanced professional training. Usually history was an avocation rather than a full-time occupation. E. A. Freeman is typical. A country gentleman for most of his life, he became Regius Professor of Modern History at Oxford only eight years before his death.[30]

The founders of the *AHR*, in contrast to those of the *EHR*, were all university professors, a reflection of the closer tie of historical scholarship to academic institutions in the United States. No one of the group can really be viewed as a leader, although George Burton Adams, of Yale, acted as a kind of coordinator. Adams had heard that

H. Morse Stephens and Moses Coit Tyler, at Cornell, were planning for a scholarly historical periodical. Ephraim Emerton and Albert Bushnell Hart, at Harvard, were doing the same. He persuaded them to give up their independent plans and to work together on one journal, arguing that the profession could not hope to maintain two similar efforts. To broaden the base of support and to ensure that the journal would represent the whole profession, Adams also brought in historians from other leading American universities, such as John Franklin Jameson, of Brown, John Bach McMaster, of the University of Pennsylvania, and William H. Coffin, of Princeton. Adams was reconstituting essentially the same group of men who had just succeeded in shifting the focus of the AHA to give more attention to the concerns of professional historians.[31]

As a group, the founders of the *AHR* were remarkably homogeneous. They were of the same generation; all had been born during the decade of the 1850s except Tyler, who was born in 1835, and Harry Pratt Judson, who missed the decade by ten days. With few exceptions, they were of New England stock and had middle-class backgrounds. These two characteristics distinguish them from their contemporary nonprofessional colleagues, who tended to be patrician and whose origins were not confined to New England. Most of the founders of the *AHR* had studied in Germany.

The founders of a scholarly historical periodical are instrumental in determining its character. By their explicit statements and through their publications in it, they establish its persona. As the years pass, the journal may change in response to new conditions or have change imposed upon it, but usually it remains close to what its founders intended it to be, at least in broad conception. The *RH, EHR,* and *AHR* are good examples of this relative stability.

The Scope of the New Journals

In theory, the three journals took all history as their province, although the *RH* qualified that by stating it was "principally dedicated" to European history from A.D. 395 to 1815.[32] Their practice has not proved to be as all-embracing as their policies. With rare exceptions, the number of articles on France in any given volume of the *RH* or on England in one of the *EHR* is larger than all the rest together. When

Mandell Creighton, first editor of the *EHR*, remarked, "I am glad to see that our range of subjects keeps on increasing: we are less purely national than any of the continental Reviews. I think we escape the charge of insularity," he was decidedly premature.[33]

The *AHR* is a partial exception to dominance by the history of the journal's own nation. From the beginning, its articles have been fairly evenly divided between Europe and America, although the United States receives a somewhat larger share. Two factors are primarily responsible for this major difference in orientation. The first is the cultural attitude of Americans, the majority of whom trace their ethnic origins to Europe. This built-in predisposition was reinforced by insecurity, which endowed the products of European culture, whether fashion or literature, with innate superiority until well into the twentieth century. In the historians' case, their craft had been defined by Germans who naturally worked on European subjects. Most of the founders of the *AHR* were European historians. The second factor responsible for the difference in geographical emphasis is the *Mississippi Valley Historical Review (MVHR)*, now the *Journal of American History*. Neither France nor England has a major historical journal devoted exclusively to national history.

Because they concentrate so heavily upon European and, in the case of the *AHR*, upon European and American history, the *RH, EHR,* and *AHR* give little space to vast areas of the globe. The *AHR* has publicly acknowledged that it is "for the most part a journal of American and modern European history."[34] The only area that is an exception to the general neglect, and a minor one at that, is the Mediterranean, about which all three journals have regularly published a small number of articles. The Mediterranean has undoubtedly received this attention because it was the birthplace of European civilization and because the classics dominated both European and American education until recently. Other areas of the world have not been so fortunate and only lately have they achieved even token historiographical recognition, as reflected in these supposedly "general" journals. The *RH* and especially the *AHR* seem to be making an effort to include the newer areas of interest.

Geographical distribution of articles is a perennial source of complaint. Every historian seems to feel that his or her field of interest is neglected: "From devotees of European history comes the complaint that too much attention is given to American history; from the devotees of American history the exact reverse."[35] Andrew McLaughlin, editor of the *AHR* from 1901 to 1905, answered a complaint about the lack of French history with a statement indicating that the journal needed to reflect the interests of its readers: "But we must remember that after all this is an American historical review and it is simply impossible for us to pay such attention as is demanded to American and English history and leave us very much space for any other particular field of European history."[36]

Topically, the three journals remain relatively traditional. Political history is dominant in all three. The *EHR* is almost exclusively devoted to political and diplomatic history. Both the *RH* and the *AHR* also have many diplomatic articles, although articles on economic and social history in the *AHR* are more numerous than those on diplomatic history. In addition, the *RH* has demonstrated a consistent interest in religious history that is not shared by the two others. Of the three, the *AHR* has the widest range and best balance. It is also alone in its regular inclusion of historiographical articles; only recently have they begun to appear regularly in the *RH*, and they are a rarity in the *EHR*.

Editorial Policy: Articles

When these journals began, the scholarly article as a format was in its infancy. It evolved in their pages. The average number of citations, for example, and those to primary printed sources and to manuscript sources increased. These journals also helped to define the proper length of an article, thereby clarifying its relationship to books. The length of articles in the *EHR* and the *AHR* has remained relatively constant, averaging between eighteen and twenty pages, but in the *RH* articles were at first very long, averaging as many as forty-seven pages, and have gradually become shorter.

Those fortunate enough to have articles accepted by one of these journals share a number of characteristics, although the inadequate biographical information available on the French and English contributors makes any very complete picture difficult. Almost all are university faculty; only the very early volumes of the *AHR* and *EHR* have more than an occasional nonacademic. Each journal consists almost exclusively of contributions from its own nationals, although the *EHR* of recent years seems to be acquiring a wider representation of foreigners. Most of them are American and Commonwealth historians who work in the area of British history, undoubtedly attracted to the *EHR* because it devotes so much space to that field.

The contributors to the *AHR* have not changed much over the years. Fluctuations occur in the proportion of tenured professors, but for the most part this group has dominated from the beginning. Almost all contributors hold the doctorate. Conclusions about contributors to the *EHR* and *RH* must be much more tentative because of the large number who cannot be fully identified. In age and position, the contributors to the *RH* seem to follow the pattern established by the *HZ;* articles have increasingly been written by well-established members of the profession. The contributors to the *EHR*, on the other hand, seem to be predominantly lecturers, a status that can denote a fair degree of seniority, but which at its highest is lower than professor. They have held the doctorate as a matter of course only since the early 1960s, a reflection of the relatively recent supremacy of that degree in England. The information available about the French contributors' education is too scanty to permit generalization.

The three journals have defined the scholarly historical periodical for their respective countries and have borne the major responsibility for establishing standards. They have done so through what they published and through what they left unpublished.

Perhaps because it is directly responsible to the AHA and therefore to American historians, the *AHR* has regularly attempted to state its editorial policy. These declarations set forth scholarly criteria and explain the particular needs of the journal. What it has published has not always met the printed standards, but they remain important as an ideal.

The preliminary circular announcing the creation of the *AHR* in 1895 provided the first policy statement on articles. It said, "The three criteria for contributions to the *Review* are: that they shall be fresh and original in treatment; that they shall be the result of accurate scholarship; and that they shall have distinct literary merit. Articles which fulfill these conditions will be welcomed on any field of history."[37] These criteria are the kind that almost any scholarly journal advocates. Later policy statements of the *AHR* have added specifics to these generalities, but have not fundamentally altered them.

Succeeding generations have restated the standards. In his April

1955 report, Boyd Shafer, the managing editor, declared: "What we need are finely written articles with sweep, vision, perspective, articles which go beyond the bare bones, the details, and show the readers how the information presented fits into the field of history, how it adds to our knowledge and how it changes previous interpretations."[38] Six months later, he amplified this. The *AHR* had officially had an editorial policy since 1939, when it was examined by the Committee of Ten, under the direction of Professor John Hicks. Shafer printed the committee's statement: "To publish only such articles as throw light upon what had been done before, or suggest new and fruitful fields of historical study and advance significant new historical interpretations." He also added more specific guidance:

> Acceptance for publication comes most often when sound research into primary sources brings new or changed interpretations and when the results of this research are couched in clear and precise English. At this time the *Review* particularly welcomes essays which attempt to answer for specific fields the questions, "Where have we been, where are we now and what are the obstacles facing us?" The chances for acceptance for this or any kind of essay will be considerably enhanced if the author has constantly in mind the question "Will the reader want to turn the page?"[39]

Another statement, in 1970, did not really differ from its predecessors. Shafer, or indeed any previous editor, could not have argued with the declaration that the *AHR* sought "articles that are intelligently conceived, carefully researched, properly documented, and clearly and effectively presented."[40] Editorial correspondence shows that narrow, technical articles, often poorly written, were most frequently submitted. The 1970 statement made clear that the journal was not at all opposed to the scholarly article per se:

> The true scholarly article—confined to a carefully argued thesis, complete in itself, provocative in interpretation, and productive of further work by others—need not be parochial; it can have an appeal outside the specialty with which its author is primarily identified. It may, for example, cut across the lines of specialties or even of disciplines; even though addressed to a subject that is at first sight highly specialized, it may evoke or suggest parallels

or comparisons with other countries, cultures, or eras; or it may provide new confirmation or criticism of broad themes that are or should be in the awareness of all serious historians. It is in such articles, not in communications addressed by specialists only to fellow specialists, that the editors of the *AHR* are interested.[41]

The editor provided a few recent examples of the kind of scholarly article he sought: one on the Moriscos that he considered a remarkable example of historical detective work, one on Enlightened government in Corsica that was really a laboratory example of institutional reform, and one on Southern violence that dealt with a matter of both historical and contemporary concern and used with profit hypotheses and techniques of scholars in other fields of the social sciences. The statement then turned to the kind of article that was unacceptable because "it may be more convincing to indicate certain types of articles that appear regularly in the morning's mail and that, in accordance with the general policy outlined above, are as regularly returned."[42] The "regularly returned" category included detailed accounts of minor diplomatic transactions, local history articles lacking some broad analytical thesis, biographical studies of the careers of second rank or lesser figures, summaries of books about to be published or unrevised chapters from dissertations or books, most pieces on methodology per se, and routine articles summarizing the state of a particular scholarly debate.[43]

Neither the *RH* nor the *EHR* formulated any such policy statements, probably expecting their intentions to be clear from the kinds of articles they published. That they had a policy is unquestionable. Examination of editorial correspondence, especially letters of rejection, confirms this conclusion for the *EHR*.

Mandell Creighton was disappointed with the quality of the second number of the *EHR*, dismissing the articles as unimportant. He had difficulty with long-winded authors; one he cut down considerably, another expressed his opinions only "at leisure." Probably Creighton would have described these articles as "indifferent," the type he found to his dismay to be the most numerous and most perplexing of those offered to him.[44]

An examination of the articles in the second number reveals some of the reasons they fell short of Creighton's standards. Davidson's on the growth of plebeian privilege in Rome[45] Creighton found the most satisfactory and used it as his lead article. It is a straightforward account covering a fairly broad time period of political history, supported by only a few footnotes. The second article[46] is a military account of King Alfred in the year 871, replete with thirty-seven citations to primary sources. In the next, Gairdner addresses the question of Amy Robsart's death[47] and takes twenty-four pages, mainly to defend Queen Elizabeth. It is the only article of the group to cite manuscript sources. Creighton considered an article on Paris under the last Valois kings[48] merely an attempt to illustrate the social life of Paris, which he included in an effort to please the general reader. The emphasis is on geography and the article does not appear to be appropriate for a historical periodical with scholarly pretensions. It used sources, but they cannot be categorized in any way. An article on Irish woolen manufacturers is almost a part of contemporary political debate.[49] Its author's intention is the exculpation of the British and his thesis is that their repressive legislation was not anti-Irish in intent. The last article is short, again a piece of political history, chiefly the summary of a diary.[50]

Creighton's dissatisfaction is understandable. Certainly, none of these articles can be described as having the sweep and vision sought by Shafer; they do not go beyond the bare bones, and no effort is made to provide perspective. By modern standards, their documentation is poor; by contemporary standards unimpressive. The writing is undistinguished. In sum, they are pedestrian, but an editor cannot print articles he does not receive. As Jameson stated, "A stream can not rise higher than its source; with our best endeavors the level our journal can attain is to some degree conditioned by the actual facts of a world, a country, and a profession in which not everyone who has something to say can say it well."[51]

To a considerable extent, the quality of articles is directly related to their availability. Insufficient information is available to determine the general pattern of the *Revue historique,* but the two other journals, after an initial, brief period of shortage, have experienced ever-increasing inundation. Wartimes mark the only break in the flow.[52] Pessimism like Creighton's proved unfounded:

The great difficulty that I foresee is a lack of new and attractive subjects. Writers whose names are known have already said their say. Though they may display much erudition which may be useful to students I do not anticipate that they will open up new fields which may attract a larger public. Younger men with new subjects will probably not offer themselves at first. I shall be deluged with papers of old writers, which have been rejected by other Reviews, and which they have on hand.[53]

The *AHR* has published statistics, which are probably typical. The increase in articles submitted can be directly correlated with the number of advanced degrees in history. During World War II the number of articles, notes and suggestions, and documents offered annually remained stable at around 80. Afterward, the number began to rise: to 88 in 1947, 92 in 1949, and 95 in 1951. By 1955 it reached 147; and by 1964, the last year for which specific figures are available, more than 200 were submitted.[54]

During those same years, the number of articles printed remained static, ranging from 12 to 16 per year. The rate of acceptance, therefore, was steadily decreasing; in 1941 it was 18 percent, in 1964 it was 10 percent. In 1944 Guy Stanton Ford, the editor, cautioned, "No one should infer that it is hopeless to submit articles when so many are rejected."[55]

Selection from articles submitted is one of a journal's most important tasks because the choices determine its character and quality. Since the results can have so great an impact on the future of an individual, the process is also highly sensitive. Statements of editorial policy represent efforts to establish criteria, but ultimately the journals depend upon the personal judgment of the individuals who make the evaluations.

The editor is central to the decision-making process. During the early years of the *EHR* and in all probability of the *RH*, with the aid of an editorial assistant, he made all the decisions. The editor of the *AHR*, on the other hand, had from the beginning an editorial board, which he consulted for advice on particular articles. Nonetheless, the *AHR*'s editor acted then and still does as the principal arbiter because he can reject an article on his own authority without consultation if he chooses to do so; he can also choose the board members to be consulted.

A recent addition to the evaluation process, especially for American and Canadian scholarly historical periodicals, is the outside referee. As history has become increasingly specialized, the editor has more often turned to an expert in the subject of a particular article to obtain an assessment, even though the expert is not formally connected with the journal. Because the practice of the *AHR* is typical of North American scholarly historical periodicals, it has been studied in detail, using 1969 as an example. In its evaluation of submissions, as in so many other respects, it sets standards and serves as a model for other American scholarly historical journals.

Although the outside referee is now regularly employed by the *AHR*, his or her role remains limited. Of 193 articles rejected in 1969, only a quarter of them were read by outside referees, and in a number of those cases they were involved only because the editor wanted to relieve himself of some of the inevitable opprobrium of rejection. The editor nonetheless is still the single most important individual in determining which articles will be published; the 1969 editor, R. K. Webb, read and dismissed without further consultation 120, or 62 percent, of those rejected.

A comparison of the reasons for the different judges' negative decisions illustrates how general editorial policies are translated into action. The most usual reason was some variation on the theme that an article was inappropriate for the *AHR*. Nearly a third of the rejected articles were considered too narrow or too specialized for it, which as the publication of a broad-based organization wished to publish articles with wide appeal. Many others were not, in the editor's widely used phrase, the "major scholarly article" the *AHR* published; some were too slight, some not scholarly enough, some not historical. Others were not articles, but essays, notes, or speeches.

Approximately two-thirds of the articles were rejected because of some inadequacy in execution. Readers criticized them because they were not significant enough. They favored articles with a broad scope and sophisticated treatment; they expected them to do something new. Occasionally, an article was criticized because the research was inadequate. Quality of writing was also a concern to the readers; many historians still consider history a form of literature, and a few articles were judged poor because of style.

A larger number were described as logically flawed. Logical flaws included diffuseness of purpose, lack of balance, arbitrary categories, loose definitions, overly simplistic analysis, and insufficient development of the material. The tone of an article also concerned readers. Judgments in this area are highly subjective, but in almost all cases authors were criticized if they were not calmly judicious. Equally difficult was the problem of articles dealing with the work of AHA leaders. The editor felt strongly that the *AHR* should not publish articles attacking former, still-living presidents of the AHA and experienced some discomfort over an article criticizing the work of a member of the board of editors. Webb did not ask him to evaluate the article, but he did send it to him after acceptance and published his response in the same issue in which the article appeared.[56]

The evaluations of articles accepted by the *AHR* varied considerably. Praise was likely to be in such terms as "adds new dimension," "documentation thorough," "significant theme with contemporary relevance," "original," "stimulating," or "avoids special pleading." "Interesting" was a favorite. If an article was criticized as well as praised, it was usually because the reasoning was not clear or the writing poor.

The mature system that produced the 1969 decisions had been evolving since the *AHR*'s beginning. The grounds for rejecting an article have remained remarkably constant, although the language describing them has become more prosaic. Jameson, for example, turned down a distinguished medievalist's article because the question of the authorship of a medieval treatise "hardly subtends a sufficiently large arc on the horizon of our readers."[57] The most noticeable change is that procedures have become systematized, and the process of acceptance or rejection has become routine.

Recent editors of the *AHR* have made efforts to explain the system, although most historians seem to accept the way it operates. Occasionally, complaints have been made. Within the last few years, a minor tempest flared when the *AHR* rejected an article dealing with the work of a member of the board on the ground that it would offend. More typical was a letter from a disappointed would-be contributor in 1958 whose article had been turned down because it was too narrow although otherwise good. He contended that other articles in the July 1958 issue were just as narrow. He concluded, therefore, that his own article was either lacking in quality, which called into question the editor's integrity, or raised the possibility that the *AHR* existed to provide a publicity medium for friends of the powers that be, a private club with a passion for mutual congratulation.[58] Such accusations of favoritism occur periodically and, given human nature, are inevitable.

Acceptance of an article by the *RH, EHR,* or *AHR* is of considerable value to a historian's career. The *AHR,* for example, is the most frequently cited scholarly historical periodical according to the Journal Citation Reports of the *Social Sciences Citation Index (SSCI).* That it is also cited widely is confirmed whenever historians' sources are studied.[59] The journals in which citations to the *AHR* appeared in 1978 include many foreign journals and cover a wide disciplinary range.[60]

Because such prestige is attached to publication in the *AHR,* Webb felt compelled to declare that "the *AHR* does not stand at the top of a pyramid of scholarly prestige, automatically to be tried first by an ambitious author before he moves on to a 'lesser' journal."[61] Most American historians probably would not agree, and many do indeed first try the *AHR* and, if rejected, submit to other journals. Approximately half of the 193 articles rejected in 1969 were published elsewhere, in more specialized scholarly historical periodicals, interdisciplinary journals, scholarly periodicals in other disciplines, and reviews aimed at the intelligent general reader.

Book Reviews, Bibliographical Notices, and News Notes

Articles are the most important part of the *RH, EHR,* and *AHR,* but they are only one section. All three from their beginning have devoted a major portion of their space to book reviews. Each was begun because no medium existed that adequately and efficiently informed professional historians of what was appearing in their fields. The journals have experimented with different formats for this function, but the traditional book review has been retained, whatever else has been tried, and continues to occupy a significant place in all three.

An analysis of the book reviews in the three periodicals reveals a primary interest in monographs. They have also regularly reviewed printed original sources, but only in the *EHR* has this reached significant proportions at any time; nearly a third of the reviews in the 1896 volume were of sources. This interest has steadily diminished. The *AHR,* for instance, now has a section "Documents and Bibliographies," which lists printed primary sources, most of which receive only this listing. Nor has any other format regularly received attention. Few reviews of essential aids to historical research, bibliographies, and other reference materials are printed. In the *AHR*, they have at least been reviewed, but this remains a minor effort.

In most aspects of its book reviewing, the *AHR* differs from the other two journals. The average length of their reviews has remained fairly stable, but the *AHR*'s have steadily decreased in length. It alone has regularly expanded its book reviewing, to such an extent that this section of an issue seems to dominate it.

The relative breadth of reviewing is difficult to evaluate. An examination of recent volumes shows that the *RH* is undoubtedly the most international of the three journals; it reviews the highest proportion of books in languages other than its own. At times, the *RH* has even reviewed more English than French books. That the *EHR* is the most insular is equally clear. In spite of Creighton's early efforts to establish a policy of regular consideration of foreign books, it reviews the fewest in numbers and percentages. The *AHR*'s reviewing of foreign books, although its percentage figures do not compare with those of the *RH*, cannot be dismissed as insignificant. It reviewed more French books than the *RH* in the most recent volumes analyzed, as well as large numbers of German, Russian, and Italian books. It is the only one that seems to be increasing its attention to German books.

The geographical distribution of reviews also shows the *EHR* to be the most insular. Reviews of books on some aspect of English history have consistently dominated, both in numbers and percentages. The *EHR*'s second interest has with equal consistency been the Mediterranean region. The pattern in the *RH* is less clear; its concentration on French history is proportionately less, but it does emphasize Western Europe, reviewing few books that do not deal with that area. The great majority of *AHR* reviews, like its articles, are fairly evenly divided between United States and Western European history; to the extent that a preference prevails, it is for European history. The considerable attention the journal gives to the rest of the world distinguishes it from its companions. Although not always true, this has been a definite feature since the early 1960s.

The book review section has produced most of the editors' difficulties. Before the journals established their reputations, they had trouble getting books from publishers. During wartimes, foreign books have been nearly impossible to obtain. Nor have competent reviewers always been easy to find. Some of the most eminent scholars, like Arthur Schlesinger, Sr., and Frederick Merk, have simply refused to review. Often another journal that emphasizes currency, like the *Times* or the *Saturday Review,* approaches the most distinguished and obvious potential reviewers first.[62]

In the selection of reviewers, European and American practices differ in important respects. It is considered proper in Europe to send an unsolicited review to a journal. Often a European editor will ask an author to suggest a reviewer. *AHR* editors, on the other hand, have never accepted unsolicited reviews and have completely excluded the author from the process. All the journals have felt that involvement with an author, personal or professional, disqualified a person from reviewing his book.

After a reviewer has been selected, many pitfalls still lie ahead. The worst is procrastination. A 1935 comment succinctly summarizes the problem: "There is, it is true, a disconcerting number of those who after consenting to review books, and receiving the volume, seem to take no further thought of the matter, sometimes being impervious to successive appeals."[63] Not all excuses have the charming simplicity of the errant Mr. Caldwell's: "Mr. Caldwell has gone trout fishing and so will not be back in time to prepare the review for the October number of the Historical Review."[64]

A published review can also produce editorial headaches. An unfavorable review of James Schouler's *Constitutional Studies*[65] was the first among many for the editor of the *AHR*. Schouler threatened a libel suit.[66] Periodically, an author or *amicus auctoris* will protest, and it is undeniably true that reviews are occasionally unfair and reviewers vindictive. Because all *AHR* editors have granted reviewers a free hand and refused to censor unless a statement is libelous, only when a reviewer has shown himself to be dishonorable in print will he be disqualified from further reviewing.[67]

Another source of difficulty is the quality of the review. The assumption behind reviews is that the reader needs guidance. The *AHR* was pleased that librarians quickly came to depend upon its reviews.[68] One librarian wanted to place a standing order for all the books the *AHR* reviewed.[69] Space limitations often prevented the probing evaluations desired;[70] and, even when space permitted, the reviewer might not take advantage of the opportunity. Jameson felt that the book reviews in the *AHR* were inferior to those in European scholarly journals. In his opinion, qualified reviewers were too few, proper acquaintance with archival resources was lacking, and too much politeness prevailed. He described the politeness as

> the well-known excess of our national amiability, heightened by the friendly and truly fraternal feelings which frequent meetings in the sessions of the American Historical Association and frequent participation in common tasks for its service, have engendered. It is a beautiful trait, rooted in benign conditions of social development, but it stands in the way of criticism.[71]

Articles and reviews have comprised the bulk of the journals since they were established, but all three have had other regular sections. All began with approximately the same parts: articles; short articles, usually called notes; printed documents; some kind of listing of the contents of current periodicals; and book reviews. Both the *RH* and the *AHR*, but not the *EHR*, also included news sections. All three have retained articles and book reviews, but the other sections have evolved differently.

The *RH* now has articles, reviews, a "Bulletin Historique," a "Chronique," and a list of articles in journals. Quite early, the "Bulletin Historique" ceased to consist of news reports and became a series of bibliographical essays. At first, these essays treated the historical research being done in individual countries, but, as historians specialized, they gradually became more topical, like the one in 1926 on the historiography of the French Revolution. Because of this change in character, it was necessary to recreate a news section, hence the "Chronique." "Mélanges," originally the documents section, later documents and short articles, finally disappeared in 1966 and was replaced by additional articles. The bibliographical component has also altered. Book reviewing was expanded when "Notes Bibliographiques," or short notices, were added before the First World War.

The *EHR* has done little experimenting. It remains, for example, the only one of the three journals to retain a documents section. It did drop the notices of articles in other periodicals for a period early in the century, but reinstated them in volume 39 (1924). In organization, volume 91 of the *EHR* is little different from volume 1.

The *AHR* began, except for its news section, with the same format as the *EHR*: "Articles," "Documents," and "Reviews of Books." It contained no separate listing of periodicals, but many were men-

tioned in its news section. The *AHR* has been the most experimental
of the major journals, although its readers have resisted almost any
change. Shafer at one point considered reducing the list of articles,
only to discover on questioning his colleagues that they really used
them.[72] Certainly in this area changes are more apparent than real.
Periodical articles have been listed from the beginning; they appeared
combined with other news under the heading "Notes and News"
until volume 42, with other publications in "Other Recent Publications" from volume 42 to 75, and since volume 75 in their own pamphlet "Recently Published Articles." More substantive changes include the cessation of the documents section in the late 1940s. The
quantity of documents had simply become too large to make it feasible,[73] and emphasis in research had shifted from a few significant
documents to massive collections. The news section disappeared in
the late 1960s, when a separate newsletter was begun. It had been a
source of perennial difficulties; because of the problem in obtaining
news from historians, it tended to concentrate on association news.

All these changes were fairly straightforward, some the recognition
of changes in the scholarly world, others perhaps the desire of editors
to leave their marks on the journals. The only real uncertainty has
been over the relationship of short notices to full-fledged book reviews. In the *RH*, the difference seems to be exclusively length. The
EHR made a distinction in that foreign books more often received
short notices. The *EHR* was also unusual because full book reviews
became a small proportion of the total reviewing effort. The *AHR*, like
the *RH*, made a distinction only in length. After it combined the two,
retaining a length distinction between more important and less
important books, it examined its total reviewing. It announced that a
decrease in middle-sized reviews (400–500 words) and an increase in
review articles could be expected.[74] Ten years later, after some rear-
rangement and renaming of sections and cutting back on categories
like festschriften, already seldom reviewed, the editors were forced to
confront the problem more directly. They decided to list rather than to
review some monographs and specialized works if, either because of
subject matter or contribution to historical knowledge, they were
marginal to the profession.[75]

These changes in composition have been accompanied by changes
in physical format. The *RH* became a quarterly instead of a bimonthly

after the Second World War. The *EHR* has remained a quarterly, and the *AHR* recently began to publish five times a year in place of four. All three have increased substantially in size because more words have been printed per page and thinner paper is now used.

The need for space forced the *AHR* to use larger pages and increase the publication frequency. Although all three journals, indeed all scholarly historical journals, have experienced the pressure caused by the publishing explosion and consequent increased reviews, the *AHR* has suffered most acutely. It began as the most truly comprehensive journal and it has retained that commitment. In 1955 Shafer proclaimed that the *AHR* had reached its limits in physical size.[76] His declaration did not stop further growth, and in the late 1960s the situation became critical. Introduced in 1971, the larger page, double-columned book reviews, narrow margins, perfect binding, and offset printing temporarily eased space and cost problems, but, within a few years, the gains had been lost as the publishing explosion continued.[77] Only within the last five years has historical publishing leveled off, though this has not reduced pressure because the *AHR* has reviewed a higher proportion of books submitted.[78]

Focus: Professional or General?

The prominence of book reviews and the great concern for them in the three journals is evidence of their scholarly character. The early editors recognized the significance of book reviews, their special importance to the professional historian, and their key role in the journals. Creighton badgered his publisher to help him get foreign books because English historians most needed information about them.[79] Foreign books continued to be a problem throughout his editorship, but he never ceased his efforts to improve their coverage.[80] Jameson faced the issue even more directly; he instructed reviewers not to hesitate to write for the specialist rather than the general reader.[81]

By such decisions, the early editors were making a choice between scholarship and popularity. In its first issue, the *EHR* posed the question directly: "Will the Historical Review address itself to professed and, so to speak, professional students of history, or to the person called the 'general reader'?"[82] Asking the question did not answer it, and the journals tried in fact to avoid doing so. Only with experience did it become apparent that the interests of the two groups were irreconcilable.

The *RH*'s definition of its purpose assumed that it would be read to some extent by nonscholars as well as scholars. Monod declared in his introduction that the study of France's past, which he expected to be the largest share of the *RH*'s task, had a national importance. Through history, as disseminated by the *RH*, the French could rediscover their national unity.[83] This goal was inspired both by the German example of the *HZ* and the positivist interest in educating the "homme du monde."[84]

Monod may have made some effort to appeal to the "homme du monde," but the journal shows little evidence of it. The articles do not seem to have been selected with any concern for their general interest, nor are there any sections that seem designed especially for the nonscholar. Probably Monod hoped they would find the *RH* of interest as it was. It existed primarily to serve the needs of the scholar.

The *EHR* made more direct attempts to attract the general reader. Creighton was pleased with the article in the first number by Lord Granville, the former foreign secretary, because it "will be new and will attract the 'general reader' of whom Bryce is so fond."[85] Within a year, it was clear that the general reader was not taking much interest in the *EHR*. Circulation remained at about six hundred, scarcely enough in Creighton's opinion, although he had never been sanguine enough to expect more than a thousand.[86] At about this time, hoping to reverse the trend, he persuaded Gladstone to write an article for the *EHR*. Unfortunately, the article, on the years 1852–60 and Greville's journals, made no appreciable difference in sales.

Creighton was forced to recognize, as J. R. Green had earlier when planning a historical journal that never materialized,[87] that "the student and the general reader are hard to combine." Creighton saw the conflict most clearly in the book review section: "The student wants to know about foreign books, the general reader has no interest in them at all."[88] The divergence was, however, more fundamental, and the *EHR* somewhat reluctantly realized that the general reader was a mirage.

Although the *AHR* made no serious effort to attract the nonscholar, some evidence exists that its founders shared the *EHR*'s illusions. The introduction speaks of the daily enlargement of the reading public;[89]

clearly the *AHR* hoped to achieve a fairly wide readership. The second editor, McLaughlin, rejected an article on the ground that it was "almost too technical and limited in scope" because the *AHR* had plenty of articles on hand that would be more apt to interest its average reader.[90] He did this in 1901, when the low circulation was causing anxiety. The journal had just been reorganized after financial problems nearly forced it to cease publication. As editor, McLaughlin was forced to bear in mind the average reader while still serving advanced scholars.[91]

The leaders of the *AHR* recognized that, although they wished the journal to serve a wide readership, it was not in fact doing so. Because leading American historians felt a responsibility for history as a whole, they became involved with the *History Teacher's Magazine*. This commercial venture, designed to serve teachers, was established in 1909. When it encountered financial trouble almost immediately, its publisher turned to Jameson for help. At its November 26, 1910, meeting, the board of editors of the *AHR* went on record that "there appears to be some need or possibly some demand in the Association for the publication of a more popular journal which would be interesting to general readers of history and useful to teachers."[92] The board then voted it $600 immediately, and Jameson raised an additional $600 for it.[93]

Challenges to the Leadership of the *RH*, *EHR*, and *AHR*

Although historians now recognize that total objectivity is impossible, when the *RH*, *EHR*, and *AHR* were founded it was considered a prerequisite to scholarship. In keeping with their scholarly orientation, all three journals duly began by abjuring prejudice. Subsequent events have made these statements something of a mockery.

The *RH* declared it intended to remain independent of all political and religious opinions[94] and then went on to become noted until the First World War as the Protestant and Republican scholarly historical periodical in France.[95] This predisposition served it well because the Republic eventually triumphed over its enemies, and, although anticlericalism grew, it was directed against the Roman Catholic Church rather than against Protestants. The *RH*'s rival, the *RQH*, was undoubtedly weakened by just these trends. The *EHR* advertised a similar intention of avoiding political and religious questions[96] and largely succeeded in doing so. The *AHR's* desire for impartiality extended beyond politics and religion: "[The *AHR*] can in no sense be an organ of any school, locality or clique."[97]

Historiographical bias has influenced the structural roles of these periodicals in a way that political and religious bias did not. The kind of scientific history to which all three journals dedicated themselves was itself an organizing principle. Its adherents, although they did not realize it, constituted a school. It was the dominant school for so long that its members found it easy to believe that all historians accepted it, but gradually other schools emerged and founded scholarly historical periodicals to publish their viewpoints. The *RH* and *EHR* were left behind, monuments to late-nineteenth-century views. The *AHR*, by making a concerted effort, managed to avoid that fate, although it remains relatively traditional. The *RH* has recently shown signs of trying to change.

Their rigidity and inhospitability to new areas of history and new interpretative schools have cost the *RH* and *EHR* the unquestioned supremacy they so long enjoyed. In many ways, they have been replaced as the leading scholarly historical periodicals of their countries, the *RH* by the *Annales: Économies, Sociétés, Civilisations* and the *EHR* by *Past and Present*. No circulation figures for the *RH* are available, but for the English journals they strongly suggest the supplanting of the *EHR*. Its circulation hovers around 3,000; that of *Past and Present*, around 4,500. Another symptom is that major disputes in English history, like those over the economic position of the gentry or the origins of World War II, have not taken place in the *EHR*.[98] Both lack that indefinable aura of excitement which characterizes the younger journals.

The *Annales* is probably the single most important scholarly historical periodical currently published. It is the only one from which a school of historians derives its name, the Annales school. The school and the journal have been immensely influential. Other historians look to them, and the *Annales* phenomenon has been so newsworthy that the popular media have reported it.[99] The *Annales* has even spawned an English language imitation, *Review, A Journal of the Fernand Braudel Center for the Study of Economies, Historical Systems, and Civilizations*, quite aside from those journals it has influenced strongly, like *Past and Present* and *Quaderni Storici*.

The *Annales* was founded in 1929 by two French historians, Lucien Febvre and Marc Bloch. Their location at that time at the University of Strasbourg is significant because Strasbourg is not Paris. The journal was conceived as an attack on establishment history, embodied in the École des Chartes. Its present editor, Jacques Revel, calls this its "black legend": ". . . a journal which, in its early years, was combative and badgering, and which defined its role as jostling a university system whose rules and customs were archaic."[100] It is no accident that one section of the periodical is entitled "Debats et Combats." In this tradition of combativeness, the *Annales* has found a source of continuous renewal, though that may now be changing.[101]

The *Annales* was not conceived only as a negative force; it also had a positive mission. This Revel has named its "golden legend." More than almost any other journal, the *Annales* has had intellectual unity. It traces this to the debate within French historiography over the nature of history and in particular to an article by François Simiand that was published in 1903 in the *Revue de Synthèse*. This article influenced the thought of individuals associated with the *Annales* and provided a theoretical matrix. Simiand took issue with the prevailing positivist school of history, which defined the task of the historian as the establishment of facts with as much certainty as possible. These facts already possessed a meaning, and to recreate the original reality was all that was necessary. Simiand substituted a long-term approach. The isolated fact meant nothing; it must be inserted in a series so that patterns could be identified. By definition, research would be comparative.[102] Simiand's article also placed history firmly at the heart of the social sciences. He believed that neither the object of study nor the methods of investigation divided the social sciences. The *Annales* was dedicated to the task of unifying the social sciences by empirical means.[103]

As the social sciences have changed, the *Annales* has changed. As Febvre expressed it: "The *Annales* change because everything around them changes: men, things, in a word, the world."[104] The unifying concept is no longer methodology but the object of study, man.

The *Annales* has been committed explicitly to economic and social history throughout its various name changes: *Annales d'histoire économique et sociale*, *Annales d'histoire sociale*, and *Annales: Économies, Sociétés, Civilisations*. Its orientation grew partially out of rejection of political history, the dominant interest of its historiographical opponents, partially from a belief in the greater importance of economic and social history. Content analysis makes clear that the dominance of economic and social history has been close to absolute; an occasional article on political history has crept in during the last fifteen years, usually via anthropological emphasis on institutions. Recently, attention has shifted to include cultural systems.[105]

During its early years, the *Annales* exhibited typical concentration on its own country and neighbors and on a few time periods. This has changed since the mid-1950s, when Braudel became editor. The *Annales* exhibits one of the most widely dispersed geographical and chronological profiles of the journals analyzed. This phenomenon is undoubtedly related to the fact that a high proportion of its contributors are foreigners. The *Annales* has sought to be truly international, a goal shared by most of those it has influenced. As the *Review* explained it: "We hope to make our journal a force that will reflect the true diversity of contemporary world scholarship."[106] The contributors to the *Annales* are also noteworthy for the number of women represented in recent volumes and for the number of dual-author articles. A theoretical conviction of the value of collaboration, deriving from its methodological interdisciplinarity, is more than a pious hope.

Over the years, the *Annales* has lost its revolutionary character and become an institution. It is now a publication of the VIe section of the École Pratique des Hautes Études, supported by the government. Its extraordinary success is apparent in such minor ways as steady growth in size,[107] but more importantly in its impact on historical scholarship. Simply enumerating the journals it has influenced demonstrates that this impact has reached far beyond France.

Like the *Annales*, *Past and Present* began as a journal that refused to conform to the historical establishment. Its founders, intellectual Marxists, began it in 1951 in the hope of reestablishing the common front of progressive historians that had existed in the 1930s. The introduction clarified the periodical's intentions; it specifically expressed dissatisfaction with the mechanical scientism then prevailing in the social sciences and the irrationalism that rejected any rational or scientific approach to history. Its Marxist outlook was deliberately omitted; nothing in the introduction can be singled out that indicates such a focus. The founders believed that the key to achieving the cooperation of Marxists and non-Marxists lay in organization on the basis of common historiographical grounds.[108]

The editorial board, composed of Marxists and non-Marxists,

quickly achieved a working consensus of what constituted a suitable article for *Past and Present*. They shared a common hostility to traditional historiography, typified by the *English Historical Review*. A critical factor in achieving this consensus was the method of management, what Hobsbawm has described as "our systematically collective modus operandi." All manuscripts were read by all board members and accepted by all. Board meetings were held regularly and eventually annual weekends were devoted to self-evaluation.[109]

Many parallels exist between *Past and Present* and the *Annales*. The editors were certainly conscious of them, both quoting Bloch and Febvre in the introduction; they shared a mission to demonstrate their theories. Like that in the French journal, the emphasis in *Past and Present* is on economic and social history, although political history is regularly included. The same internationalism, a broad spread of articles over the world and many foreign contributors, is apparent in both journals. Several historians of the *Annales* school have contributed to *Past and Present*. The latter also shares the same interest in the social sciences; its editorial board includes representatives from them. Its approach to historical fact is similar; the accumulation of facts does not matter, but an understanding of how change took place does.

Some differences also exist. *Past and Present* is not quite the institution the *Annales* has become. As it has evolved, it has not taken on the character of a journal of communication. Unlike the *Annales*, it has dropped what little book reviewing it did rather than expanding it. *Past and Present* has always tried to attract the nonspecialist by avoiding specialist jargon in the interest of readability and liveliness. *Annales* addressed itself to the professional historian and social scientist. Nor has *Past and Present* become a part of the historical establishment in quite the way the *Annales* has. It remains independently financed. Individual scholars associated with it have achieved great success and even renown, but there is no equivalent to the tight little world of the VIe section in Paris.

The biggest similarity between the two journals is success. *Past and Present* was described in the *EHR*, true to the British tradition of fair play, as "one of the most heartening as well as exciting features of recent historical scholarship . . . its impact has already been distinctive and influential."[110] Such praise is not overstated. *Past and Present* captured the historiographical initiative and profoundly influenced the discipline.

These two journals were able to replace the major periodicals in their respective countries, but the *AHR* has not been so eclipsed. To some extent, the reasons are to be found in the different traditions of the American historical profession. The *AHR* was and is the organ of the AHA, a body that embraces almost all American historians. A major controversy within the AHA in 1915 established the *AHR* editorial board's accountability to the association membership. Accountability required the board to be sensitive to the membership's changing interests; when insurgent groups have arisen, they have been coopted.

Past and Present and the *Annales* benefited from their own strengths and from the weaknesses of the *RH* and *EHR*. They managed to attract the ablest of the younger generation of scholars, individuals who became leaders of the profession. That indefinable but useful characteristic, the trend of the times, was on their side.

Since World War II, the world has been deeply concerned with economic and social questions, and the *Annales* and *Past and Present* have addressed themselves to these areas of history. They have encouraged the use of the techniques of the social sciences, the glamour disciplines of our age. At the same time, the *RH* and *EHR* could muster no comparable advantages. Braudel remarked that the force of the *Annales* was enhanced because it came at a time of "satisfied and widespread mediocrity in French historiography."[111] Harsh though this judgment may be, its truth seems indisputable. The combination of intellectual malaise and institutional rigidity of the older journals encouraged the small revolutions *Past and Present* and the *Annales* represent.

Management

The example of the *AHR* is a particularly pointed illustration that success or failure is not only a matter of intellectual outlook, but that management can also be highly influential. The editor has a central role, and the *RH*, *EHR*, and *AHR* were all fortunate to have capable, strong-minded, and dedicated men as their first editors. From the beginning, their organizational patterns differed somewhat.

The unfortunate absence of editorial correspondence for the *RH* makes it impossible to be certain about Gabriel Monod's style. What can be said with assurance is that he was a strong editor. His obituary notice and other testimonials leave no doubt that he shaped the *RH* and participated actively in its direction. He frequently contributed articles and regularly wrote for the "Bulletin historique" column. His role was probably similar to Sybel's: he made major policy decisions but an assistant was responsible for the routine work. Such a pattern was typical of European periodicals at the time.

Mandell Creighton became the first editor of the *EHR* because, in addition to the more obviously necessary qualities, he occupied a position of some eminence in the historical world. Such a standing was considered a prerequisite. When Creighton resigned, his assistant editor, Reginald Lane-Poole, could not succeed him because, as a mere lecturer at Jesus College, he lacked it. Poole would continue to do the work and provide the motive power, but Samuel Rawson Gardiner was a necessary figurehead.[112] Poole did not become editor in his own right until ten years later.

As editor, Creighton seems to have enjoyed almost absolute freedom. The group that established the *EHR* retained no formal responsibility for it, although its members may have served as an informal editorial board. When Gardiner was appointed, Bryce commented, "Indeed we could find no other with any general hold on the historical world."[113] The use of "we" indicates participation in the selection. On the other hand, the *EHR* has never printed any listing of a board of editors. Whether or not a board, formal or informal, existed, Creighton turned to and received most of his help from Acton. Poole continued this tradition, although to a lesser extent.

Creighton may have felt the lack of informal advice, but he was not fettered by unwanted suggestions. He could shape the *EHR* as he felt appropriate, to be "scientific and special," although Bryce found it "needlessly heavy" and hoped Gardiner would be able to find more lively material.[114] Creighton selected the content, provided overall direction, and sometimes involved himself more directly by rewriting.[115]

The contributions of Monod and Creighton are impressive, but J. Franklin Jameson was even more important to the development of his nation's journal and historical profession. He was the editor of the *AHR* for twenty-nine years and also headed the Carnegie Institution's Bureau of Historical Research during much of that period. He was the one historian in the country whose primary responsibility was the entire field of historical scholarship. Sooner or later, almost every project passed through his hands. Sometimes he used the resources of the *AHR* to help advance other causes; he was able, for example, to give the World War I National Board for Historical Service more publicity than it could otherwise have acquired.[116]

The praise from the board of editors on Jameson's resignation does not seem fulsome in the light of his accomplishments: "By the happy choice of our first Board of Editors, in 1895, it fell largely to this young scholar, still in his thirties, to set the high standards which have gained the *Review* its enviable reputation at home and abroad."[117] A more personal appreciation comes from the autobiography of Dexter Perkins, testimony to Jameson's wide knowledge: "I was impressed by the fact that he was able, despite years of research on my part, to point out an article on my subject in one of the French historical periodicals which I had not read. He gave me excellent criticism."[118]

When Jameson accepted the appointment as editor for the first time in 1895, the terms of the agreement between him and the board of editors were set forth in a memorandum. The general policy of the *AHR* was to be determined by the board, whose members would review the proposed contents of each number before publication. The managing editor was to represent them in correspondence. He was to sift articles and reject the "manifestly unsuitable." He thus exercised absolute power of rejection, but he could accept an article only after it had been read by one member of the board and approved by the entire board.[119] Although this appears to be a rigid structure, in practice it allowed Jameson considerable operational latitude. Because he alone was in day-to-day contact with the journal meant that board meetings soon became sessions in which his reports were accepted with little question.

Although the *AHR* was chronologically the first of the scholarly historical periodicals in France, England, and the United States to have a board of editors, it was not for that reason innovative. By 1895 a board of editors was common for American scholarly journals, and the *AHR* was simply adopting the general practice. The resolution of the conference that established the *AHR* indicates that the only real debate was over words, not whether the *AHR* should have a board. It called for "An Executive Committee of _____ to take all future action (including selection of editor); or a board of advisory editors with similar powers."[120]

Throughout Jameson's years as editor, the board of editors bore substantial responsibilities. Until 1915 it held legal title to the *AHR*. Some members were more influential than others. George Adams, for example, continued his Nestor-like role and was regularly consulted on all manner of issues.[121] As problems appeared, the board made policy.[122] It might even be called upon for its judgment on the suitability of the title page,[123] although this kind of judgment was rarely necessary after the *AHR* survived its first growing pains. The board's greatest opportunity to shape the *AHR* came through reviewing articles. Until the 1930s, members evaluated almost all articles. Individuals were selected for the board to cover the necessary specializations, although their geographical location was also a factor.

The system worked smoothly until 1915, when a group of dissidents within the AHA challenged the board and the managing editor. Their charges were the classic attack of an out-group upon an in-group: monopoly of and abuse of power. The conflict dominates the correspondence of 1915. Such complaints are not unique to the American situation. In the memoir of Goronwy Edwards, editor of the *EHR* from 1938 to 1959, his successor mentions occasional grumbles over Edwards's domination of the English historical profession because he edited both the *EHR* and the *Bulletin* of the Institute of Historical Research.[124] The 1915 episode reached such large proportions only because it took place within the AHA, a supposedly democratic organization.

The semiofficial relationship of the *AHR* to the AHA began in 1898, when the original guarantees expired and some new method of financing the *AHR* had to be found. The AHA voted a subsidy; a year later, the agreement, which remained in force in 1915, was concluded. The AHA paid the publisher of the *AHR*, Macmillan, $2 for each of its members; in return, each of them was to receive a copy of the *AHR*. The council of the AHA was to have the right to fill vacancies on the board of editors. Macmillan contributed $2,400 for editorial services. In 1903 the Carnegie Institution of Washington began its support of the *AHR*. Andrew McLaughlin, managing editor, was coming to Washington to head the institution's Bureau of Historical Research. It was agreed that, as part of his duties, he would continue to edit the *AHR*, thus relieving its treasury of any responsibility for the salary of the managing editor.[125]

In December 1913 Dunbar Rowland, director of the Mississippi State Department of Archives and History, began the assault with a speech at the Charleston meeting of the AHA; later he sent to members a pamphlet entitled "The Government of the American Historical Association: A Plea for a Return to the Constitution." In July 1915 Rowland, Frederic Bancroft, a member of the council of the association, and John Latané, a professor at Johns Hopkins, published a pamphlet in which they accused the council and board of editors of robbing the association for their own private gain. When this pamphlet evoked little response, Bancroft sent a letter to the *Nation*, published September 16, that repeated essentially the same charges. This letter was followed by others in the *Nation* from Ulrich B. Phillips, Latané, Edward P. Cheney, and A. B. Hart, and by the "Historical Statement" from the board.[126]

The particulars of the accusations centered around the monopoly of power because so many members of the board of editors were on or went on to the council. Bancroft describes them frequently as a "ring," and the Boston *Herald*, reporting on Bancroft's September 16 letter, declared that the *AHR*'s "methods of control make the ways of Tammany look rather feeble and circumspect."[127] Another admirer of Bancroft's wrote to him, agreeing: "I have been a member of that organization for a dozen years or more, during all of which time I have never had the slightest doubt that strong-arm work was being done to keep out all interlopers from the sacred circle."[128]

The second part of the charges was more specific; the group accused the board of editors of taking money from the association. The *AHR* had established the custom of paying railway fares and expenses of the editors to their meetings, so it is perfectly true that they were indirectly receiving money. But the charges were worded to imply high living and corruption. On this subject, Bancroft was sanctimonious: "My point is not against paying the expenses of poor men who come from a long distance, but against paying the expenses of men in comfortable circumstances like Turner, Jameson, Haskins, Burr and others, who get much honor and prestige out of the Association."[129]

The self-appointed crusaders seem to have expressed a fairly general resentment. Clarence Alvord, at the University of Illinois, pointed out to Jameson that they spoke for a large constituency: "You said you believed that the dissatisfaction with the way the association is run is not great. The true fact of the case is that there is no danger of a revolution but the dissatisfaction is almost universal."[130] A year later,

Alvord, a "reformer" himself, analyzed the situation in more detail. The method of control had been efficient and had, on the whole, "guided the Association towards the highest ideals of scholarship." He was willing to accuse the clique only of poor judgment; they had held on to offices for themselves. They had not realized the importance of securing new men who were rising in reputation but were unconnected with members of the clique. The leaders of the Western school had not received the recognition that was their due.[131]

Bancroft, Rowland, and Latané may have spoken for the Westerners, but they themselves were little different from the men they attacked. Rowland, it is true, shared none of the Eastern, New England background of those he opposed, but Latané was a professor at Johns Hopkins, an early leader in historical scholarship. Bancroft, ironically, could have been editor of the *AHR* had he chosen.[132]

Had these reformers been less vituperative, they might have gained more support. Bancroft did not trust Rowland as a leader: "He has an inordinate ambition for offices for which he has no fitness."[133] Two years later, Guy Stanton Ford characterized Latané as "a chronic sorehead with practically no following of any sort in the historical profession."[134] Temperate men like Alvord had to part company with the dissidents when they indulged in personal attacks and language like "ring" and "childish greed."[135] The events of 1915 mark an irrevocable break with the tradition of scholarly gentility. Differences had existed within the group; Hart, for example, had no use for George Adams, but no historian had mounted a personal public attack. As Jameson commented rather sadly, "We had all been friends."[136]

Many of the effects of the attempted reformation were more apparent than real for the *AHR*. In 1917 the AHA formally became its owner.[137] Well before the contretemps, new men had begun to join the circles of power within the AHA. As Jameson pointed out to Alvord, George Garrison had served as a member of the council; Eugene Barker of Texas was then on it.[138] The board of editors of 1925 exhibits slightly more diversity than that of 1915, but not much. In 1915, besides Jameson, it consisted of Carl Becker, of the University of Kansas, George Burr, of Cornell, Edward P. Cheney, of the University of Pennsylvania, James H. Robinson, of Columbia, and Frederick J. Turner, of Harvard. The 1925 members were Evarts B. Greene, of Columbia, Guy Stanton Ford, of Minnesota, Francis A. Christie, of the Meadville (Pa.) Theological Seminary, William E. Dodd, of Chicago, Sidney B. Fay, of Smith College, and Jameson. Jameson remained the editor.

In some ways, the reformers did the *AHR* a service. The episode put it on notice that it must be responsive to the entire membership of the AHA. This heightened awareness almost certainly helped it to retain its position as the leading historical periodical in the United States. It would need to accept newer kinds of history and involve rising young historians or run the risk of more unpleasantness.

Finances

By 1915 the *AHR* could present to the world a well-fed aspect that gave color to the suspicions of peculation raised by Bancroft. Such substantiality had not always been the case. Both the *AHR* and the *EHR* encountered financial difficulties in their early period; the survival of each was questionable. The two were supported in different ways. Ultimately, of course, the founders planned that each would be self-supporting, but until that was achieved some means of subsidy needed to be found.

For the *EHR*, the necessary support was obtained, reluctantly, from the publisher, Longmans. Within a year of its first number, the nature of the *EHR*'s problem was clear; interest in history was not sufficient to support a specialized periodical. The founders had seriously overestimated the prospects of the new review; 2,000 copies of the first number were printed. The steady decline, from 2,000 to a printing of 1,500 for the second number, 1,250 for the third, 1,000 for the fourth, 900 for the eighth, 800 for the tenth, before stabilizing at 750 with the eleventh, tells its own story.[139] As Creighton explained it, "Longmans was doubtful about going on a second year but we dragged him to that point. Our circulation tends to settle down to about 600 copies—which is scarcely enough, though I was never sufficiently sanguine to expect more than 1000."[140]

For perspective, these figures can be compared to those of the *Edinburgh Review,* one of the most important of the quarterlies Longmans published. At that time, its runs averaged around 3,000 per number.[141] Using Creighton's circulation figure of 600, income must usually have failed to balance costs. Had Longmans received the full face value of 5s. per copy, it would have received about £150 per number, but many of the copies were retailed by news dealers who bought them for 3 or 4s. Only small revenues from advertising could be added to the sales receipts.

To enable the *EHR* to continue publication, several schemes were adopted, the most helpful of which was strict economizing. Cutting the number printed from 1,500 to 750 reduced costs from £169.6.10 to £130.15.1.[142] Agreeing to keep the printer's bill as low as possible, Creighton gave up much of his freedom to make corrections to the proofs. A payment of £50 to the editor was reduced to £25 by January 1890. What this payment represented is unclear. According to Reginald Lane-Poole, Creighton's assistant, both Creighton and his successor, Samuel Gardiner, received no recompense. Most probably the payment covered the expenses of the editor and in the early days included payments to writers, although those later had to be sacrificed to the need for economy. The fixed nature of this payment probably contributed to Creighton's uncertainty when he wrote to Poole, "Personally I think I am out of pocket by it."[143]

The *RH* was probably financed in the same way. No publisher enjoys losing money, but a learned journal confers prestige, and most European scholarly journals of the period were supported by commercial publishers. The absence of records makes it impossible to be certain that the *RH* was indeed subsidized as needed by Germer Baillière, its first publisher, but other candidates are distinctly lacking. No organization of historians existed, the state had not yet taken on the responsibility of assisting scholarship, and no trace of an individual patron like the *RQH*'s Marquis de Beaucourt can be found. The publisher was the only alternative.

Like those of the *EHR,* the *AHR*'s financial difficulties during its early years nearly put an end to it. Its first three years were subsidized by individual guarantors, each of whom agreed to contribute a sum if the journal should require it. For example, among those Hart obtained was A. Lawrence Lowell, future president of Harvard.[144] The guarantees were exhausted, the *AHR* had not become self-sufficient, and another method had to be found. The relationship with the AHA was the solution. Aided by an annual subsidy from the publisher and soon afterward substantial support from the Carnegie Institution, the *AHR* prospered. Its circulation had dropped from 1,077 to 780 during its first three years, but the affiliation with the AHA immediately brought it up to 1,310 in 1898–99, and thereafter growth was steady.[145] The *AHR* did not, of course, assume immediately the international position it holds today. Its 1897 subscription list included only three European subscribers and two Canadian,[146] although exchanges did distribute it more widely.

Bancroft had impugned both the AHA support and the Carnegie assistance. To him, it appeared that the AHA was giving much and receiving nothing from its support of the *AHR*. That such a charge could have the color of truth is a measure of the change between 1898 and 1915 in the *AHR*'s position; in 1898 the AHA had not wanted to assume ownership and therefore liability. Bancroft also failed to appreciate that the Carnegie arrangement conferred benefits with no obligations.

Transfer of legal ownership in 1917 to the AHA had no real effect upon the *AHR*'s financial position; the ending of the generous Carnegie support in 1928[147] and the coming of the depression did. Jameson had resigned the year before, and the combination of events for a time raised the specter of cessation. It was difficult to find a replacement for Jameson; at least one candidate, Victor Clark, declined the editorship.[148] It was even more of a problem to make alternative financial arrangements. Economies were made: the reviews were cut to 80 pages and a limit of 825 pages per volume was imposed.[149] This kind of economizing could not compensate for the loss of 6,000 Carnegie dollars, and the *AHR* was forced to explore the possibility of university sponsorship. Duke made an offer that the *AHR* was on the verge of accepting when the librarian of Congress proposed that the editorship of the journal be combined with the new half-time consultant in European history at the library, who was funded by the Rockefeller Foundation.[150] The *AHR* accepted this plan eagerly; it solved the problem of the editor's salary and enabled the publishing operation to remain in Washington.

The loss of Carnegie support in 1928 was a major blow, and the ensuing condition was exacerbated by the depression. Membership in the AHA fell, and considerable contraction of advertising occurred, which forced further cuts. The executive secretary attributed the decision of the board of editors in 1934 to stop paying reviewers directly to this loss of revenue.[151]

The most recent financial crisis for the *AHR* was produced by the inflation of the late 1960s and the 1970s. No periodical was untouched by these conditions; the only special feature of the *AHR*'s predicament is that it has been described more clearly. The main factor is simple: income failed to keep pace with rising costs. To fight the problem, the *AHR* has used several different tactics.

Cutting costs is receiving a major share of attention. Economies have been effected in printing costs by changing the format and design. The average cost per copy was $1.06 in 1968–69, the last of the old system, and $0.95 in 1970–71, the first year the *AHR* used offset printing and the new format. Canceling one of two meetings of the board of editors, cutting travel funds for the staff, and spreading operational improvements over a longer period of time than originally planned also helped to save money.

The amounts saved by such methods, although useful, were small. In 1969 the *AHR* increased its resources on a comparatively large scale when it terminated its contract with Macmillan and became its own publisher. Macmillan had continued to make its annual $2,400 contribution for editorial expenses, but by 1968 it was receiving $7,000 in agency fees and $30,000 as its one-third share of the income. When the *AHR* became its own publisher, this money was immediately available for such things as staff expansion and salary improvement.

Another major change in 1975 was the move of the *AHR* from Washington, D.C., to Indiana University at Bloomington. Although its new location meant that the *AHR* could serve as a training institute in scholarly editing, helping to prepare graduate students for alternative careers in a tight job market, the primary impetus behind the move was financial necessity. The editor would become half-time, holding at the same time a tenured position with half-time teaching and research obligations in the Indiana History Department. The professional editors of the Washington staff would be replaced by faculty and graduate students.[152]

Although the *AHR* is the largest and most expensive operation in the AHA, it also produces large amounts of income. Subscription revenue[153] in 1972 was $140,000 and advertising income approached that figure. These two sources cover approximately 70 percent of the total cost. If income from other sources—book sales, permission to reprint articles, promotional activities—is added, the proportion rises. These calculations do not include an indeterminable sum, a just proportion of the membership fees that would otherwise be subscription income. On the whole, the *AHR* is nearly self-supporting.[154]

A recurring question has been to pay or not to pay. Like the *EHR*, the *AHR* began with the idea that contributors would be paid for articles and reviews. It was honored in the breach rather than the observance until Carnegie began its support. As early as the 1895 planning conference, James H. Robinson had indicated that, based on his experience with the *Annals* of the Academy of Social and Political Science, he thought articles could be obtained without paying for them.[155] This proved to be the case, though payments to authors of articles began with the coming of Carnegie assistance. Reviewers were paid continuously until 1934.[156] The absence of consecutive documentation makes it impossible to declare that payments for articles were uninterrupted until 1972, although this appears to be the case. A limit of $30 was established in 1917, only to be abolished in 1919.[157] By the time payments were eliminated by the financial difficulties of the 1970s, they had reached $5 per page.[158]

*   *   *

The historians responsible for the *RH*, *EHR*, and *AHR* worked so hard to ensure their survival because they believed the journals could make an essential contribution to their profession. Their colleagues would doubtless have agreed, although it is impossible to find personal testimonies. Historians, when they write memoirs, simply do not address themselves to the subject "What the *Revue historique*—or *EHR* or *AHR*—has meant to me." Probably the best confirmation that these journals fill a real need is the silent witness of their long survival and reactions like those encountered by Shafer in 1958. He sought suggestions from historians for the improvement of the *AHR* and found that readers wanted more of the same.[159] Individual testimony can also be found. Creighton modestly claimed for the *EHR*, "It does not produce any startling novelties; but I find simply in my own work that it produces a body of matter to which I often refer."[160] This same need is confirmed by the objections of readers to change and by the large numbers of subscribers.

The impact of the three journals has been substantial. They were part of the domestication of the German model of professional scholarship. By existing, they helped establish historical scholarship on a national basis. By surviving, they strengthened it. They helped to raise the quality of scholarship by enforcing standards that represent a collective judgment. If the products of this approach have more often been "solid"[161] than brilliant, the overall level has nonetheless improved. Having looked to the *HZ* as model, these periodicals have in turn served as models for later scholarly historical periodicals in their own countries.

For all their many similarities, the three journals also have important differences. All have served as a means of communication, but it was communication for different purposes. Because professional scholarship in France and Britain was relatively undeveloped at the time the *RH* and *EHR* were founded, they could further its institutionalization in their countries in a way the *AHR* could not. The *AHR*, published in a country where professional scholarship already existed, quickly became a tie among widely dispersed historians. The journals have become more dissimilar because French, British, and American higher education have evolved so differently; they cannot be separated from their contexts. It has been significant for the *AHR* that it is a publication of the AHA, that American universities are hospitable to new approaches,[162] and that the numerous universities are widely dispersed. It has been significant for the *EHR* that higher education has remained relatively elitist and that doctoral education in history has been unusual until recently.

The importance of context is even more apparent by contrast. France, Britain, and the United States are all part of the same cultural area, but much of the world is outside it. Not all countries have followed the German pattern with their first professional journal: taking a wide area of history as its scope, publishing independently, and achieving almost instant success. In Albania, for example, history has yet to achieve a periodical of its own; probably the most important "historical" periodical is the Bulletin of the State University of Tirana, begun as the *Boletin për Shkencat Shoqërore* (Bulletin of the Social Sciences).[163] The Soviet Union now has a journal of universal history, *Voprosy istorii*, but it only gradually assumed leadership among scholarly historical periodicals.

The *RH, EHR,* and *AHR* were a response to the needs of French, British, and American historical scholarship in the late nineteenth century. They represented the first stage of development of scholarly historical periodicals in their own countries. Their success encouraged the next generation of historians to create journals to serve their own somewhat different needs; their scope and character influenced the nature of those successor journals.

FOUR ❦ GEOGRAPHICAL SPECIALIZATION ❦ THE DEUTSCHE ZEITSCHRIFT FÜR GESCHICHTSWISSENSCHAFT, THE MISSISSIPPI VALLEY HISTORICAL REVIEW, AND THE JOURNAL OF SOUTHERN HISTORY

Specialization is inherent in scholarship, and the patterns of development are similar in all fields. Scholars seek the company, approval, and criticism of those who understand what they are doing; the closer the specific subject area of one scholar to that of another, the better the two can understand each other. When a field or discipline begins to emerge, its scholars must be satisfied with the collegiality of those working in related but distinctively separate areas. As time passes, the members of a discipline who are interested in similar, closely related topics increase. They develop close intellectual bonds. When a sufficient number define their field of endeavor in the same terms, a subfield, a specialization, has been created. Subfields may in turn generate their own subfields, but all are part of the same system. Scholars have, nevertheless, found less and less in common with those working outside their own specialized subfield.

In history, it is impossible to assign precise dates to the beginning of specialization because every historian is in some sense a specialist. A mature discipline, in which various subfields have replaced the field in general as the area of activity, in which subfields have established priorities and historians are working on the problems, is a product of the second or third generation of professional historians. Only then do they think of themselves as American historians or economic historians rather than as historians.

Dating specialization is so difficult because it is the product of interacting forces rather than a single identifiable event, a matter of degree rather than a discrete state. In many ways, scholarly historical periodicals are the best indicators. A specialized journal in itself is a statement that a specialty exists and has reached the point where it needs a medium of communication. In Germany, where professional history first evolved, specialization came earliest, during the last quarter of the nineteenth century. In the United States, it appeared in the first quarter of the twentieth.

The emergence of particular specialties is closely connected to numbers. To establish itself as an identifiable separate field or subfield of endeavor, a specialization must have a certain number of scholars working in it. The rise of African history is a good example. A dramatic increase in the number of historians who concentrated in this area preceded the foundation of the two journals of African history in 1960. An even larger increase preceded that of the *African Economic History Review* in 1968.

In almost all countries, but especially in the United States, during the 1960s and 1970s a large increase has occurred in the number of specialized periodicals as new areas of research have attracted attention and specialization has expanded. As one example, in the United States two journals, the *East European Quarterly* and *Central European History*, now replace the *Journal of Central European Affairs*, which ceased publication in 1962. One journal is even devoted to East Central Europe. The proliferation of periodicals dealing with African and Asian history is also noticeable. England, a country in which specialization developed largely after World War II, now has such journals as the *Journal of American Studies* and the *Journal of Latin American Studies*. Several of the specialized journals were founded to serve research in newfound areas of interest, but the situation is to some extent reminiscent of the spread of imperialism in the late nineteenth century. Any portion of the globe not already claimed was taken into custody.

Although professional history has specialized in almost every country, the patterns vary considerably. A rational progression would be from the general to the specialized to the more specialized. In the United States, African history did proceed from the *American Historical Review* (general history) to the *Journal of African History* and *African*

Historical Studies (both African history) to the *African Economic History Review* (a specialization in African history). American history advanced from the *AHR* to the *Mississippi Valley Historical Review* (*MVHR*), a journal of American history, to the *Journal of Southern History* (*JSH*). Progression has not always been so rational. Specialized periodicals in Germany in the form of the *Preussischer Jahrbücher* were contemporaneous with the general, the *HZ*. In the USSR, a number of specialized periodicals emphasizing proletarian and revolutionary themes, such as *Proletarskaia revoliutsiia* (Proletarian revolution), *Krasnyia arkhiv* (Red archive), and *Letopis' revoliutsii* (Annals of the revolution), preceded a general scholarly historical periodical. In France, relatively few specialized scholarly historical periodicals of any kind are published.

Specialization is not only a matter of periodicals. What advancing specialization in research meant to the individual historian is also revealed by a comparison of the major publications in book form of the founders of the *AHR*, the *MVHR*, and the *JSH*. Among the founders of the *AHR*, George Burton Adams wrote *The Constitutional History of England*, *The Growth of the French Nation*, and *The History of England from the Norman Conquest to the Death of John*. Albert Bushnell Hart wrote *The Formation of the Union, 1750–1829*, and John Bach McMaster an eight-volume history of the United States from the Revolution to the Civil War. Clarence Alvord, the first editor of the *MVHR*, published *The Mississippi Valley in English Politics*, and Orin Libby, a member of the *MVHR*'s first board of editors, *The Geographical Distribution of the Vote of the Thirteen States on the Federal Constitution*. Walter Posey, a member of the *JSH*'s first editorial board, prepared a history of Methodism in the old Southwest between 1783 and 1824 and another on the Presbyterian church in the same region and approximately the same period. Although the biographies written by historians associated with all three periodicals represent to some extent an exception, their research indicates progression from broader to narrower topics.

Trends in the teaching of history reinforced specialization. In many American institutions before the turn of the century, history had been part of another department. It achieved autonomy and the status of a department of its own. Separate history departments that already existed grew in size and brought in new people with differing interests. The expansion of graduate education profoundly influenced the socialization of both student and teacher. Identification as a specialist in German, American, or Southern history was more evident for the faculty member who was teaching seminars and directing dissertations in one of those subjects than for one who taught only an occasional lecture course in it together with courses in other areas.

Despite the pervasiveness of specialization and the consequent profusion of specialized periodicals, some influences discourage it. It lacks a well-articulated intellectual justification, for historians have rarely considered it in its own right, although it was implicit in Ranke's statements on method. When they have examined it, they have usually criticized rather than praised. Many historians, especially Europeans, argue that history should concern itself with the sweep of events, seeking patterns and meaning, not with small-scale events. This widely shared conviction has helped to retard the spread of specialized periodicals in some European countries, where they tend to be confined to areas of traditional interest, like the Mediterranean, or to areas formerly controlled as colonies.

Historians have criticized the profusion of specialized periodicals, arguing that it does not serve the reader as effectively as the writer. A Polish historian expressed dismay that his country should have nearly a hundred periodicals,[1] and historians in other countries share a similar concern. Too many periodicals hinder rather than help communication. Historians' chances of missing a worthwhile article in their fields increase. Another danger is that the sheer quantity of material tempts them to confine their reading to their immediate specialties, thereby losing the breadth of perspective that comes with wider knowledge.

The specialized periodicals studied in depth in this chapter, the *Deutsche Zeitschrift für Geschichtswissenschaft* (*DZG*), the *MVHR*, and the *JSH*, antedate the explosion of them that has so exacerbated the problems. The first issue of the *DZG* appeared in 1889; the *MVHR* in 1914; and the *JSH* in 1935. The *DZG* and the *MVHR* pioneered specialization in Germany and in the United States. All three survived long enough to solve initial problems and establish themselves among the strongest journals in their countries.

The *DZG* was begun by Ludwig Quidde, a professor at the University of Königsberg but still a young man of thirty-one. It was very much his personal undertaking. At the end of 1888, he wrote to Paul Siebeck, head of the J. C. B. Mohr (Paul Siebeck) Verlag, proposing that Siebeck publish a journal he would edit. Siebeck, a publisher who combined sound business instincts with idealism, was receptive to the idea. The firm was already publishing religious, economic, and legal history, and Quidde's proposed journal neatly fitted his concept of specialization.[2]

Clarence Alvord, a professor at the University of Illinois, was the principal mover behind the *MVHR*. As soon as the Mississippi Valley Historical Association (MVHA) was organized in 1908, he began urging it to publish a journal.[3] In October 1912, Alvord, as chairman of a committee appointed by the president of the association to investigate the feasibility of a journal, wrote to a number of his Midwestern colleagues. His chief concern was whether they would be willing to contribute enough articles to fill its pages.[4] He had already been assured of financial support. When most of the replies were favorable, the committee presented its report to the association, which authorized a journal. Alvord became the first editor, and an editorial board including representatives from each of the major participating states was appointed.

The *JSH* was also largely one man's creation. Wendell Stephenson, a professor at Louisiana State University (LSU), "nourished a consuming desire to establish an outlet for the writing and dissemination of southern history."[5] The call to organize a Southern Historical Association at the Atlanta meeting of the Southern Political Science Association in November 1934 triggered the events that transformed his hope into reality. He and a young colleague, Edwin A. Davis, immediately began to prepare a prospectus. At about the same time, Stephenson was discussing with a group of LSU friends known as "Hokum Kollege," which was dedicated to eating, drinking, history, and storytelling, a suggestion that the university publish a magazine of history through its History Department. Stephenson prepared a proposal, Davis a budget, and presented them to the "Hokum Kollege" group.[6] After lengthy discussion, the two then persuaded the president of LSU to guarantee the expenses of the editorial office. Armed with this proposition, Stephenson persuaded the organizing members of the Southern Historical Association to sponsor the journal.[7]

The founders of these specialized journals, though of a different generation, were superficially similar to the founders of the first scholarly historical periodicals in their countries. Like the founders of the *HZ* and *AHR*, most of them held doctorates in history and all were unversity professors. But, as members of a different generation, in the case of the *JSH* of a third generation, they did not perceive the profession in the same way as their elders. A crucial difference was that they considered themselves German historians or American historians rather than historians. They saw additional needs and were prepared to meet them. They depended upon the *HZ* and *AHR,* but were ready to build on the foundation those periodicals provided.

In contrast to the founders of the *HZ* and the *AHR,* all the founders of these geographically specialized journals were outsiders. They were not members of the historical establishment in the same way as their counterparts of the *HZ* and *AHR.* Most of them had not obtained their educations at the most prestigious institutions nor did they teach at them. Königsberg, Illinois, and LSU, although important work was done at them, were not Berlin, Harvard, and Yale.[8] The founders of the specialized journals viewed themselves as outsiders, especially in the case of the *MVHR.* They were the "Westerners" whom Jameson and other leaders in the AHA and the *AHR* stood accused of excluding in the 1915 controversy.

Although the founders of these geographically specialized journals did not view the historical profession from precisely the same perspective as the men who established the first scholarly historical periodicals, their goals were remarkably similar. Essentially, they were hoping to accomplish for the branch of history in which they worked what the earlier groups had hoped to accomplish for the discipline as a whole.

The primary purpose of the geographically specialized journals was to provide a place to publish, for their founders believed that existing publications did not pay sufficient attention to the subjects in which they were interested. At the same time, they were convinced that, at least potentially, good articles in the subject existed for which there were not enough places to publish. In his introduction, Quidde declared that only a few articles on German history were being printed and that there ought to be a place for articles other than those by scholars who were already well known.[9] Alvord's introduction to the *MVHR* quoted a letter from Professor H. L. Osgood, of Columbia: "I am in sympathy with your project because I do not think that the *American Historical Review* furnishes a sufficient outlet for the volume of historical work which is in progress in this country. We need more avenues of publication."[10] To underscore Osgood's point, Alvord cited the growing number of historians in the West who were interested in American history and the consequent demand for "more avenues of publication."

The founders of the first scholarly historical periodicals had also believed that appropriate places to publish were insufficient, but the founders of specialized periodicals were even more persuaded of a deficiency. Since the foundation of the first scholarly historical periodicals, scholarship had become more professionalized and more institutionalized, thus increasing both the need and the desire to publish. The Ph.D., a degree that prepared historians to do research and persuaded them that they should do it, was more and more widely held. The growth in the number of scholars meant that an interested audience existed, if only it could be reached. Because professional historians were now almost invariably affiliated with universities, they had a practical incentive to publish. "Publish or perish" was not yet the rule, but a leading route to academic prestige has always been publication.

Belief in the need for more outlets of publication was characteristic of the second phase of historical scholarship, even in areas that did not immediately acquire specialized journals. George B. Adams, one of the founders of the *AHR* and a specialist in English history, was involved in an unsuccessful plan for a review of European history, which was discussed at intervals between 1911 and 1921. In 1916 he expressed sentiments about English history similar to those of Osgood on American history. In the process, he unintentionally clarified one of the inherent problems of specialized historical periodicals: "The demand for the new Rev[iew] is a writers', not a readers' demand. . . . There is no place in this country where technical articles in European history can expect publication—dry-as-dust articles, if you will, the results of special scholarship which few will want to read, and which ought on scholarly grounds to be published."[11]

The bibliographies of the historians who helped found specialized periodicals indicate some justification for their belief that outlets for publication were inadequate. In the early twentieth century in the United States, the lack of appropriate journals was forcing historians to publish in nonhistorical journals, foreign journals, or journals that did not reach a wide scholarly audience. An article by George B. Adams, "The Origin of English Equity," appeared in the *Columbia Law Review*. Bernadotte Schmitt, the first editor of the *Journal of Modern History*, a journal for European history founded in 1929, was published in such diverse places as the *Bulletin* of Western Reserve University, the *Mid-West Quarterly,* the *Revue politique internationale,* the *Texas Review,* and the *Political Science Quarterly,* as well as the *AHR.*[12] Articles by Frederic Paxson, an American historian, appeared in many of the Midwestern local history society journals, the *History Teacher's Magazine,* the *University of Colorado Studies,* the *World Review,* and the *Proceedings* of the State Bar Association of Wisconsin.

Providing space for publication was the principal motivation of the founders of the specialized periodicals, but they had other goals as well. Quidde wanted to provide better coverage of the scholarly literature in German history,[13] a desire shared by Alvord for American history, to judge by the issues of the *MVHR.* Alvord also hoped to use the new journal to raise the standard of historical work in the West,[14] just as Stephenson hoped to improve the quality of work in Southern history through the *JSH.*[15]

A geographical area would seem to be largely self-defining, but each of the journals studied in this chapter experienced some difficulty in defining its scope. Quidde was caught between two conflicting goals, as he stated in his introduction. He wanted the *DZG* to be the journal for German history, ignoring that the *HZ* was really such a journal in practice if not in theory. At the same time, he sought to clarify the relation of the German historical experience to that of other lands,[16] a desire that required at least some attention to non-German history. His first volume contained articles on medieval Florence; Mary, Queen of Scots; and sixteenth-century English economic development. His immediate successors at least partially eliminated the inconsistency when they changed the journal's name to *Historische Vierteljahresschrift (HV),* which abandoned the implied exclusive interest in German history.

Quidde's historiographical position influenced the definition of the *DZG's* scope. His interest in establishing relationships is one indication that he was not an adherent of the historicist school, even though an interest in German history was typical of historicists. His explicit commitment to a scholarship uninfluenced by political circumstances is another and suggests that he was, in fact, antihistoricist. The presence of Professor Baumgarten, an opponent of Sybel's, on his board of editors is additional evidence of the antihistoricist position of the *DZG* from its earliest days.

Content analysis of the *DZG/HV* makes clear that the scope of the journal was never really clarified. German history was its primary interest, although articles dealing with other geographical areas occasionally appeared. These usually concerned Central Europe or the Mediterranean, but in 1929 one on Turkey was published. Chronologically, articles concentrated on the seventeenth century or early periods. Only in the last volumes before the *HV* ceased publication in 1939 were the nineteenth and twentieth centuries represented. Topically, most of the *DZG/HV*'s articles were political history. The major secondary interests were military history, religious history, and historiography. Diplomatic history was almost completely absent.

The *MVHR* gradually expanded its scope from the Mississippi Valley to the entire United States, but the forces that brought about its expansion were quite different from those of the *DZG*. Like the *DZG*, it formalized the change by a new name, becoming the *Journal of American History (JAH)* in 1964. The *MVHR* owed its beginning to strong regional feelings and a certain anti-Eastern bias. Almost as soon as it began publication, it was under pressure to become a journal for the history of the entire nation, although some years elapsed before it succumbed. No scholarly journal of American history existed, and historians felt a need for one. In many respects, the pressure was also a tribute to the *MVHR*'s success in establishing itself as a scholarly journal.

In January 1915, less than a year after the first issue, Alvord turned down "The Committee on Colonies in the Constituent Assembly" because it was "too far afield" from the Mississippi Valley.[17] A letter later in the same year makes clear the nature of the debate within the editorial board:

> I wish to say that your paper opens an issue which has been up before the board several times. It has been made desirable by pressure from prominent historians that we do not confine our pages to articles on the Mississippi Valley. On the other hand there has been considerable objection to every attempt to go outside of the Mississippi Valley, and on the whole I think the board is very conservative in this matter, much more conservative than the managing editor who has no objection to taking issue over your paper.[18]

On this occasion, the board of editors chose to reject the paper, on the reopening of diplomatic relations between the United States and Holland, and adhere to its original intentions, which they had already compromised. In the third number of its first volume, the *MVHR* published "Some Aspects of British Administration in West Florida," and only by a very generous definition does West Florida fall within the Mississippi Valley. Ten years later, it went even further afield with "The Peace Movement in North Carolina." By no stretch of the imagination is North Carolina in the Mississippi Valley.

By the 1940s, when Louis Pelzer was editor, the *MVHR* had established itself as the scholarly journal of American history and was being pushed to expand even further. One member of the board of editors argued that it should be exclusively "American," but he defined American to include countries bordering on the United States.[19] One of Pelzer's successors even received an article on Hegel's philosophy of history, which he immediately rejected.[20] In practice, the *MVHR* has confined itself to the history of the United States.

Content analysis of the *MVHR* shows that it has published more articles on the United States as a whole than on any single part of it. The remaining articles are distributed fairly evenly except that there are somewhat more on the Southeast than any other region. This strong interest in the Southeast continued after the founding of the *JSH*. Topically, most of the *MVHR*'s articles are in political history, but interest has also been continuing in military, economic, and social history as well as in historiography. In recent years, intellectual history seems to be attracting more attention. The volumes analyzed contained no article on agriculture, which has always been vital in Midwest life. Chronologically, most articles deal with either the eighteenth or the nineteenth century. The twentieth has been almost completely ignored.

Just as the editors of the *MVHR* had difficulty in trying to decide what territory was included in the Mississippi Valley, the editors of the *JSH* periodically debated how much southernness was required for an article to be Southern history.[21] The journal did publish a number of articles dealing with United States history as a whole, usually written from the Southern perspective. More articles are about the Southeast region as a whole than about any single part of it; the part that has received the most attention includes Alabama, Tennessee, Mississippi, and Louisiana.

Chronologically, the majority of articles deal with the nineteenth century; in more recent volumes, those on the twentieth are appearing with increasing frequency. An analysis of the first fifteen years of the *JSH* reveals that, of 215 articles published, 76 of them focused on the three decades before the Civil War, twenty-nine on the Civil War period, and eighteen on Reconstruction. These 123 articles represent 57 percent of the total, or an average of 27 per decade for the period of sectional crisis.[22]

Topically, some clustering has also occurred. The *JSH* carries more articles on political history and on economic and social history than on other topics. Additional areas in which it regularly publishes are military history, intellectual history, and historiography.

With minor exceptions, the contributors to geographically specialized journals were very similar to those of the *HZ* and *AHR*. The *DZG* contributors were almost entirely university faculty who held doctorates. Their principal distinction from the contributors to the *HZ* was that, like the founders of the specialized journals, they were rarely at the most prestigious centers of German historical scholarship. Instead, they were at unversities like Graz, Greifswald, and Königsberg. The *MVHR* contributors, like those to the *AHR,* included during the early years some who were not professional historians, but they soon disappeared. The *MVHR* contributors differed slightly from those of the *AHR* in some respects. A somewhat larger number of them held the doctorate and were junior faculty. Their ages were almost invariably lower, even in the first volume, for which Alvord had mobilized the leading historians of the Mississippi Valley. The *JSH* contributors were overwhelmingly university faculty who held the doctorate. Their only difference was a noticeable concentration at Southern universities.

Before the *MVHR* began publication, Alvord had feared he could not obtain sufficient articles to fill a journal, but even then he did not contemplate opening it to anything except scholarly contributions. His preliminary inquiry about willingness to contribute went to his fellow college and university teachers, the professional historians. Ida Tarbell, the famous muckraking journalist, was one of the few non-professional historians to whom he wrote. Soon after the first issue, it became apparent that his fears were groundless. At the same time that he was trying to collect some of the articles that had been promised earlier, he was writing to the members of the editorial board that articles were "coming in extremely well."[23] By mid-1915 he was "becoming embarrassed by A-#1 articles and have pledged myself to so many more that I don't know what I am going to do."[24] There have been temporary shortages since, but the need for a journal of American history was real.

The frequent repetition among the contributors to the *DZG*[25] suggests that Quidde was operating in the typical European fashion of the time by persuading his friends and acquaintances to contribute, rather than depending like the two American journals on unsolicited submissions. Quidde did not, therefore, face the problem of rejection of unsuitable material. He did not, on the other hand, enjoy the freedom to return articles.

The criteria for acceptance by the *MVHR* and the *JSH* were very similar to those of the *AHR*, qualified always by either American or Southern. From the beginning, *MVHR* articles were required to cover sufficiently broad themes, be scientific, use footnotes, and be complete in themselves. One member of the board of editors was especially caustic on the scientific requirement. He described one paper as more suited "to a Monday Club pink tea."[26] Alvord rejected another article because "it is one of those philosophical essays enjoyed by the general reader, which present no novelty to the special student."[27] Wendell Stephenson rejected articles for the *JSH* on various grounds, such as: the subject matter was too local and not important enough,[28] content and style were not suitable,[29] and a wider body of material needed to be treated.[30]

The evolution of the refereeing systems for the *MVHR* and the *JSH* followed the same pattern as that of the *AHR*. Both began with editorial boards whose members were selected to represent the participating states and to achieve a spread of subject expertise. Originally, the editors consulted only members of the editorial board for opinions on articles, but gradually they also began to use outside readers. For the *MVHR*, the change from dependence only on an editorial board to the more complex system used today can be dated fairly precisely. In 1941 Louis Pelzer, the editor, invited Francis Wiesenburge "to serve temporarily on the board of editors" so that he could review a paper.[31] By the time of William Binkley's editorship (1953–63) a fully fledged system, indistinguishable from that of the *AHR*—coordinating editor, editorial board members, and outside referees—was operating without such subterfuges as "temporary" membership on the board of editors.

The most important feature after articles in each journal has been bibliographical material. The *DZG/HV*, *MVHR*, and *JSH* have all printed book reviews, and the *DZG* published in addition a detailed systematic bibliography of German history, which Quidde judged to be a particularly valuable contribution. Alvord intended to add each year to the regular book reviews several in-depth reviews of fifteen to twenty pages of particularly significant books. These extended reviews did not survive for long. One of the first, a review of John Bach McMaster's *History of the People of the United States*,[32] received sharp criticism for its use as the lead article when so much had already been written about it.[33]

The traditional brief book reviews have changed little through the years, except that in both the *MVHR* and the *JSH* they have increased in number. Partly to accommodate this increase, the *MVHR* added in the mid-1950s a "Book Notes" section for shorter reviews. A similar increase did not take place in the *DZG/HV*. The explanation is probably to be found in the uncertain economic conditions in Germany during the years analyzed, rather than in the productivity of German scholarship or the intentions of the journal.

The reviewing patterns of these specialized journals differ slightly from those of the general journals. They are, for example, more likely to review source material. They have also been, except for the *DZG*, remarkably monolingual. Of the 1,193 titles analyzed from seven volumes of the *MVHR*, only six are in a language other than English. A 1957 study of the entire *MVHR* found only some dozen and a half foreign language titles among approximately ten thousand books reviewed.[34] The *JSH*, in the analyzed volumes, reviewed no foreign language titles. The specialized journals differ from the general in another respect: the geographical distribution of their book reviews is often broader than that of their articles. The *MVHR*, from its beginning, reviewed books on areas of the United States outside the Mississippi Valley and went even further afield to review works on South America and non-United States North American history. The *JSH* reviewed three books dealing with South America in its 1974 volume.

The book reviews in these specialized journals produced the same kinds of problems as those encountered by the general journals. Alvord had hoped for incisive reviews,[35] but the reviews in the *MVHR* did not escape the general American scholarly tendency toward blandness.[36] The editor really exercised little control over this situation. Alvord, for instance, had requested Justin Smith to review

Riva's *The United States and Mexico, 1821–1848,* only to have Smith refuse because he was tired of making enemies gratuitously and being accused for writing "true and needed criticisms."[37] More than a quarter of a century later, Milo Quaife, himself a former editor of the *MVHR,* would withdraw his offer to review the *WPA Guide to Michigan* when he found the book "a mess."[38] A reviewer for the *JSH* asked to be excused from reviewing a book because "I find it so poorly done that I should have to write a devastating review."[39] She felt that such a review would be "so ungracious an act to a sister institution in Baltimore" that she did not want it to be printed.

The problems presented by the systematic bibliography of the *DZG* were of a different order. It was expensive, its compilers were inevitably late, and it always seemed to be larger than it should be. A relatively independent operation, its compiler had his own contract. As early as August 1889, less than a year after the *DZG* began publication, Quidde was writing about his effort to bring Siebeck's concern with Dr. Liebermann, the compiler, under control.[40] By 1892 both Quidde and Siebeck recognized that the problem was intractable; in spite of the best efforts of publisher, editor, and compiler to keep it within bounds, the bibliography kept growing. As Quidde reported to Siebeck, Dr. Liebermann regretted that German scholars found it impossible to be moderate, but he could not halt the size if he was to carry out his obligations.[41]

In spite of all the headaches, both Quidde and Siebeck cherished the bibliography. The *HZ* had long since abandoned any effort at systematic bibliographical coverage, and the *DZG*'s bibliography was truly unique in its comprehensiveness and currency. Quidde felt that a large part of the journal's success depended on it and so convinced Siebeck. Siebeck opposed changes that the next editors tried to make,[42] and only after the *DZG* moved to another publisher was the bibliography altered. At that time, the new editors dropped it from the journal, although they continued to publish it separately. The separate bibliography finally ceased publication in 1929, ten years before the journal itself.

Besides articles and book reviews, each of the three geographically specialized journals discussed in this chapter included a news section when it began publication. When the *DZG* began in 1889, the *HZ* did not have such a section, although the *Historisches Jahrbuch* did. A few years later, the *HZ* added a similar section and a listing of the current contents of periodicals, a change Quidde credited to the competition from the *DZG*.[43] The *MVHR* had in addition to a regular news section articles that surveyed recent historical activities in a region. The authors found these difficult to write because those involved were reluctant to respond to queries.[44] The first three issues of the *MVHR* printed such surveys, but they then became much more infrequent and were soon abandoned.

The two American journals also had a documents section when they began. Alvord found that the *MVHR's* section gave him more trouble than any other.[45] Both journals have since dropped them, probably for the same reason as the *AHR:* the change in emphasis in historical scholarship from single, high-interest documents to collections.

In spite of the obvious dominance of scholarly considerations in both the planning and management of the *DZG* and *MVHR,* both Quidde and Alvord hoped to attract nonprofessional readers. Quidde expressed the hope in his introduction that a nonspecialist, a "Nichtfachmann," would be interested in much of what the *DZG* published, although at the same time he declared that this audience could not determine the selection and treatment of material.[46] Quidde was honest enough to recognize later that his periodical did not offer much appeal to the wider public.[47] Alvord and members of the *MVHR's* board of editors expressed similar hopes for a general audience,[48] but Alvord, too, refused to let pursuit of the nonscholarly subscriber influence editorial policy. The complete absence of discussion about nonspecialist readers in the correspondence of the *JSH* and in the published materials about it indicates that by its time, 1935, scholarly journals had abandoned the attempt to attract them.

Quidde, Alvord, and Stephenson were all strong editors, and their gifts were crucial to the establishment of their geographically specialized journals. Each had a clear vision of what he wanted the final product to be, the willingness to concern himself with the myriad details, and the intelligence to recognize the consequences of individual decisions. The following tribute to Wendell Stephenson could apply as well to Quidde or to Alvord: "For seven years he was the *Journal*."[49]

Other statements clarify the nature of Stephenson's contribution and demonstrate how central a position the editor holds. When Stephenson was reluctant to preside at the annual dinner meeting of the Southern Historical Association in 1935, William Binkley, later an editor of the *JSH*, wrote to him, "As editor of the *Journal* you probably have more to do with determining the standards of our work than does any other individual in the group."[50] Another colleague credited Stephenson with having "lifted the writing of southern history from a condition of defensive mediocrity and regional provinciality onto the high plane of penetrating investigation and literary craftmanship."[51] He used the *JSH* to educate: "A whole generation of young southern historians, and many of the older ones, learned what it meant to take a second and even a third look at citations, quotations, and sentence structure."[52]

The ways in which the editors of these journals were selected depended upon the nationality of the journal and whether or not they were published by associations. The publisher decided who would succeed Quidde on the *DZG* just as the *HZ*'s publisher decided on Sybel's successors. Quidde suggested Karl Lamprecht and Erich Marcks as editors, and they were eager, but Siebeck made the final decision. For the *MVHR* and the *JSH*, the officers of the associations that published them made the decisions.

The *MVHR* shows patterns of selection similar to the *AHR*'s. The officers of the MVHA, acting on their own, replaced the early editors. Later, they appointed special search committees to advise them.[53] The *MVHR*'s changes of editors, however, illustrate something more as well. While selection procedures were becoming more formal, the choice of editor was becoming less dependent on the financial offers made by potential sponsoring organizations. Unlike the *AHR*, which has been subsidized by a university only during the last decade, the *MVHR* has been dependent on such sponsorship for most of its career.

The survival of the entire correspondence of the 1940–41 search committee makes possible a detailed examination of the process. Headed by John D. Hicks, of the University of Wisconsin, the panel included Louis Pelzer, of Iowa, Jonas Viles, of Missouri, James Randall, of Illinois, and Homer Hockett, of Ohio State. They needed to find an institution willing to subsidize the *MVHR* at a certain level that could also present an acceptable candidate as editor. Hicks wrote to various institutions in the Mississippi Valley asking if they would be interested in supporting the *MVHR* and soliciting their proposals for editor.[54] After some negotiation, the committee chose among the offers. It completed its work within four months.

The final choice of Pelzer was more complex than this brief account suggests. The Hicks committee started with two major disadvantages: everyone on the committee with the possible exception of Hicks wanted the appointment, and the former editor's assistant was to go with the journal. In a letter to the successful candidate, Hicks said he thought the decision had aroused no ill feeling, but he suggested that Pelzer eventually include on his editorial board most of his unsuccessful competitors.[55] The assistant presented more of a problem. She was "extremely unpopular with a large section of the association."[56] They felt she took too much upon herself, although both the treasurer of the MVHA, Clara Paine, and Hicks felt that she might do better with a new editor who would give more attention to the job.[57] One of the arguments against Hockett had been that he would leave too much to her.[58] Fortunately, she eventually resigned, but only after Iowa had been persuaded to accept her. The committee was also subject to some outside pressure. William Binkley, a friend of Wendell Stephenson, was one of the candidates, and Stephenson wrote to several of his colleagues in Binkley's support. Stephenson also offered to write to James Randall,[59] one of the members of the committee he knew rather well, but Binkley, "a very modest fellow," was reluctant to undertake any campaign.[60]

The Hicks committee chose Pelzer for two reasons: the financial advantages of the offer made by his university, Iowa, and recognition of his long service to the *MVHR*. Binkley's university, Vanderbilt, had offered support for only a half-time assistant in place of the full-time incumbent.[61] More important was the conviction "that Pelzer's deep interest in the *Review* over a long period of years seemed to make his appointment almost a necessity."[62] He would have had a right to feel deeply hurt had he been passed over, especially because he had not been chosen in 1930 when Arthur Cole was made editor.[63]

Once selected, the editors enjoyed varying degrees of independence. Although Quidde appointed an editorial board with an ancient historian, two medievalists, and two German historians, he seems rarely to have consulted them. He and his successors were primarily accountable to the publisher, but Siebeck gave them almost complete freedom, involving himself only when expenses became

excessive. Lamprecht and Marcks, for instance, did Siebeck the courtesy of consulting him when the third man of their editorial triumvi-
rate died and had to be replaced, but the two of them chose Gerhard
Seeliger as managing editor and general factotum.[64] On more routine
matters, neither Quidde nor Lamprecht, Marcks, and Seeliger consulted Siebeck on anything except minor points.

The editorial boards of the *MVHR* and the *JSH* were far more active
than that of the *DZG* and fulfilled the same functions as that of the
AHR. John Hicks may have felt that the *MVHR* editors consulted their
editorial board too seldom,[65] but most of them used their boards
regularly. In Alvord's time, the members of the board raised money,
chose reviewers, evaluated articles, and rushed to the rescue in
emergencies. Frederic Paxson, for example, untangled the chaos left
by the sudden death of the *MVHR*'s treasurer, Clarence Paine, in
1916. Stephenson depended on the members of the *JSH*'s editorial
board for similar assistance. They advised him on policy; and he had
them review articles, suggest book reviewers, and solicit subscriptions.

Because both the *MVHR* and the *JSH* were published by an association, their management, like that of the *AHR*, had an additional dimension. They have been fortunate in that neither has experienced a
crisis similar to the *AHR*'s in 1915, undoubtedly because that one
established for all American scholarly historical periodicals published
by associations their accountability to the membership. The relationship to the events of 1915 is especially clear in the case of the
MVHR, which was directly affected by them. Dunbar Rowland, the
leader of the attack on the *AHR* was at the time president of the
MVHA. He signed a joint letter with the other reformers, using his
title, president of the Mississippi Valley Historical Association, after
his name, an act that Alvord and other members of the *MVHR*'s board
of editors found to be offensive.[66] Claude Van Tyne resigned from the
board[67] after Rowland refused to make a statement that he was not
speaking for the association and the association refused to censure
him.[68] Petty as these events were, they did cause the *MVHR*'s board
of editors to decide that the immediate reelection of members should
be prohibited.[69]

Although both the *MVHR* and *JSH* were published by associations,
initially they depended heavily on outside sources of funding. While
he was inquiring of scholars about their interest in writing for a new

journal, Alvord was also canvassing possible guarantors. He had originally set $1,500 as the minimum necessary to begin publication, but by March 1914 $2,050 had been pledged and the board of editors raised its sights to $2,500. The guarantors were divided between individuals and institutions. Men like the industrialist Cyrus McCormick, the physician Otto L. Schmidt, of Chicago, and the author Justin H. Smith, of New York, as well as the universities of Chicago, Illinois, and Nebraska, and several of the state historical societies in the Mississippi Valley contributed amounts between $50 and $200. Because the *MVHR* was not self-supporting when the guarantees ran out in 1917, Alvord undertook a new round of searching.[70] Not until volume 39 (1952/53) did the last contributor, Mark Morton, of Chicago, disappear from the title page. The *MVHR* had begun creating an endowment fund from surplus in the early 1920s[71] and was investing heavily in war bonds during the Second World War.[72]

In addition to the guarantees, the *MVHR* received subsidies in a different form from the institutions with which its editors were associated. When Alvord became the first editor, neither he nor anyone else seems to have considered that the University of Illinois would be contributing to the support of the new journal. When Milo Quaife resigned as editor in 1929, he pointed out that the Detroit Public Library was contributing services of monetary value in providing him with two assistants plus office space and supplies.[73] Since then, the relative value of offers made by different universities has entered into decisions when the MVHA chose a new editor.

The *JSH* also derived strong support from universities. For its first three years, LSU paid all printing and editorial costs. Gradually, the Southern Historical Association was able to contribute more, and by 1938 LSU paid half the printing costs and provided the editorial staff. In 1942 a new LSU administration undertook to retrench and cut back the *JSH*'s subsidy to a token amount. Usually, university sponsorship is discussed in vague terms of prestige and service to scholarship, but Stephenson endeavored to put the issue in concrete terms the president, an ex-military officer, could appreciate. He hit hard at the benefits that the *JSH* and two other journals the administration was eliminating had brought to the university:

They have attained national recognition; they have established enviable reputations in their respective literary and professional fields; they have been significant factors in maintaining a scholarly respect for the university in years of internal scandal and public denunciation. These are intangible services the magazines have rendered the University during the darkest days of political and financial debauchery—services that cannot be measured in dollars and cents.

The seventy-five or eighty exchanges which brought to the university library free of cost "all of the historical magazines of the country" were more tangible rewards.[74] The president was not convinced, and the *JSH* was forced to search for a new sponsor. In 1942 it moved to Vanderbilt.

The *DZG* on the other hand depended upon the Siebeck firm for support. When he undertook publication, Siebeck established a *Garantiefons* of 2,000 M at the disposal of the editor, from which Quidde was expected to cover all editorial costs of the first five volumes, including such items as authors' corrections and payments. In addition, the editor received an honorarium of 1,000 M per year and twenty copies of the periodical.[75]

Subscriptions were a major element in financing the three journals. Quidde took an especially active interest in marketing and was continually writing to Siebeck with new suggestions. One day, he proposed giving a free copy to public libraries in foreign countries; another, sending circulars to the major political reviews.[76] When he left after six years as editor, the subscribers numbered approximately four hundred.[77] Both the *MVHR* and the *JSH* achieved larger circulations within their first six years, but they were both tied to membership in an association. Their editors, too, worked hard at increasing subscribers, and one of the first activities of the *JSH* was a subscription drive.

Many aspects of the establishment of geographically specialized journals were the same as or similar to those of the more general journals, the *HZ, RH, EHR,* and *AHR,* which had been founded earlier. One factor, probably the most influential, was different: the existence of other scholarly historical periodicals. The *DZG, MVHR,* and *JSH* had to accommodate themselves to an established pattern. Unlike the first scholarly historical periodicals, they lacked the freedom to appropriate an area of scholarship and make it their own, yet they had to accomplish something that was not already being done.

There were some compensating advantages. Probably the biggest was the concept of a scholarly historical periodical that had been established by the first journals. The new geographically specialized periodicals were able to adopt features that the early scholarly historical periodicals had been forced to discover through experimentation. They might receive benevolent assistance from the editors of established journals, but those same editors might also try to impede them.

The geographically specialized journals fulfill different functions within the profession from those of the general scholarly historical periodicals. By definition, they attempt to reach only a part of the profession and bear correspondingly diminished responsibilities. They do the same things as the general scholarly historical journals, but on a smaller scale. The major qualitative difference is that they do not have the same responsibility to the intellectual foundations of the discipline. In a limited way, the specialized journals serve as a training ground for the less specialized. They provide additional outlets for publication of research by potential authors of articles for the less specialized journals. Their editors may go on to become editors of more general journals.

Geographically specialized scholarly historical periodicals are an integral part of the mature professional communications network in history. They provide historians with an easily identifiable focus for their activities; they enable them to obtain the benefits of specialization without losing all breadth; and, though they limit their scope to one geographical area, they publish material on various topics relating to it. Most historians feel they are the most useful type of periodical.

FIVE ❦ TOPICAL SPECIALIZATION

❦ THE ZEITSCHRIFT FÜR SOZIAL-

UND WIRTSCHAFTSGESCHICHTE, THE

CATHOLIC HISTORICAL REVIEW, AND

THE JOURNAL OF THE HISTORY

OF IDEAS

Specialization in historical scholarship may take many forms besides geographical, including topical specialization, specialization by time period, by ethnic group, by major event, and by famous individual. In each of these areas, research is conducted, courses are offered in universities, and associations are organized.

Topically specialized history, like geographically specialized, arose in the nineteenth century and blossomed luxuriantly in the post-World War II period. The most usual forms in which it first appeared were economic and social, religious, and scientific history. The major European countries and the United States, for example, acquired scholarly journals of religious history relatively early. The *Zeitschrift für Kirchengeschichte* was founded in 1876, the *Revue de l'histoire des religions* in 1880, and *Church History* in 1932. British journals on the history of science show how thoroughly an area can be covered. Britain shared *Isis*, the influential international review of the history of science that began in 1912, with the rest of the world. In 1922 the *Journal of the Newcomen Society,* which treated the history of engineering and technology, was established; the *Annals of Science* in 1936; *Ambix: The Journal of the Society for the Study of Alchemy and Early Chemistry* in 1937; the *British Journal for the History of Science* in 1962; and the *History of Science,* also in 1962. In the United States, where specialization has admittedly gone the farthest, there are now journals of railway history, forest history, spelean history, family history, labor history, psychohistory, burlesque history, the history of biology, the history of philosophy, the history of medicine, the history of dentistry, the history of the behavioral sciences, the history of the social sciences, and of sport history, to name only a selection.

Although many historians specialize in a specific time period, the periodicals have not divided up the chronology of the world's history in quite the same systematic way they have apportioned the earth's surface. Some scholarly historical periodicals, like the *Berliner Blätter für Vor- und Frühgeschichte* and the *American Journal of Ancient History,* do focus on particular time periods, but this type tends to be interdisciplinary. *Speculum,* the journal of the Medieval Academy of America, is only one example among many. These periodicals are probably more often interdisciplinary because relatively few scholars specialize in these areas and because the educational requirements for them have more evenly balanced language, literature, and history than do most geographical specializations. In addition, the very concept of a time period implies interdisciplinarity.

Closely related to specialization by time period is that by major event, another fairly rare specialization among scholarly historical periodicals. The relative infrequency of these journals probably results not from a lack of such events but from the existence of so many other kinds of specialized periodicals that comprehend great events within their scope. The United States does have *Civil War History* and Germany the *Archiv für Reformationsgeschichte,* but this form of specialization is most characteristic of France, which has fewer specialized periodicals than other countries whose historical professions are comparably developed. Several periodicals have taken as their province the French Revolution, and at least one the much less momentous Revolution of 1848.

Another kind of specialization, most common in the United States, is by ethnic group. Many of the periodicals in this category are at best only semischolarly; the roots of ethnic history are similar to those of local history, and many of its practitioners are members of the ethnic group but not necessarily professional historians. Some periodicals whose scope is the history of an ethnic group have sought to be and are scholarly. The earliest of these was the *Journal of Negro History* (*JNH*), founded in 1916 by Carter Woodson. His principal motivation was the same as that of the founders of most nonscholarly ethnic historical journals of the period: to show what his group had contributed to America. Other black historical periodicals were begun in the

1960s, but their purpose was fundamentally different: to reshape the black past.[1] Mexican-American periodicals show the same division; the *Journal of Mexican-American History* took the *JNH* as its model,[2] and *Aztlan* demonstrates its orientation by using *Chicano* in its subtitle.

Specialization by famous individuals is the most recent and most unusual type among historical periodicals. Biography is one of the most frequent forms of historical writing, but periodicals devoted to one person, however significant, are rare. Towering historical figures are relatively infrequent, and too many are not entirely admirable. Two who have journals devoted to them are Napoleon and Abraham Lincoln, both of whom have attracted considerable amateur interest.

Amateur interest is characteristic of the different types of topically specialized periodicals and is the principal characteristic that distinguishes them from other types of specialized historical periodicals. Many of them have roots in some kind of social activity, similar to those in which local history associations engage. The introduction to the *Journal of Industrial Archaeology* proclaims that "the study of the physical remains of an enormously rich and varied industrial past has proved an attraction to engineers, historians, economists, photographers, railway devotees, geographers, antique dealers, schoolboys, professors, industrialists."[3] When the journal was founded, industrial archeology was not an academic concern; except for the Department of Archaeology at the University of Southampton, those in Britain dealt solely with prehistory. Amateur interest was widespread, manifest in such ways as the popularity of industrial museums, and the new journal could use it as a base. Similarly, *Civil War History* grew out of its founder's involvement with the Chicago Civil War Round Table. This organization gave dinners and conducted annual battlefield trips. On these occasions, Clyde Walton, a rare books librarian at the University of Iowa, met the many scholars and other individuals who were interested in Civil War history and became convinced that a journal would be possible that would appeal to amateurs yet meet scholarly standards.[4]

The amateur component is especially prominent in periodicals that are specialized by ethnic group or by famous person or by an area with which an individual can feel personal identification. Tradition is also important in areas where the support of individuals whose only qualifications are interest and enthusiasm is vital; professional historians have only recently, for example, begun to interest themselves in the history of leisure-time activities. Significant amateur involvement, particularly in management, influences many features of the specialized journals.

The three journals that will be studied in depth in this chapter were selected because they represent different types. One is German, two are American; two are topical, and one specializes in a religious group. Two are exclusively scholarly; one shows some amateur involvement. They were founded in different periods, and all have been significant in their respective fields.

The oldest of the three is the *Zeitschrift für Sozial- und Wirtschaftsgeschichte* (ZSWG), now the *Vierteljahresschrift für Sozial- und Wirtschaftsgeschichte* (VSWG). It was begun by four men, three of whom were associated with the University of Vienna; the fourth was a friend of one of them. One of this group has stated that Paul Siebeck, publisher of the *DZG*, suggested the idea to them,[5] but in fact it was one of their number, Emil Szantó, who in December 1891 proposed it to Siebeck, who had recently published a book for him.[6] Vienna was at the time a center for economic and social history. As early as 1847, Joseph Chmel, a canon at the monastery of St. Florian in Upper Austria, had proposed that economic history should be studied, but the real impetus came from Karl Theodor von Inama-Sternegg's 1877 address to the Vienna Academy on the sources of German economic history. Economic history became a subject for regular university lectures. Social history was less advanced in 1891, but it had made a beginning. Its founders recognized that social history and economic history studied different aspects of the same events and thus made a natural combination.

The group that proposed the idea for the ZSWG consisted[7] of Ludo Moritz Hartmann, professor of Roman and medieval history at the university and probably the leader of the group; Szantó, a privatdocent whose specialty was ancient history; Stephan Bauer, the youngest of the group and both the secretary of the Handels- und Gewerbekammer in Brno as well as a privatdocent at the Technische Hochschule there; and Carl Grünberg, a privatdocent for political economy at the University of Vienna. Active involvement with the social and economic problems of the Austro-Hungarian Empire stimulated their interest in such a journal. Hartmann, for example, was a leader in the adult education movement and in later years, 1918–20, would be the representative in Berlin of the newly founded Austrian Republic. The group shared a liberal, even socialistic, outlook that sought to find the key to the explanation of historical revolution in the dialectic of economic development. They belonged to the universal school of history, which concerned itself with more than traditional political history.[8]

The *Catholic Historical Review* (CHR) was the creation of one man, Peter Guilday, who in 1915 was a young professor at the Catholic University of America. He had studied at the renowned Catholic university at Louvain, where he had obtained his doctorate only the year before. He had then joined the faculty at Catholic University at the request of the rector, Thomas J. Shahan, who hoped to establish the university as a center of Catholic historical scholarship.[9]

In 1915 Catholic historical scholarship was well established in Europe, although in the United States little progress had been made. In Europe, it could trace its roots to the Benedictine monks of St. Maur in the eighteenth century. During the next century, it had provided some of the most important opposition to the historicist school in Germany, had founded periodicals, organized specifically Catholic education in history, and produced significant research. Guilday was part of this great European tradition.

One man was also the founder of the third and newest of the periodicals, the *Journal of the History of Ideas* (*JHI*). He was Philip Wiener, an instructor in the Philosophy Department at City College, in New York. He conceived the idea for such a periodical, organized scholarly and financial support for it, and eventually became its first managing editor.

In 1938, when Wiener first proposed the new journal to Arthur O. Lovejoy, a distinguished professor of philosophy at Johns Hopkins University, the history of ideas was not a recognized specialty. Wiener needed to refer to Lovejoy's classic work, *The Chain of Being*, to explain what he had in mind. Those who wrote in the area of the history of ideas were scattered among philosophy, history, English, and other departments.

The founders of these specialized periodicals gave reasons for beginning them that frequently echo those given by the founders of other types of scholarly historical periodicals. Prominent among them was the need for a place to publish. Wiener, for example, in his initial overture to Lovejoy, spoke of his own difficulties in getting articles published and of the long delays once they were accepted because of lack of space.[10]

The founders of topically specialized historical periodicals had additional reasons not shared with the founders of other types. Probably the most important was to define the specialty. A geographical specialization is self-defining, and most of the areas have long been recognized as entities. But, for a topical specialization, scholars must often impose the unity. The introduction of the *ZSWG* expressed the desire to create a focus for economic and social history and to influence and advance their study.[11] Similar statements can be found in many other topical journals.

In some ways, the need to define and shape the specialization is a variation on the theme of a place to publish. Before the *ZSWG* began, articles on economic and social history appeared in journals like the *Hansische Geschichtsblätter*, the *Zeitschrift für gesamten Staatswissenschaften*, and especially the *Jahrbücher für Nationalökonomie und Statistik*.[12] Guilday would have had available the *AHR* and the various historical periodicals published in Europe. Wiener's problem was not the inability to publish, but the delays, which in his opinion were excessive. The true need seems to have been less an absolute need than one for more space than was available, and for a journal that would give special consideration to the particular topic.

Sometimes a topical journal is the only institution furthering its specialty. The *Journal of Transport History* (*JTH*) was responsible for opening that field. It can almost be said that, to the extent that such a field exists, it is the journal. Before the *JTH* began, few articles on transport history had been written; had they been, they probably would not have been published. During the early years, the editors frequently encouraged authors to write articles.[13] Today, few courses on transport history are offered; and, though associations of railway and aviation history have been organized, there is none in the field of transport history. There remains the *JTH*.

A historical periodical that focuses on a particular religious or ethnic group usually has an implicit or explicit interest in furthering the interests of that group. The principal motives for founding the *CHR* were "to reflect in its pages the past glories of the Church as well as to promote the intellectual standing of Catholics of the present."[14] The *CHR* would help Catholics attain recognition by presenting the church's contribution to civilization. It would also educate its members: "No better means could be devised of instilling intelligent love of Church and country into the hearts of Catholics than such a periodical."[15] *Hispania Sacra*, a publication of an Augustinian-sponsored research institute, saw itself as fighting the evil forces of positivism;[16] *Historia Judaica*, anti-Semitism in the United States. *Historia Judaica's* statement on the subject is one of the most intelligent on what a historical periodical can contribute:

> Not only had prejudice risen to alarming heights in the United States, but it was being bolstered and propagated by a vast amount of conscious and unconscious misrepresentation of Jewish life, history and influence. Correction was called for, and it had to be more solidly based than the type of information available for use by the existing defence organizations and publications. It was imperative for the American Jewish community to have a periodical devoted to the promotion of "scholarly research in the field of Jewish anthropological, economic, political and cultural problems."[17]

The three periodicals studied in depth in this chapter all began under circumstances similar to those previously discussed. A publisher and four interested scholars began the *ZSWG;* a faculty member, backed by the resources of his university, began the *CHR;* another, similarly supported, the *JHI*. More recent topically specialized historical periodicals trace their origins to conferences, workshops, and other group experiences unknown to the academic world a generation ago. The *Historical Methods Newsletter* (1967) grew out of a special conference on historical analysis of quantitative data, sponsored by the Inter-University Consortium for Political Research and funded by the National Science Foundation. The participants recognized the desirability of creating a permanent channel of communication.[18] The origin of the *African Economic History Review*, both topically and geographically specialized, is remarkably similar, in its case a special seminar at the University of Wisconsin supported by the Ford Foundation.[19] The *History of Childhood Quarterly* (1973), now the *Journal of Psychohistory*, owes its origin to a research project sponsored by the Association for Applied Psychoanalysis that brought together historians and psychoanalysts.[20]

Defining the scope of the specialization is a fundamental part of the task of almost all topically specialized historical periodicals; consequently, the content of the published journal matches the original intention less often than in other types of scholarly historical periodicals. The contract between the editors and publisher of the *ZSWG* stated the journal's scope clearly: it was to present historical questions as they related to national economic and social politics, presenting articles on all lands and all peoples.[21] In the application of these specifications, problems arose that eventually proved serious enough to be a major factor in breaking up the original editorial group.

As Carl Grünberg's letters reveal, the issue was whether the journal was to exist for the national economists, although it might also be read by historians, or whether it was to involve historians directly. He and Szantó intended that, if historians might write for the *ZSWG*, their contributions would be economic history governed by the discipline of economics. Hartmann wanted to recruit historians,[22] who would presumably be working on their own terms. The terminology perhaps conceals the sharpness of the division. Grünberg wanted to maintain the existing approach to economic history as exemplified by articles that had appeared in journals like the *Zeitschrift für gesamten Staatswissenschaften*, the *Jahrbücher für Nationalökonomie und Statistik*, and the *Jahrbuch für Gesetzgebung, Verwaltung, und Volkswirtschaft*.[23] Hartmann was looking toward the opening of a new field.

Grünberg argued that, after the few articles by historians in the first volume had appeared, the editors could find no more historical articles. Historians concerned themselves only with political history. All the articles on hand or promised had been written by national economists. Except for a piece by Charles Andrews,[24] Grünberg had himself obtained all those that had appeared.

Hartmann, Grünberg's principal opponent, never presented his side. His close associate, Stephan Bauer, indicates in a memoir that the issue of scope was in reality a disagreement over whether the *ZSWG* should take a political stand. The editors had agreed that "strictly scientific method required the rejection of every political inclination."[25] Hartmann and Bauer were convinced that only by basing research on historical sources could the journal avoid becoming a medium for argument and propaganda. Hartmann was not renouncing what was really the fundamental political aim of the *ZSWG*; his argument was that "objective, correct knowledge would be better propaganda for socialist thought than any other kind."[26]

Although Grünberg and Szantó withdrew from the editorial group in 1894, their absence did not eliminate the problems of the *ZSWG's* focus. The relationship of economic to social history, and their relationship to legal and legislative history, to the affairs of the guild, and to administration were resolved only with the passage of time and the acceptance of articles. Economic history has dominated the *ZSWG/VSWG*. In an effort to justify its title and to encourage the lagging growth of social history, Hartmann and Bauer added a sequence of supplements in 1897, "Sozialgeschichtliche Forschungen," the first of which was the oft-cited "Geschichte der Fugger'schen Handlung in Spanien," by Konrad Häbler. The title of this separate section prevented any uncertainty over the focus of the journal.[27] Its articles also indicate that the editors defined economic and social history quite narrowly. Only a few scattered articles on the political, religious, or intellectual aspects of economic or social history and only a handful on historiography have appeared.

Despite the contractual obligation that the journal should cover the peoples of all lands, the geographical spread of the articles has been minimal. In 1905 the editors reiterated their commitment to an international journal, but at the same time declared their intention to give special preference to Germany on the ground that economic history flourished there more than elsewhere. The majority of articles in the *ZSWG/VSWG* have dealt with either Germany or Western Europe. The few others involve Central Europe, the Baltic, and the Mediterranean. Chronologically, the spread of the articles is too diffuse to establish any pattern, unlike most other scholarly historical periodicals analyzed.

The *CHR* also experienced some initial difficulties in establishing its focus, although its problems were practical rather than intellectual. When he began the journal in 1915, Guilday intended it to be a journal for American Catholic history. Some years later, he was advocating that its scope be expanded to all Catholic history. Several considerations prompted him to encourage the change. New journals dealing with American Catholic history, such as the *Illinois Catholic Historical Review* and the *St. Louis Catholic Historical Review,* had commenced publication; the subscribers were pressing for such an expansion; the interest of the American Catholic Historical Association, which had assumed responsibility for the *CHR*, was the whole of church history. The proposed enlargement would bring the journal more into line with its parent organization's purposes.[28] Guilday also admitted privately that his old teacher, Canon Cauchie, was disappointed with the content.[29]

Guilday succeeded in persuading the editorial board to enlarge the scope of the *CHR*. It became a journal for all church history in fact as well as in theory; United States Catholic history does not dominate. Although few articles dealing with Latin America, Africa, or the Far East have appeared in it, it has to be considered relatively well balanced in view of the history of Catholicism. It is also well balanced chronologically. As in the *ZSWG/VSWG*, the dispersion of articles by period is too broad to identify any concentration.

The characteristics of contributors of articles to topically specialized periodicals vary from periodical to periodical. Contributors to the *ZSWG/VSWG* and the *JHI* are almost exclusively university faculty who hold the doctorate. Those to the *CHR* and to the *JNH*, an ethnically specialized historical journal founded only a year after the *CHR*, include many nonprofessional historians. This was true not only during their early years, when, like the *AHR* and the *MVHR*, they accepted articles by nonacademics, but has remained true since, although to a lesser extent. Articles by nonhistorians and individuals in related fields, like archivists and secondary-school teachers, have continued to appear. Fewer of the contributors to the *CHR* or *JNH* hold the doctorate than do those who contribute to the *AHR*, *MVHR/JAH*, *ZSWG/VSWG*, and *JHI*.

The standards for acceptance in the topically specialized historical periodicals are somewhat different from those in the general and geographically specialized journals, partly because of the strong amateur element, partly because of manuscript supply problems. Most of the topically specialized journals strive to be scholarly and would say that they adhere, except when inappropriate to their scope, to the same standards as the *AHR*. The differences arise from the relative rigor with which these standards are applied. The *CHR* might turn down an article because it was not based on archival research,[30] but Guilday relied heavily on conference papers to fill his pages. Because of their different goals, most editors would agree that their articles usually do not entirely satisfy scholarly criteria.

Because of their implicit role as advocates, topically specialized scholarly historical periodicals that deal with the history of an ethnic or religious group encounter a unique problem with scholarly objec-

tivity. The *CHR* illustrates the difficulties. In spite of avowedly religious goals and comments in articles such as "It reminds us that
Divine Providence has Its own way of shaping the destinies of men
and in accomplishing through events that are untoward, Its merciful
designs for the salvation of souls,"[31] Guilday did not wish the *CHR* to
be overwhelmed by its Catholicism. In a letter to J. Franklin Jameson,
he remarked, "It has been a hard fight to save historical study here
from becoming a species of Catholic chauvinism."[32]

Although no clearly defined hierarchy of status of topically specialized periodicals exists like that of the *AHR, MVHR,* and *JSH,* few
of them enjoy the same prestige as the general or leading geographically specialized scholarly historical periodicals. Consequently, they
do not attract as many scholarly articles. The *JNH* printed an article
previously rejected by the *JSH.*[33] Such an occurrence is not unusual
among topically specialized journals. The increase in number of historians since their establishment has obviously meant more choices for
established periodicals like the *JNH, ZSWG, CHR,* and *JHI,* and they
have improved their overall quality. Nevertheless, limited selection is
inherent in all specialized journals, and the topically specialized seem
to suffer the most. All three of the periodicals studied in this chapter
were handicapped, at least in their early years, from an inadequate
number of the right kind of articles, and many other topically specialized scholarly historical periodicals face a similar problem.

The journals contribute to their own manuscript supply problems
because, with few exceptions, they are quarterlies and print three to
five articles per issue. "Quarterly" seems to be almost part of the
definition of a scholarly historical periodical, and the difficulties are
most apparent with the topically specialized. They prefer to interpret
their standards less rigorously than to publish less often or to cease
publication, perhaps hoping that the existence of a journal will encourage more scholarly activity in the area and that supply will increase. One rare exception to this trend was the *Abraham Lincoln Quarterly,* whose editor and the board of directors of its sponsoring
organization chose to cease publication when it began to run out of
material rather than allow it to degenerate into antiquarianism and
trivia.[34]

Topically specialized periodicals follow the practices established by
the general journals with respect to articles so far as they are able;
they follow their lead on other sections as well. All the topically

specialized periodicals studied in depth included book reviews when they began publication. The two American journals also had separate sections for documents and announcements. The *ZSWG* had a "Miscellen" section, which was used for short articles, documents, and news. In the years since, the *CHR* and *JHI* have dropped their document sections, and the *ZSWG* has added a section of review essays.

The book reviews in the *ZSWG/VSWG* and the *CHR* follow patterns similar to those in the general and geographically specialized periodicals. They have increased the number of reviews, but not on quite the same scale as the *AHR* or *MVHR/JAH*. The *ZSWG/VSWG*'s have steadily decreased in length, probably to accommodate the growth in numbers. Both the *ZSWG/VSWG* and the *CHR* have regularly reviewed foreign books and in recent years have noticeably increased the percentage of them. To review so many foreign publications is not typical of topically specialized historical periodicals. Among those in which they are rare are the *JTH*, *JNH*, *Dix-septième siècle*, and *Civil War History*, only some of which specialize in topics where books in languages other than the language of publication would be unusual. Another respect in which the *ZSWG/VSWG* and *CHR* are atypical is the range of their book reviews. The subject spread corresponds fairly closely to that of their articles. Other topically specialized periodicals often review books on subjects peripheral to the focus of their articles.

The *JHI* handles book reviews quite differently. When it began, it printed five or six per issue, approximately one page each, all of which were of English-language books. When almost all other scholarly historical periodicals were increasing the number of reviews, those in the *JHI* decreased. During the 1960s, usually only one was included in each issue. In the early 1970s, the *JHI* completely abandoned book reviews and replaced them with review essays. The topics tend to be fairly comprehensive, like Marc Saperstein's "Current Israeli Scholarship on Medieval Hebrew Literature" (volume 41, April–June 1980). The essays include coverage of foreign-language publications.

In addition to its book reviews, the *ZSWG* made another contribution to bibliographical control in its field. Before its suspension in 1900, it had published a bibliographical survey. When it resumed publication in 1903, the survey was continued in the most complete form possible, including selected references to foreign items, such as Russian, Hungarian, Italian, and French. The survey soon became an independent supplement, compiled by the Internationale Institut für Social-Bibliographie, in Berlin.

A brief analysis of the component parts of these journals leaves the impression that they are scholarly. This reaction is quite correct, and further investigation only sustains it. The editors of the ZSWG never envisaged it as anything but scholarly and never sought to be anything but that. Guilday hoped to involve amateurs in the CHR, and the contributors and news notes while he was editor show some evidence that he did, but since that time it has been exclusively professional. Wiener hoped the JHI could attract the nonprofessional reader and believed that it had a better chance to do so than "more specialized journals,"[35] although he never let this hope influence his editorial policies.

The relative balance between scholarliness and popularity is determined to some extent by the nature of the topic; economic and social history, Catholic history, and the history of ideas are all scholarly topics. Catholic history established itself early in the twentieth century as a subject of interest to professional scholars, who gradually took over leadership in the field. The other two areas began as academic pursuits, and their journals have maintained a scholarly character from the beginning. Many topics and topically specialized periodicals are following the course of Catholic history and the CHR. As professional scholars widen their areas of inquiry and teaching to include such subfields as sports history, they begin to publish in the appropriate specialized historical periodical, and gradually its character changes.

The editor and management structure of a journal also help determine its character. The first editors and their successors of the ZSWG/VSWG, CHR, and JHI have been professional historians. The original editors of the topically specialized periodicals, like those of the general and geographically specialized scholarly historical periodicals, defined their journals' purposes by applying general principles to day-to-day decisions.

Because most topically specialized periodicals are small operations and many lack strong institutional support, the editors are even more crucial to their fortunes. They must provide intellectual direction that goes beyond the setting of standards, which all editors must do. What was said of *Historia Judaica* and its first editor is more apt to be true of topically specialized than of any other kind of scholarly historical periodical: "It does not represent the joint work of a staff, but rather the efforts of one man . . . it inevitably carries his imprint, to wit, the accuracy and diligence that mark the entire scholarly work of Guido Kisch."[36]

The generally inadequate support of most topically specialized scholarly historical periodicals requires of the editor "unceasing work, constant devotion to the 'cause,' and readiness to sacrifice to it."[37] The editors are apt to find themselves acting as their own clerical assistants, like Kisch of *Historia Judaica*, Hay of the *African Economic History Review*, and Wiener of the *JHI*. Only periodicals like the *CHR* that are connected with an institution are provided the normal complement of assistant editors, editorial assistants, graduate students, and clerks. Some editors find the manifold demands exhilarating, others bear it with grace though not enthusiasm. Guilday obviously brought to editing considerable gusto, describing it as "a burden of the pleasantest kind."[38] In contrast, Wiener felt that "an editor's lot like Gilbert and Sullivan's policeman's is not a happy one."[39]

The first editors of the *ZSWG*, *CHR*, and *JHI* were self-appointed; since then, different methods have been used in the selection process. The editors of the *ZSWG/VSWG* have usually picked and groomed their successors.[40] The administration of Catholic University chooses the *CHR*'s editors, and for the *JHI* the editorial board makes the selection. Presumably, some kind of informal search is made, but in all cases the process is much less formal and more personal than that of the search committees of the *AHR* and *MVHR*.

The management structures of the three periodicals differ in several key respects, but at the same time display many similarities. All experienced some difficulties in that area. The *ZSWG* began with a quadrumvirate as editor, responsible to itself and to a limited extent to the publisher. Only after its suspension and resumption in 1903 did the *ZSWG*, renamed the *VSWG*, acquire an editorial board. Aubin refers to its creation as a means of securing the cooperation of distinguished scholars,[41] but their "cooperation" seems to have been limited to the use of their names. The presence of Georges Espinas, of Paris, Giuseppe Salvioli, of Palermo, Henri Pirenne, of Ghent, and Paul Vinogradoff, of London, on the editorial board reinforced the *VSWG*'s claim to be an international journal, but they apparently never participated in important decisions.

The original four-man team quickly proved unworkable and soon dissolved. In addition to fundamental disagreement over the scope and purpose of the journal, several of the editors were personally antagonistic. Awkward administrative arrangements compounded the difficulties.[42] The group had apportioned responsibility among themselves: Szantó, Greek and Oriental antiquity; Hartmann, Roman antiquity and the Middle Ages to the fifteenth century except for agriculture; Bauer, England and America, again minus agriculture; and Grünberg, everything else.[43] In these areas, the respective editors had total authority for everything from finding and accepting articles to revising proof.[44] To make his own life easier, Siebeck appointed Grünberg as managing editor and routed all correspondence through him. Grünberg felt that he was doing 90 percent of the work, and Hartmann found the arrangement to be intolerable. The original contract had not called for a managing editor.[45]

Hartmann was not the easiest of men. He had Bauer, his ally and childhood friend, threatening repeatedly to resign. Hartmann was frequently unnecessarily sharp with Siebeck; whether disagreeing over Grünberg as a managing editor or asserting editorial control over layout, he verged on rudeness. He achieved it when he informed Siebeck that, as soon as Siebeck ceased to refer to the *ZSWG*'s contributors in a familiar and impolite way on postcards, particularly a man like Mommsen, Hartmann would send his criticism of Siebeck's printing shop under cover.[46] Siebeck had referred to Mommsen in a less than adulatory way on a postcard to Hartmann, and Hartmann had disparaged Siebeck's printing shop on a document the craftsmen would see.

Less than two years after the *ZSWG* began, Grünberg and Szantó were gone. Siebeck, Grünberg, and Bauer had all made efforts to save the journal as it was originally conceived, but none succeeded. By volume 4, Hartmann and Bauer were sole editors and were trying to extricate themselves from the contract with Siebeck. The main point of discussion was the deficit, and Siebeck, after his difficulties with the group, was not inclined to be accommodating. By May 1894 he was flatly refusing to negotiate further.[47] The new publisher, Emil Felber, finally resolved the impasse by reducing the deficit by Siebeck's minimum settlement, 1,000 M.[48]

The most important fact about the administration of the *CHR* is that it is published by and responsible to Catholic University. Many of the members of its editorial board have traditionally been on the faculty of the university. Service to the journal was considered part of the responsibility of those in the History Department. When Leo Stock, a longtime associate of the *CHR*, resigned from the university, he wrote to the editor, John Tracy Ellis:

> If my connection with the University is thus severed, I shall not, of course, be available for any further work on the *Review*. I would do anything for you, Ziegler, and McGuire personally, but the journal is the University's project and I would be a fool to give any further time and effort to an institution which after 22 years of service would toss me aside so casually.[49]

The administrative problems of the *CHR* were predominantly personal rather than structural like the *ZSWG*'s. In 1921 the Reverend Patrick W. Browne took over as editor from Peter Guilday. Seven years later, Browne yielded the position back to Guilday. As editor, Browne had been inadequate in many respects. A revealing letter from his printer charged Browne with not allowing reasonable time to set foreign languages, making changes in an article at the proof stage that should have been made in typescript, and proofreading in a careless manner. Worst of all, Browne lacked tact. As examples, the infuriated correspondent pointed to his rude remarks about a linotype operator on proof sheets where that operator could not fail to see them as well as Browne's tendency to exhort by threats.[50] Other evidence points to more substantive deficiencies, but most of it comes from Guilday, who was not exactly a disinterested party. Guilday must have distressed Browne by remaining as an active associate editor during his tenure; the printer, for example, sent Guilday a copy of his angry letter to Browne.

The *CHR* was also sponsored by the American Catholic Historical Association, although more in name than in substance. In 1919 Guilday had organized and founded the association, which was then predominantly an association of amateurs. One of his main purposes had been to provide support for the *CHR*, which officially became the association's publication; subscriptions were tied to membership, but the *CHR* retained its close ties with Catholic University.[51]

The *JHI*, like the *CHR*, was sponsored by a university, but City College of New York never regarded the *JHI* as its own in the way Catholic University did the *CHR*. City College's commitment was indirect, to Wiener as managing editor of the *JHI* rather than to the journal itself. Several other universities interviewed Wiener, and, had he left, the *JHI* would have gone with him.[52] The editorial board was active from the beginning as was the editor in chief, Arthur Lovejoy. The role of the editor in chief depends on the journal. The *CHR*'s editor in chief when it began, the rector of Catholic University, Bishop Shahan, was only a figurehead. What he did as editor in chief he would have had to do in any case in his capacity as rector. As editor in chief of the *JHI*, Lovejoy screened prospective manuscripts, suggested candidates for the editorial board, and kept an eye open for possible material. After his retirement from that position, he remained as a consulting editor and was frequently called on by the managing editor.

The *JHI*'s administrative problem centered on John Randall, the chairman of the editorial board in the late 1940s. Seeking to make the *JHI* his journal, Randall accepted manuscripts without consulting the board and also independently appointed a replacement for himself when he was to be absent for a semester. When Randall added to these actions perennial lateness and gross discourtesy to potential contributors, Lovejoy concluded that he had to be removed.[53] Shortly afterward, Randall became honorary chairman rather than chairman of the board.

The implications of sponsorship are as profound for a journal's financing as they are for its management. The financial arrangements of the *ZSWG* with the Siebeck firm were similar to those Siebeck had made with Quidde for the *DZG*, although they were not as clearly set forth in the contract, an oversight that caused problems when the periodical parted company with Siebeck. The editors had considerably overspent the *Garantiefons*. That Siebeck was willing to settle for 1,000 M gives some indication of the size of the figures.[54]

The *CHR* and the *JHI* were sponsored by their universities, but their financial arrangements were quite different. During its early years, the *CHR* received money directly from the university. The editing of the journal was also defined as part of the editor's academic appointment. City College made no direct grants to the *JHI*, but it permitted the necessary subsidy to be solicited from alumni. In return, it was granted the position of managing editor and one other position on the editorial board for its faculty. Not until some years later did the college allow the managing editor a slight reduction in his teaching load.

Periodicals associated with an ethnic or special-interest group have been able to draw upon its members for financial help. A gift of $200 from Hugo Bulova enabled *Historia Judaica* to publish its first issue, and the periodical received continuing support from "scholarly-minded, thoughtful friends." A number of rabbis appointed themselves as fundraisers.[55] *Recusant History,* the journal of English Catholic history, benefited from the devotion of its business manager, Francis Allison. Through his Arundel Press, he made available to the periodical an office staff to handle without charge subscriptions, correspondence, accounts, and publicity.[56] Because of the general poverty of the black community, Carter Woodson of the *JNH* was unable to concentrate his efforts on a few wealthy contributors. Instead, he was forced to solicit from his subscribers continually. Donations of sums like $5 and $8 were usual, although Cleveland Dodge, a socially prominent New York merchant who was interested in educational and humanitarian projects, gave $400. One man donated $25 in two consecutive years, to be paid in fortnightly installments of $5.[57]

Topically specialized periodicals have also been able to interest foundations, and some European journals have obtained help from governmental sources. The *JHI* received $300 from the American Council of Learned Societies to help begin it.[58] *Historia Judaica* acknowledged support for its twenty-third volume from such diverse organizations as the Conference on Jewish Materiel Claims against Germany, the Alexander Kohut Memorial Foundation, and the Jewish Community Federation of Cleveland.[59] A subsidy from the Centre National de la Recherche Scientifique enabled the *Revue d'histoire moderne et contemporaine* to begin publication fourteen years after its predecessor, the *Revue d'histoire moderne,* was forced to cease because of World War II.[60]

Most topically specialized like most other kinds of scholarly historical periodicals regard foundation support as a temporary condition. They must aim for self-sufficiency, which can be achieved only through subscriptions, but their circulations tend to be low. The *VSWG* now has 1,100 subscribers; when it left the Siebeck firm it had only 165, which exacerbated its other problems. Of those 165, 108 were in the German Empire; Italy, 6; Holland, 5; the United States, 2; and France, Sweden, and Bulgaria, one each.[61] The *CHR* now has a circulation of 2,110 and the *JHI* 3,700, but many journals have fewer subscribers. The *JTH* has only 450.

Subscription drives are a recurring feature. Ethnic and religious periodicals are particularly well placed to conduct them. The *CHR*, for example, mounted such a campaign in 1917 after its initial resources were exhausted. At least sixty Knights of Columbus groups were persuaded to subscribe.

Topically specialized journals rely more heavily upon institutional subscribers than other types of scholarly historical periodicals. Many, such as *Recusant History*, attempt to stay within the financial reach of the individual subscriber,[62] but price seems to have little effect. Three periodicals that have acknowledged their dependence upon the library and institutional market are *Historia Judaica*, the *JTH*, and *Textile History*. The two presently being published, *JTH* and *Textile History*, are among the least expensive of scholarly historical periodicals.

Topically specialized periodicals are in general among the least expensive scholarly historical periodicals. The *VSWG*, at 88 DM per year, is an exception, but that 1982 price compares with the 106 DM 1982 price of the *HZ*. The *CHR* is $16 and the *JHI* $10. The *AHR* price to individual subscribers depends upon income. The maximum is $50 for those who earn more than $30,000 annually; only for the individual earning less than $10,000 is the price comparable to that of topically specialized periodicals, $15.

Evidence of what a journal means to its readers is just as sparse for the topically specialized as for any other type of scholarly historical periodical. Praise or criticism is usually very general. Wiener reported to Lovejoy after a trip to Minneapolis in 1955 that he found "great interest in and high respect for *JHI*."[63] The *JNH* was able to print in its second issue a number of endorsements from prominent historians and others. Typical was Frederick Jackson Turner's: "It is a credit to its editors and contributors and I hope it may continue to preserve high standards and prosper."[64]

The character of nonprofessional response to ethnic and religious periodicals is quite different. It is usually phrased in terms of the individual's pride in the group. A Singer sewing-machine importer in Lagos, for example, wrote to Carter Woodson about the *JNH*: "I am pleased to know that it was edited and published by my own colour."[65] A subscriber to the *CHR*, in response to a 1925 questionnaire, stated that he subscribed because he was interested, but, had he not been, he would still have subscribed because he valued the study of history from the Catholic point of view. He did not find the journal to be a practical source for sermons on church history, but thought a section of sermons in synopsis with a bibliography would be welcomed.[66] To proceed in this direction would have diminished the scientific character so carefully fostered by Guilday and suggests a conflict in expectations between group member-subscribers and scholarly editors.

The *ZSWG/VSWG, CHR,* and *JHI* demonstrate that topically specialized journals may strive to emulate general scholarly historical periodicals but certain characteristics set them apart. They do the same kinds of things as other scholarly historical periodicals—offer publication space, set standards, and provide a formal mechanism for communication—but their professional role is somewhat different. The difference arises from the nature of topical specialization. As it proceeds to ever narrower subdivisions, the community of fellow specialists becomes smaller, and the individual journals affect directly fewer professional historians. As a group, the periodicals do contribute to professional history by publishing the results of what Higham calls "the exercise of craftsmanship and the accumulation of professional finesse."[67]

The frequent involvement of amateurs further dilutes the professional influence of some journals. Their participation means that a journal cannot always be as scholarly as the purist might wish. The *JHI,* unremittingly scholarly, does not involve amateurs, but it is edited by philosophers. It is highly professional, but on its own terms, and should be considered interdisciplinary as well as topically specialized.

These characteristics are in part responsible for the insecure economic status of many topically specialized periodicals. They frequently encounter difficulty in securing institutional support because of their limited sphere of influence. Topical historical associations are comparatively few in number, and they are for the most part weaker than general or geographical associations. Some give the impression that they exist solely to publish a periodical. Such journals would be more firmly based if they represented a response to professional activity and demand.

The proliferation of topically specialized periodicals since World War II suggests an almost exponential growth rate. A few have voluntarily ceased publication because of paucity of suitable material, but the death rate does not appear to be higher than that of other scholarly historical periodicals. Adverse economic conditions may increase the rate, but specialized journals, although the topics to which they are committed may change, would seem to be an essential accompaniment of historical research, at least so long as journals of any kind remain the accepted publication medium of scholarship. Higham maintains that·"a traditional vision of pushing the boundaries of inquiry outward in space and downward in society has apparently reached its limits. Further extension of the horizons of history no longer seems credible."[68] If he is correct, the rate of proliferation of topically specialized periodicals may decrease.

Specialization is an inevitable trend in any area of scholarly activity, but equally important are unifying ideas and integrative concepts, the elements of theory. The divisions in history are now methodological, chronological, regional, and thematic. According to Pflanze, "the invasion of social science into history has not filled the breach, but instead threatens to split history itself into warring camps."[69] History gives the appearance of narrowing scope and diminishing effectiveness; it has become a dangerously fragmented discipline because its philosophy has not kept pace with its practice.[70]

Specialists have lost sight of or ignored the necessity to place their research in a larger framework. The ideas and concepts dominant since the beginning of the century may no longer be tenable, but "a discipline that uses up its big ideas invites exhaustion." Refocusing them or formulating new ones "suitable to an age of limits" is the task of historiography.[71]

The topical specialists and their journals, with the possible exception of *History and Theory,* are not likely to play a major role in the effort. The more general journals undoubtedly will, and the *AHR* has made a specific commitment: "The *American Historical Review* will seek not only to present history in all its bewildering variety, but to contribute to the next synthesis, if indeed there is a new paradigm of history struggling to be born."[72]

SIX ❦ INTERDISCIPLINARY
SCHOLARLY HISTORICAL PERIODICALS

Although the term "interdisciplinary" has come into general use only during the last fifty years,[1] as an idea it is contemporaneous with the growth of specialization. Webster's dictionary defines interdisciplinary as "involving two or more academic disciplines,"[2] and other dictionaries agree. The imprecision of this definition reflects the imprecision with which the term is usually employed. It has been a catchall word used to describe any kind of mixing of disciplines. Sophisticated educators prefer to reserve it for interaction between two or more disciplines, which may range from communication of ideas to the mutual integration of organizing concepts, methodology, procedures, epistemology, data, and organization of research and education. Interaction is crucial; the mere juxtaposition of disciplines is properly described as multidisciplinary rather than interdisciplinary. Successful interdisciplinary activity usually leads to something more. The whole is greater than the sum of its parts. This meta-interdisciplinarity is usually called transdisciplinary and means that a common system of axioms for a set of disciplines has been established.[3]

The practice of interdisciplinarity, in an unspecific sense, is as old as human thought. The Greeks regarded knowledge as a unified whole, an attitude that survived into the modern period, even though the unifying concepts changed. Education remained unspecialized, and learned men were scholars first, not mathematicians, political scientists, or historians. One individual could make substantive contributions in different areas.

All this changed during the nineteenth century; first in Germany, then in other Western countries, higher education was reorganized. New scientific subjects, such as chemistry and engineering, became topics for academic instruction; the humanities differentiated themselves; and the various areas of the social sciences emerged. No longer did all students study the same things; they pursued different courses of learning. When they became mature scholars, they were specialists, not generalists. An exact date cannot be assigned to the change, but Goethe, often called the last of the "universal men," who was born in 1749 and died in 1832, can serve as a symbol.

Many good reasons obviously exist for organizing education and research on a disciplinary basis, but it is equally true that such organization has drawbacks. Not all problems worthy of intellectual investigation fit neatly into a disciplinary category. Some of them, whatever their disciplinary origin, can benefit from the insights of other disciplines. Individual scholars, especially in the Continental European countries, early recognized these difficulties, and some sought to escape the restrictions imposed by the institutional constraints. It is, for instance, difficult to categorize men like Thorstein Veblen and Ernst Troeltsch. Several disciplines claim them.

History had barely succeeded in establishing itself as a discipline before it was challenged for its narrowness. Karl Lamprecht, who had hoped to succeed Heinrich von Sybel as editor of the *HZ*, was one of the first historians to question in a systematic way the theoretical assumptions of traditional history of which Sybel was a leading exponent. Lamprecht and others, like Henri Berr and Émile Durkheim in France and later the advocates of the "New History" in the United States, argued that the discipline was not meeting the needs of modern society. Research confined itself to too narrow a sphere in concentrating on political, diplomatic, and military events. Historians should concern themselves with the life of the masses and try to discover the underlying social processes. The critics also questioned some of the epistemological assumptions of the practitioners of traditional history and no longer accepted their assertions of objectivity. History should become a social science, "seeking historical explanations with the help of generalizations gathered from the social sciences."[4]

In Germany, Lamprecht achieved little beyond provoking a reaction that defended and consolidated the theoretical position of conventional history, but in other countries the challenge had a more lasting effect. One of the most important figures is Henri Berr, a French philosopher who was concerned with the theory of historical knowledge. He founded a journal intended to stimulate reform, the *Revue de synthèse historique*. His ideas profoundly influenced Lucien Febvre and Marc Bloch, founders of the *Annales*. In several significant ways, especially those relating to the interdisciplinary approach, the *Annales* perpetuated ideas first presented in the *Revue de synthèse historique*. In 1903 the latter published an article by François Simiand, "Methode historique et science sociale," that defined the nature of the relationship of history to the other social sciences. The theses presented in this article were integral in the philosophy of the *Annales*.[5]

In his essay to mark thirty years of publication of the *Revue de synthèse historique*, Berr described its program. Because the essay is both retrospective and current, the evolution of his thinking is difficult to trace, but the major themes of the journal are present. Criticizing specialization, Berr accused it of treating historical phenomena in isolation and thus losing sight of their true significance. Learning had become an end in itself, the sterile satisfaction of accumulating detail after detail, a substitute for the broad and productive desire for knowledge. The concept of history must be broadened. All the diverse activities of man were its proper study, and they should be studied with an approach that was enriched by the other social sciences. Berr especially sought enlightenment in sociology.[6]

Underlying his arguments was Berr's concern with the theoretical aspects of historical scholarship. He wished to replace the then current philosophy of history, "Geschichtsphilosophie," with "something completely scientific."[7] Synthesis should be based on analysis, not speculation.[8] Historians should use hypotheses. Individual historians would not themselves be capable of synthesis; that would require teams of scholars from relevant disciplines.

The activity of the *Annales* school is an application of some of these ideas, but in the English-speaking world interdisciplinary activity has preceded rather than followed theory. The search for a theory and a structure to accommodate attempts to reestablish intellectual links has been relatively recent; one writer traces it to C. P. Snow's lecture propounding his "two cultures" theory.[9] The English-speaking world also differs in that much of its interdisciplinary activity has been stimulated by practical problems. Some examples are the Tennessee Valley Authority project and the expert advisory groups appointed to study bombing attacks during World War II. The interdisciplinary committee, commission, or task force has been characteristic of American and English culture for several generations.

Whatever the relationship of theory to practice, whatever the value of interdisciplinary cooperation in certain types of research, it is still a relatively small segment of scholarly activity. Universities have been rigid, and the young scholar doing interdisciplinary work has experienced difficulty in obtaining the recognition necessary to advance his career. Tenure, for example, is almost invariably awarded by a department, not by an interdisciplinary program. It is also easier to publish conventional research in disciplinary journals. Referees more readily appreciate the value of familiar types of work. Too often what should be of interest to two fields is judged by both to be inappropriate for their journals.

Interdisciplinary periodicals in which history is an element differ from purely historical scholarly periodicals in almost all aspects, from scope to financing. Those selected for intensive study here are the *Slavonic and East European Review* (*SEER*), founded in 1922 as the *Slavonic Review,* and *Victorian Studies* (*VS*), established in 1957. They are representative of some of the more important variations within the group. The *SEER* is an older, multidisciplinary journal with a geographical focus; *VS* attempts to achieve true interdisciplinary interaction in its articles and has a temporal focus.

The primary motivation for the foundation of interdisciplinary periodicals is the same as that for all interdisciplinary activity: the hope of achieving, as the *Journal of Interdisciplinary History* explains, new breadth, sharpness, and methodological sophistication. The terms for the result of the process may differ, but the idea is the same. The editor of the *Jahrbuch für Amerikastudien* spoke of the "Beleuchtung," the illumination to be shed upon the total cultural phenomenon of the United States by contributions from the disciplines of sociology, philosophy, and law as well as the more traditional history, language, and literature.[10]

The founders of interdisciplinary periodicals more often than those of other types of scholarly historical periodicals hope to broaden their own understanding. The editors who established *VS*, for example, were very conscious of their inability to understand English literature fully without better knowledge of its context.[11] Those of *Eighteenth-century Life* clearly state this idea:

Eighteenth-Century Life was born one convivial evening last December when two "enthusiasts," one an historian the other a student of theater, met to discuss common interests in *le siècle des lumières*. Emboldened by their discovery of how much they had to say to each other, and aware of how infrequently such ex-

changes occur, they drew up an announcement of a new interdisciplinary newsletter, sent it off to bulletins in their respective
fields, drank a toast, and waited on events.[12]

The motives for the foundation of interdisciplinary periodicals are
not always purely intellectual. Sometimes a desire exists to offer a
different approach. *Business and Society* expressed hope that it would
provide relief from the intense preoccupation with management that
characterizes most business periodicals.[13] *Amistad* viewed interdisciplinarity as a means of escaping the racism of the traditional
disciplines of the humanities and social sciences.[14]

Interdisciplinary periodicals rarely claim their purpose to be the
providing of "space for publication," so familiar in other types of
scholarly historical periodicals. This important variance in approach is
the result of the strikingly different professional role of interdisciplinary periodicals. They cannot claim to provide a place for publication
because the pressure to create such an outlet rarely exists prior to
their beginning. Other types of scholarly historical periodicals hope
to stimulate research in their fields by their existence, but to create
activity from scratch is different. Interdisciplinary activity in an area
often results from the existence of the periodical. *Speculum,* one of the
oldest multidisciplinary journals, hoped to become a "rallying point"
for the study of the Middle Ages.[15] When some activity already exists, it rarely has a sufficiently organized voice to bring pressure.

The factors that explain the absence of the motive to provide space
to publish also account for the relative scarcity of truly interdisciplinary articles, factors of which few new periodicals display any
awareness. The *Journal of European Studies* was one of the exceptions:

> The *Journal of European Studies* seeks to promote studies of an
> interdisciplinary kind relating to the Literature, History and
> Thought of Europe. While we do not intend to solicit work which
> is strictly confined to the topics and methodology of traditional
> disciplines we shall not exclude work of a "specialized" kind if it
> happens to offer an important contribution to European Studies.[16]

Clio was another. It described itself as "an interdisciplinary journal of
literature, history, and the philosophy of history." Its editors recognized that, "much as we should like to foster a true interdiscipli-

nary atmosphere in which non-specialized polymaths communicate," most of its articles would fall into one of its three categories. True synthesis would be rare.[17]

The fundamental problem of scarcity of appropriate articles is indicative of the obstacles faced by interdisciplinary journals. Timing is therefore more crucial for them than for other types of scholarly historical periodicals. Both the *SEER* and *VS* were begun during periods of economic expansion. Until the 1960s, the 1920s marked a high tide of economic prosperity in the Western world. From the perspective of the *SEER*, those years offered the additional advantage of a lively interest in things Slavic. Russian ballet, literature, and music had begun to make an impact on the British intelligentsia before 1914, and World War I had forced Eastern Europe upon the attention of the public. No existing periodical was devoted to that area.

The *SEER* was begun in 1922 by Sir Bernard Pares and R. W. Seton-Watson, both recognized leaders in their fields. Pares had been head of the only Russian program in the United Kingdom before World War I, the School of Russian Studies at the University of Liverpool. Between 1914 and 1917 he had been attached to the Russian army and in 1917 to the British ambassador in Petrograd, for which services he was awarded a knighthood. Seton-Watson had published a series of books that had established him as the leading authority on the Austro-Hungarian Empire and on the peoples of the Hapsburg lands. He was particularly known for *The Southern Slav Question and the Habsburg Monarchy*, which had appeared in 1911. A third man, H. W. Williams, a brilliant linguist who held the doctorate, participated in planning the review, but his interests were not essentially scholarly and he returned to newspaper work before it began.

Both Pares and Seton-Watson brought to the new journal considerable editorial experience. The Liverpool school had published the *Russian Review* between 1912 and 1914, and Pares had been one of the editors. Seton-Watson had edited and published a magazine, *The New Europe*, from 1916 to 1920. Both these journals were multidisciplinary and both were scholarly in the broad sense but nonacademic in their intentions. The *Russian Review* hoped to further the development of "sane and intelligent public opinion" in Russia and to make accessible to the English public the work and views on various subjects of Russians of diverse opinions. The political aims of *The New Europe* were even more explicit: to help achieve victory and to prevent discord among the Allies. The audience of both was the same: "people who mattered," governmental officers, members of Parliament, universities, libraries, and editors of leading journals.[18]

The *SEER* was an integral part of the organizational plan of the School of Slavonic Studies at King's College of the University of London. Seton-Watson wrote to Ronald Burrows in 1915: "When you return, I shall have a parallel scheme to show you, for the creation of a British-Slavonic League—my idea being that *it* will cover the political field, your School of Slavonic Studies the academic, and a possible monthly review the literary—all absolutely distinct, yet working in sympathy with each other."[19] When the *SEER* came into existence seven years later as "an organ of the School of Slavonic Studies," it more clearly shared the goals of the new school. It was "to be devoted to the history, institutions, political and economic conditions, and also to the literature, arts, learning and philology of all the Slavonic nations, and in a lesser degree to their neighbors and associates in the former Russian Empire and in the former Dual Monarchy." Pares and Seton-Watson did not intend the journal to be exclusively scholarly, but felt it should combine scholarship with *The New Europe*'s tradition of political involvement. The *SEER* would be a publication for all those who had Slavonic interests or sympathies and desired to promote good relations between the Slavic- and English-speaking worlds.[20]

Because the focus of *VS* was English culture of the Victorian period, its aims were more clearly historical. In view of the continuing strength of some Victorian values within the culture of its audience and contributors, *VS* played a large role in interpretation and appraisal, or perhaps more accurately reinterpretation and reappraisal, a purpose not shared by the *SEER*. The first issue of *VS* made clear that it sought to be truly interdisciplinary in its approach. The prefatory note recognized that "this hope is more likely to be realized through the coordination of academic disciplines than in departmental isolation."[21]

In the fall of 1955, the three men who were to found *VS* all arrived at Indiana University in the English Department. All young, eager, and specialists in the Victorian period, they felt that they should take advantage of this unusual occurrence[22] and looked for a project. They examined several alternatives, but soon settled upon a journal and within a year convinced the university to support it.

VS had more in its favor than the general climate of economic growth when it was founded. Indiana's administration was ambitious and wanted to enhance the university's scholarly reputation. A fund to subsidize projects that could not easily find other support had been created from the overhead money from all grants. The chairman of the English Department was sympathetic, eager to see his bright young men succeed, and strong enough to restrain the objections of senior colleagues.[23]

The three founders, Philip Appleman, William Madden, and Michael Wolff, were a fortunate combination of talents and temperament. They described themselves in an automotive metaphor: Wolff was the accelerator, Appleman the steering wheel, and Madden the brake. They were joined in 1956 by Donald Gray, who served as the book review editor and lent quiet support.[24] In 1959 George Levine became part of the group and contributed additional eagerness, competence, and flair.[25]

The founders of *VS* were unusually systematic in their preliminary organization. They devoted much effort to developing contacts in the scholarly world and created a master file of 2,000 names of individuals who were potentially interested in Victorian studies. They sent brochures and covering letters, each with a personal note, to all these people. They distributed 600 brochures at the Modern Language Association meeting in December 1956. They studied fourteen standard learned journals, such as *American Literature* and *Speculum*, for format, page arrangement, cover, binding, contents, and editorial arrangements.[26]

The contents of interdisciplinary journals tend to be somewhat more diverse than those of other types of scholarly historical periodicals. The *SEER*, for example, especially in the years when Pares was editor, often printed translations of prose and poetry in addition to traditional articles and book reviews. Pares, a skilled translator, took a special interest in this aspect of the periodical and enjoyed his responsibility for the poetry section.[27] Many of the translations were drawn from the literatures of the smaller nations and would not otherwise have become known to the English-speaking world. Pares felt this endeavor offered an opportunity to set high standards of translation.[28]

Geographically, Russia has received the most attention in the *SEER* in keeping with the editors' introduction, which promised that it would be devoted to the Slavonic nations and "in lesser degree" to their former neighbors and associates in the Russian Empire and in the Dual Monarchy.[29] An informal arrangement also seems to have existed whereby Seton-Watson was given a third of the space for "his subjects."[30] "Subjects" were always conceived geographically rather than topically. The necessity to master a language was such a significant barrier that specialization was along ethnic lines.

Chronologically, the emphasis of the *SEER* is on recent times, although growing attention seems to be given to earlier periods. Articles have been in a broad range of disciplines, all traditional areas: literature, political history, economics, and religion. Strong and apparently increasing emphasis is accorded to linguistics. To a certain extent, the focus shows some evidence of changing with editors, although this is largely coincidental rather than intentional and reflects the changes in the kinds of articles submitted. Under W. K. Matthews, editor from 1950 to 1958, the emphasis was clearly upon literature and history. Between 1963 and 1966, when R. Auty was chairman of the editorial board, history dominated, and when F. L. Carsten succeeded him in 1966 languages and linguistics were given a new prominence. Auty and Matthews were philologists; Carsten, a German historian. Literature and history have remained staples throughout; only occasionally does an article appear outside these areas, which can usually be traced to the interest of a member of the editorial board, like that of Dr. Georgette Donchin in art.

An unusual feature of the *SEER* was its almost journalistic interest in contemporary events, which derived in part from its political predecessor, *The New Europe*. In 1922 no other journal devoted significant attention to current events in the area and their worldwide importance, and it was natural that the *SEER* should treat them. It retained this interest so long as the original editors continued to lead it. Pares's connection ceased only with his death in 1949; Seton-Watson's, because of his retirement in the same year. As time went on, this interest became less and less compatible with the *SEER*'s academic and scholarly focus, but Seton-Watson remained a strong defender: "A decision to omit political material would be absolutely fatal, and would stultify our whole effort." He described the alternative: "The best illustration of the alternative 'academic' policy has been provided by our American cousins, who in some of the Nos. produced by them seem to have been actuated by an escapism so extreme that the war was virtually excluded and nothing of the slightest *practical* value appeared."[31]

Pares, on the other hand, increasingly wished to see more of the *SEER* devoted to historical rather than contemporary problems. In 1937 he confessed: "I myself feel least comfortable when we are dealing in the Review with current controversial questions of detail which, especially with foreign writers, are so likely to take the form of propaganda."[32] To a certain extent, Pares felt that the inclusion of political material created administrative problems. A year later, he wrote: "At the same time I am quite clear that we have overdone the space which we have given in the Review to controversial subjects. . . . On current political subjects, we have run more than a risk in the case of some of the nations represented in the School of appearing all around and uncompromisingly hostile."[33] Pares further argued that criticism of the policies of governments had been possible when Britain had been regarded as a "universal umpire," but such was no longer the case. That some of the foreign governments in question gave money to the school was an additional deterrent. Pares still, however, wanted the *SEER* to treat "major" subjects in an "authoritative and objective way."

Seton-Watson was posing a real choice, although the division was not quite along the British-American lines he envisioned. In volume 22 of the *SEER*, edited in the United States because of the war, the May 1944 number contained four articles that were clearly political: Louis Adamic, "Yugoslavia and the Big United Nations"; Samuel H. Cross, "American-Soviet Relations"; Oscar Halecki, "Post-War Poland"; and J. B. Kozale, "The Future of Czechoslovakia." The journal regularly carried four articles per issue, and the proportion of the political was not usually so high, but the Americans can hardly be accused of ignoring current events. They continued this tradition once they established their own journal. The 1952 volume of the American *Slavic and East European Review,* now the *Slavic Review,* included such "practical" pieces as "Can Communism and Democracy Coexist? Beneš's Answer," "The Soviet Urban Housing Problem," and "Old Russia, the Soviet Union, and Eastern Europe." A more valid contrast is between the *SEER*'s prewar and post-1950 numbers. The later volumes by any standards are almost exclusively academic in tone. An article like K. M. Smogorzewski's, "The Polish Economy under Soviet Control," which appeared in the June 1954 number of volume 32, is so rare that it underlines the academic nature of the journal. Similarly, articles on contemporary affairs have gradually disappeared from the *Slavic Review.*

These changes in focus parallel the creation of alternative journals in which to publish and the dramatically heightened interest of popular magazines and newspapers in Eastern Europe and Russia. Particularly significant was the founding of *Soviet Studies* in 1949, which was "designed to promote the systematic study of the society functioning and developing in the Soviet Union." Its editors noted that, because most work on Soviet Russia had been done in Russian departments, the result had been a disproportionate emphasis on linguistics and literature; this implied that their journal would provide a different emphasis.[34] A division of labor between the *SEER* and *Soviet Studies* is now apparent. Articles on the Soviet Union tend to appear in *Soviet Studies,* which now bears the subtitle *A Quarterly Journal on the USSR and Eastern Europe.* Its articles are scholarly also, but primarily in the social sciences; economics is especially prominent. Nonscholarly articles on Eastern Europe and the Soviet Union appear frequently in the mass media.

VS has published a wide range of articles, not all of them traditional staples, to which the categories of content analysis do not do full justice. They have varied from the truly interdisciplinary, a rare category, to the history of science, art, architecture, economics, and drama. Topics that do not fit more traditional publications, such as history of sport and history of children, have been given considerable space. Martha Vicinus, who became editor in 1970, was determined to broaden the scope. During the 1970s she included such topics as feminist history and oral history. She was also interested in publishing more on new theories and approaches. Despite all the conscientious effort to achieve diversity, literature and history continue to dominate the pages of *VS.* To a large extent, this dominance is inevitable; the largest numbers of scholars interested in the Victorian period are located in departments of English and history.

VS couples a very high rejection rate, approximately 90 percent, with a continual search for appropriate articles. Several people associated with the journal independently stated that the supply of good articles is never sufficient. From time to time, the editors have commissioned them, but this has many drawbacks, the most important of which is the loss of editorial authority. The principal alternative in times of shortage is a letter to members of the editorial board urging them to look for and encourage articles in the area needed. During a period of scarcity of history articles in the mid-1960s, Michael Wolff tried this method, and Martha Vicinus used it during a later shortage in the same field.[35]

The refereeing system of *VS* is unusually thorough; only from a quarter to a third of the manuscripts are rejected outright. Each of the remainder is sent to at least two outside readers chosen from the field file, an elaborate indexing system that organizes potential manuscript readers, reviewers, and contributors by specialty. The editors have made a determined effort to avoid a clique of house reviewers.[36] They take into consideration readers' recommendations, but they make the final decision.

VS places heavy emphasis upon revision. The referee's form, which is designed to encourage suggestions, contains questions like "Can the paper be made more suitable for VS? Alternatively, if it is unsuitable, do you have any criticism of which the author might take advantage?" Few articles have been printed without revision, and those rejected are often returned with elaborate suggestions for improvement.

VS's biggest editorial difficulty has been the achievement of interdisciplinarity, which has never been as successful as its editors would have liked. The number of truly interdisciplinary articles, however, has been increasing as studies in this field have become more common and better understood in recent years. One member of the editorial board commented: "I agree, not that articles are too 'literary' but that they are too one-disciplined. The history articles are too 'history' too."[37] It is not coincidence that the editors can cite the genuinely interdisciplinary articles by name.

The editors of *VS* have tried to maintain a rigorous definition of interdisciplinarity. When they began, they hoped for articles which would deal with the period as a whole; which would straddle the conventional disciplines; or which, if from those disciplines, would illuminate other disciplines. Most of the published articles have come from the last category because most of the submissions have been standard fare. Inevitably, few contributors have been able to make *VS*'s individualistic interests their primary consideration during the writing stage. Scholars prepare articles that can be published elsewhere if *VS* does not accept them, nor is *VS* necessarily their first choice for submission. Its editors, therefore, look for articles that can be read with profit by anyone interested in the Victorian period. If a traditional, one-discipline article is good, they ask the author to "frame" it by providing opening and closing paragraphs that place it in proper perspective.

From time to time, *VS* has published special issues devoted to a theme, a fairly rare occurrence among scholarly periodicals. The first, in 1968, focused on the Victorian city; the second, in 1969, under Vicinus's direction, on the Victorian woman. Since she became editor, several more theme issues have been published: the Victorian child, Victorian leisure, imperialism. These issues were planned because the thematic approach seems to encourage interdisciplinarity. Several of the themes have involved new areas of history, and publishing issues on them has enabled the journal to encourage innovative work. The issue on the Victorian child was also planned with the idea that women scholars would be likely to contribute in this area; Vicinus sought more women and minority contributors.

The thematic issues, except that on the Victorian child, have been highly successful. That one suffered because not enough scholars were interested in the subject. Publication had to be delayed twice, and the editor was finally forced to use one article not originally intended for the issue.[38] Two of the others, on Victorian cities and on the Victorian woman, have been separately reprinted. Generally speaking, the editors feel that the thematic-issue approach is rewarding.

Unlike *VS*, the *SEER* seems never to have sought interdisciplinarity in the modern sense of interaction. From the beginning, it has remained a forum for various specialists. As Seton-Watson expressed it: "The Slavonic Review was founded of necessity on a hybrid basis and had to serve as a receptacle for many different subjects: and this was its main point of attraction insofar as it did attract."[39] This approach corresponds with the organization of the School of Slavonic and East European Studies, its parent, where linguistics, history, and other areas of study are taught in relative isolation. The *SEER* achieved what Seton-Watson described as "the very thing which Professor Struve desiderates, 'a sort of encyclopedia of things Slavonic.' "[40] It can be called interdisciplinary in the sense that it has achieved a balance among various areas.

Because articles by and for disciplinary specialists are abundant compared to interdisciplinary articles, the *SEER* has never, except possibly during the war years, suffered from a shortage. In 1923 Pares reported that "the Slavonic Review could be filled two or three times over with first-class contributions."[41] Their availability tempted the editors to expand the size of the *SEER*. A few years after its founding, Pares wrote to Seton-Watson, "I am sure you won't mind my saying that I am getting seriously alarmed at the length of the Review. I am sure we must really impose limits on ourselves and stick to them; our good intentions seem to fail us each time."[42] Even in the depression year of 1933, Pares could remark, "I think there is as little danger as ever of our being short of material."[43]

In 1980, the *SEER* accepted fifteen articles and rejected twenty-one, or 58 percent, of the submissions; in 1981 the figures were nineteen accepted, twenty-five, or 56 percent, rejected.[44] The refereeing system is less rigorously structured and complex than that of *VS* and more nearly resembles that of many other scholarly historical periodicals. The editorial board makes the final decision, but the advice of one or more outside referees may be sought. Articles may be handled entirely by the board if one or more of the editors is felt to be in a position to pass judgment.[45]

The *SEER* shares with *VS* a characteristic of all interdisciplinary and multidisciplinary journals: the attempt to achieve balance. As one editor of *VS* explained, in each issue it tries to publish one article on literature, one on history, and one on something else.[46] Interdisciplinary seems to be defined in practical terms as some form of equal space. Editorial preferences contribute to unevenness of coverage, but the supply of articles is a major factor. The *SEER* has found that those on history are the most frequently submitted;[47] *VS*, that history and literature alternate.

VS and the *SEER* both have an unusually high proportion of foreign contributors. In *VS* about a third have regularly been non-Americans, most of them British. The first editors made a real effort to involve British scholars, for they wanted *VS* to be seen as a journal that happened to be published in the United States, not as an American journal that accepted an occasional British contribution, and this tradition has continued.[48] The *SEER*'s figures are less consistent over time; in the first and eleventh volumes, 75 percent and 44 percent were foreign contributors, respectively; the forty-first and fifty-first, 40 percent and 25 percent. The foreign contributors in the early volumes fall into two groups. One reflects the *SEER*'s interest in contemporary affairs; the other the fact that so many scholars of Slavonic languages and history, though resident in Britain, are of Slavic origin. The first group contains names like Tomas Masaryk, a close personal friend of Seton-Watson, and Josef Pilsudski; the second, the less-recognized Dragutin Subotić and Jan Hanák. In the post-World War II volumes, "foreign" only rarely means Slavs or other East Europeans. Most of the later foreigners are American or Commonwealth scholars.

That both journals deal with the culture of an area other than the country in which they are published is only partly responsible for the high proportion of foreign contributors. *French Historical Studies*, another publication whose focus is the culture of a country other than that in which it is published, only rarely has French contributors. Their absence may be at least partly by design because one reason for the periodical's foundation was to counteract French neglect of American scholarship on France. The *Journal of Hellenic Studies*, which explicitly stated a welcome to Greek scholars, has also failed to publish more than an occasional token article. The editors of *VS* and the *SEER* not only issued a welcome, but they also worked hard to achieve real participation.

Both *VS* and the *SEER* have the standard contents of scholarly journals—articles and book reviews—but each has also attempted to accomplish something more. During its early days, the *SEER* published, besides poems and short stories, chronicle notes, a kind of chronicle of events; economic notes, current information on economics; and, to supplement the reviews, bibliographical notes. The economic notes had been discontinued by the fifth volume; the chronicle notes were published until the American-produced World War II volumes. Stories and poems lasted into the 1950s, but became rare. The disappearance of these elements produced an increasingly academic tone.

The additional items in *VS* are somewhat different from those in the *SEER:* a notes section, devoted to comments and queries; and the annual Victorian bibliography. Both continue. The notes usually consist of news about forthcoming events, conferences, and special issues; the Victorian bibliography is an essential part of the journal. Whatever headaches the bibliography causes, and they are many, obtaining it from *Modern Philology* guaranteed the establishment of *VS*.

The book reviewing procedures of *VS* are systematically organized.

Several times a year, the editor circulates to the editorial board a list of books whose titles he or she has collected from *Publishers Weekly* and the *Bookseller*, the journals of the American and British book trades, and asks for suggestions on the books to be reviewed and for names of reviewers. The editors then make the final decision. They have tried to avoid the obvious names, the top specialists in any given field, and to involve younger scholars, but an important book is given to a recognized scholar. Ideally, the editors hope to find someone who can evaluate a book and put it in its larger, interdisciplinary context.[49]

The topical range of books reviewed is similar to that of the articles. *VS* reviews appropriate interdisciplinary works and also major works in the individual disciplines. Literature is the largest identifiable category. The book review section is often used to provide balance for an issue when its articles are dominated by one disciplinary area.[50]

Much less information is available on the book reviewing practices of the *SEER*. Pares dismissed the reviews with the comment: "Our section of reviews, I must say at once, was never properly organized and was redeemed only by the contributions of the brilliant Seton."[51] Since the early volumes, reviews have tended to be short and to occupy a small proportion of the journal in comparison to *VS* and most other scholarly historical periodicals. The books reviewed are predominantly in the areas of history and current events.

A striking feature of the *SEER*'s reviews is the relative absence of books published in the Slavic languages, which has been a consistent pattern. The majority of books reviewed are in English, with a smattering in other Western European languages, but those in the languages of the countries being studied are rare. The *SEER* receives few books from East European publishers and does not review all those it does receive, although every volume sent to it, East European or Western, is listed under "Publications Received."[52] The Soviets publish extensively in history and literature,[53] the *SEER*'s primary interests, but they neither offer anything for review nor do they review books in English in their own journals. Because it is difficult for a journal editor to ask a person to review a book if he can offer neither payment nor a copy of the book, East European literature is rarely reviewed.[54] This omission may be less of a loss to scholarly communication than it appears because Westerners often find that Soviet works and those published in other Communist countries are as much propaganda as scholarship.

The audiences of *VS* and the *SEER* reflect their interdisciplinary character. Their composition by discipline is in approximately the same proportion as that of the articles they publish. For *VS*, scholars of English literature are the largest group, and the readers of the *SEER* are about evenly divided between language scholars and historians. A large number of libraries subscribe to both journals. *VS*'s subscription list is approximately two-thirds institutional; the *SEER*'s, approximately 95 percent.

Both *VS* and the *SEER* are affiliated with universities and display a number of the characteristics in their administration and management of other journals published by universities. Both have an unusually close relationship to the educational programs in their respective universities. The *SEER* was an essential component of Pares's and Seton-Watson's comprehensive plan for the development of the School of Slavonic and East European Studies. At Indiana, *VS* preceded rather than followed the related educational program in Victorian studies. The program offers several graduate assistantships for the *VS*, and some students who have held them have gone on to editing positions of "prestige and responsibility." Ironically, a period of financial retrenchment in the late 1970s led to the curious situation of replacing a graduate student book review editor by a faculty member for several years.[55]

Neither *VS* nor the *SEER* is the organ of an association, but they perform many functions of such a journal. *VS*, for example, carries news notes. By their existence, both publications contribute to the definition of their respective fields and to the cohesiveness of scholars working in them. An editor of *VS* commented that he viewed the *VS* office as the secretariat for a nonexistent Victorian Studies Association.[56]

Both *VS* and the *SEER* have editorial boards, which have varied in importance. When Pares and Seton-Watson edited the *SEER*, they made all the decisions. More recently, the other members of the board have assumed greater responsibility and have achieved something like a division of labor.[57] The editor, whose title is now more accurately chairman of the editorial board, is selected by consultation among the board; the School of Slavonic and East European Studies and its director, an ex officio member of the board; and the governing council of the school.[58] The board has always consisted largely of faculty members of the school, although it now includes representatives from other universities. In the early days, editorial business was part of the agenda of staff meetings.[59]

VS's arrangements are more complicated. It has both editorial and advisory boards. There has been no clear division of labor between the two, although since 1982 a distinction in membership has been made: the editorial board consists of Indiana University faculty and the advisory board of non-Indiana faculty. The journal has always made a particular effort to involve distinguished scholars in its activities through the advisory board. The first three editors established criteria for membership on it.[60] And Indiana faculty have always been important as advisers whether or not they were members of either the editorial or the advisory board.

When Wolff became sole editor in 1963, he established the editorial board. It was intended to be smaller than the advisory board and to participate more actively. By 1975, when Vicinus became editor, the system tended to reduce the editorial board to the same level of activity as the advisory board. She decided "to return to the old format of just four or five people on the Editorial Board, and a longer, more honorary list of names for the Advisory Board." The editorial board would represent *VS* at conferences, encourage scholars to submit manuscripts, and prepare symposia on particular issues.[61] The editor has felt free to call more frequently upon editorial board members and has made a point of regular communication. Both Wolff and Vicinus worked hard to make the editorial and advisory boards as effective as possible, and the editorial board particularly has the reputation of participating actively.[62]

The first editors of the *SEER* and *VS* made determined efforts to involve both American and British scholars in their management. Although American Slavic scholarship lagged behind the European in the 1920s, both Pares and Seton-Watson maintained contact with American scholars. When Pares spent a semester at the University of California (Berkeley) in 1924, he discovered that the Americans "wish to make use of our review rather than make one of their own."[63] Various forms of affiliation were considered and eventually Archibald Cary Coolidge, a professor at Harvard and its librarian, decreed that three American contributing editors would cover various subjects and districts of the United States. Coolidge named Samuel Harper, who had worked with Pares at Liverpool and who represented the University of Chicago and Russia; Robert Lord, Harvard and Poland; and

Robert Kerner, the University of California (Berkeley) and Czechoslovakia. Each was to seek appropriate articles and encourage subscriptions. Kerner would periodically supply Pares and Seton-Watson with bibliographies and notes on American publications.[64] This arrangement worked successfully, and, when World War II prevented the publication of the *SEER* in Britain, a group of American scholars undertook its production. After the war, American Slavic scholarship had matured to a point where the Americans founded a journal (now the *Slavic Review*) of their own, closely modeled on the *SEER*. An earlier journal founded by American scholars, whom Seton-Watson characterized as "(fortunately inferior) slavists," had unsuccessfully challenged the *SEER*.[65]

The cooperation of British scholars was indispensable if *VS* was to become the leading journal in its field. Its Indiana founders wrote to the senior British Victorian scholar, George Kitson-Clark, asking him to recommend a British editor. He suggested Geoffrey Best, who served as associate editor until 1963 and sat on the editorial board from 1963 to 1971. Wolff worked particularly hard to strengthen the British connection, and during a sabbatical arranged the first meeting of the British members of the editorial board. At one time in the 1960s, there was talk of a tripartite arrangement involving Indiana University, Leicester University, and Western Ontario, each of which was to take responsibility for particular issues.[66]

This elaborate plan never materialized, but Leicester did act in a fairly independent fashion during the late 1960s and early 1970s, which caused frequent delays and occasional loss of manuscripts. In 1971 a prospective British contributor wrote to the Bloomington office, which had never heard of him, inquiring about the status of his manuscript. This event led to a reevaluation of the dual editorial system and greater centralization of operations in Bloomington.[67] The most lasting British involvement has been the continuing presence of British scholars on the editorial and advisory boards. A conscientious effort has been made to maintain equal representation on them between American and British, including some Commonwealth, scholars.[68]

The two sole editors of *VS* operated quite differently: Vicinus independently, Wolff as a self-styled "impresario." Under Wolff, day-long editorial meetings were held at which all details were thoroughly discussed. Vicinus discontinued them when she became editor and at the same time defined and limited the editorial board's role. The goals under Wolff were on a larger scale, "creative editing"; under Vicinus they were more limited and specific. To a certain extent, their respective temperaments and visions were appropriate to the times. Wolff benefited from the expansive mood and free spending of the 1960s. Vicinus was forced to adjust the journal to straitened circumstances.[69]

Pares and Seton-Watson jointly shared the editing of the *SEER,* but Pares himself was ultimately responsible. He was answerable first to King's College and later to University of London authorities for the *SEER's* expenditures. Pares did much of the routine work himself, reading all articles, querying authors when necessary, making all decisions for the poetry section, even doing much of the translation. He also provided the general oversight any journal requires.[70]

Relations between the two men were not always smooth, and editorial sessions "though always friendly, were sometimes fierce. . . . But the net result was that each number showed a balance and a wholeness, which since 1939 we have never been able to recover."[71] Seton-Watson was shy, diffident, rather deliberate in thought and action—almost the exact opposite of Pares.[72] Pares, according to Samuel Harper, was a difficult man with whom to cooperate, but completely loyal to his coworkers: "It was just that his loyalty was sometimes qualified by his sense of mission, in the name of which he would rush ahead, regardless of the consequences to others."[73] Pares and Seton-Watson did share complete dedication to a scholarly cause. Pares described their relationship:

> Rubs and conflicts—and we seemed almost to live on them— could only be welcomed in the vitalizing partnership with such a man. Most fortunately, before we ever met, we had arrived independently, not only at the same general objectives in our task, but also at a kinship on most of the major issues that face political thought and temper.[74]

Both the *SEER* and *VS* have labored under a difficulty that is often the lot of editors: problems with the printer. Lateness has been a recurring embarrassment to both. In 1935 Pares found that, of the preceding nine issues, only one had been on time; one had been twenty-four days late. The production of the *SEER* was tied to the university calendar, and, if an issue were late, colleagues were not available for corrections. Pares himself could not oversee distribution and sales without cutting into his own holiday:[75] "For him the Varsity Cricket match and the ensuing Eton-Harrow meeting were something sacred; he wanted to be there and with 'a mind of peace.' "[76] *VS* has resorted to a chart of the various production stages that involve the printer, although the editor lacks any real leverage. The university requires competitive bids on all contracts, and the decision is not made in the editorial office. Occasionally, craftsmanship has not been what either journal would like. Pares detected more than fifty misprints or other errors in the *SEER*'s April 1923 issue. He was particularly annoyed because some of them had been corrected in the proof stage.[77]

The editors of *VS* and the *SEER* have been fortunate to be relatively free of financial worries because in each case the sponsoring school has made a continuing commitment. Each enjoys a respectable circulation, but that alone would not maintain it. Financially, interdisciplinarity can be a disadvantage. Neither journal can rely on an obvious association to come to the rescue as the AHA did for the *AHR*; the Modern Humanities Research Association, "a body which exists to promote scholarship in many fields," was persuaded to do so for the *SEER*.[78] It is more difficult to convince an individual scholar whose primary allegiance is to a discipline to subscribe on the basis that the journal is indispensable for his particular interest. Similarly, at the institutional level, a history department will feel that its library must have a copy of a historical but not necessarily of an interdisciplinary journal.

VS and the *SEER* have been subsidized continuously. The *SEER*'s subsidy from the School of Slavonic and East European Studies originally drew considerable criticism from within King's College and the university. The money came from a larger governmental grant to the school, a part of which was originally designated specifically for publication. Later grants seem to have been less specific.

This money was crucial. During the early 1930s, two-thirds to three-quarters of the *SEER*'s resources came from the governmental grant and one-third to one-quarter from subscriptions. The *SEER* would occasionally apply to other sources, such as the London County Council, the Czech government, the Rockefeller Foundation, and individuals, but the British government remained its chief supporter. At one stage, Seton-Watson, who had private means, would come to the rescue when it exceeded its allotted length.[79]

The school also subsidized the *SEER* by less direct means, which did not appear on any account sheet. Work on the *SEER* was expected from all members of the school; contracts required participation in "any publication work of the School." The school also provided and continues to provide the kind of services that are made explicit only when a periodical moves from one sponsor to another, such as space and typing assistance.[80]

VS's only source of assistance has been Indiana University. Indiana's Research Committee made a starting grant that was essentially total; since then, the proportion of grant support has decreased to approximately 35 percent of running costs. As of 1979 the university also provided a staff of one work-study person, a secretary, and two graduate assistants on eleven month half-time appointments. The editor is also a half-time appointment.[81]

VS benefited periodically from the openhandedness of the 1960s, including, for example, a generous unrestricted fund, but in the 1970s it had to economize. In 1972 the budget increase was limited to 3 percent, but the post office raised its rates well above that figure. An effort was made to increase advertising to raise the necessary revenue. The next year, the budget was not cut, but it was not increased. This forced *VS* to regain additional costs from subscriptions. A more recent economy measure was the elimination of one graduate assistant position. Other "savings," cosmetic in character, have been achieved by budgetary legerdemain. The secretary, for instance, has been moved from the *VS* budget to that of the English Department.[82]

One of *VS*'s biggest financial assets has been a solid subscription base. Its strength was apparent even before publication began, a tribute both to the need for such a journal and to confidence in its quality. The founders had hoped for 250 subscribers before the first issue, but they achieved 350 individual subscribers and 100 libraries, without soliciting the latter. The prepublication total was, except for *Modern Fiction Studies*, greater than that of any other humanities journal not supported by an organization. A year after publication began, *VS* had 1,065 subscribers, 646 individuals and 419 libraries. Because it had done so well on subscriptions, the university continued its subsidy.[83]

VS has maintained its healthy position. The only noteworthy change has been the reversal of the ratio of individual to library subscriptions. As of 1979, two-thirds of approximately 3,000 subscribers were libraries, a much more usual pattern for a scholarly humanities journal. When last analyzed, three-quarters of *VS's* subscriptions were from the United States, a rather high percentage for a humanities journal. The foreign nations with the most individual subscribers were Canada, Britain, Australia, and Japan; those with the largest number of institutional subscriptions were Great Britain, Canada, and Germany, which has fifty to Australia's forty-eight.[84]

The subscription position of the *SEER* has never been so sound. In 1981 its circulation was 1,100, in contrast to *VS's* 3,000. During its early years, it struggled constantly. In 1922 Pares felt that the most promising prospects were British libraries, but he hoped for 100 American subscriptions. In 1923 he made plans to send a reminder to subscribers who were delinquent in their renewals and two years later toyed with the idea of a package deal on the *SEER* plus the dictionary that the school was publishing.[85] None of these efforts was successful, and in 1930 the *SEER's* new publisher, Eyre and Spottiswoode, attempted to increase subscriptions: "The figures, however, which Miss Galton gave me regarding the subscribers were very startling and suggest very strongly that something ought to be done and could usefully be done, to increase the total number of subscriptions." The professional approach did not help much—the early 1930s were not exactly promising years—and the 1931–32 volume received only £237 from some 285 subscribers. In 1933–34 the figures fell to £144 from 180 subscribers.[86]

VS and the *SEER* rarely paid for articles. *VS* commissioned and paid the person who made the survey of Victorian studies programs. The *SEER* did somewhat more commissioning, although the editors did not call it that and only rarely was the question of payment raised. Pares urged Seton-Watson to "write to the other people whom you would like to write for the new March number, so as to get them all going." When an author suggested that Constance Garnett's secretary translate his essay, Pares felt some remuneration would need to be offered. On another occasion, the president of Russian House, a relief agency for Russian exiles, when submitting an article by a refugee, suggested that "some small remuneration would be very acceptable, as I learn that the author is greatly in need."[87]

Financial difficulties did not prevent the *SEER* from becoming the leading journal in its field in the English-speaking world and in maintaining this position for a long time. In 1937 Pares considered it the best known of the school's activities and its success the reason foreign governments wished "to have a footing" in the school. The *SEER* has also been cherished by individual scholars. When World War II interfered with its publication, George Noyes, of the University of California (Berkeley), said he was "deeply grateful" it was to continue. Lucy Textor, of Vassar, sadly missed it and hoped it would achieve the same high standards under the American committee. Her praise was an endorsement of Pares's and Seton-Watson's editorship: "As published under your auspices it meant more to me, far more, than any other journal."[88] Such general comments, however gratifying to an editor, do not give much indication of why the *SEER* was valued. Noyes did explain that his gratitude was rooted in the fact that its continuation meant that an article in which he took a particular interest could still appear.

VS has also received commendation of a general nature. Its editor was able to point out to the vice-president of the Bloomington campus of Indiana University that over the years it has been praised by leading British and North American scholars. When it was formally evaluated by outside scholars in 1971–72, it was graded among the best journals in the humanities and the leader in its specialty. No less a personage than Dean Acheson, the former secretary of state, wrote in its praise. Specific favorable comments have been made. In their report at the end of the first year of publication, the editors arranged their correspondents' reactions under interdisciplinary significance and foreign reputation, credit to Indiana University, and general congratulations. Even more impressive are the reactions of the editorial board ten years later when it was asked to suggest improvements. Such terms as "quality" and "enlivening" were used.[89]

Like the praise, much of the criticism of *VS* derives from its interdisciplinary character. One member of the board, a literary scholar, felt that its formula, though well suited to history and the history of ideas, was less appropriate to literary studies. The literary articles published by the *VS* he dismissed as "pompously or vacuously wide."[90] Such a reaction is not atypical of interdisciplinary activities. Interdisciplinarity is fine—for other people's subjects.

Interdisciplinary periodicals perform a considerably different professional function, at which the above personal reactions only hint, from that of other scholarly historical periodicals. Professionally, they still remain relatively peripheral, as significant as other forms of interdisciplinary scholarly activity. A notable exception has been the *An-*

nales, whose professional influence in history has been highly significant. True interdisciplinary periodicals like the *Annales* remain rare compared to the multidisciplinary, in which the particular disciplines do not give up any independence in the interest of a common goal. Articles in multidisciplinary journals remain disciplinary in nature, judged by their standards. Many interdisciplinary and multidisciplinary journals give the impression of less stability than other types of scholarly historical periodicals, especially those with a relatively uncertain subscription base. That neither *VS* nor the *SEER* has moved from the institution where it was founded is also suggestive, but the position of inter- and multi-disciplinary journals outside the institutional structure can offer advantages. Because they are not so closely tied to academic rigidities, they enjoy greater freedom.

Their professional importance is not necessarily a measure of their intellectual importance. Interdisciplinary journals are trying to accomplish something new, something that goes beyond the familiar. In their pages, new questions are asked and new approaches brought to old questions. They do not always succeed in their endeavor, but when they do they are intellectually exciting.

SEVEN ❦ POLITICS AND
SCHOLARLY HISTORICAL
PERIODICALS

Because its past is the foundation for the self-concept of any group—family, church, nation, or any other—history is not a subject that can be divorced from present concerns. The cliché that each generation must rewrite history contains a profound truth. Current issues inevitably affect historians' perceptions and influence all aspects of their work—from the problems they consider worth examining to the interpretations of their findings.

Political considerations are particularly prominent in the historian's world view. The frequent focus of historical scholarship on political history makes for equally frequent retrospective application of present politics. Thucydides had an Athenian point of view, Machiavelli was ostentatiously pro-Medici, and Catherine Macaulay's *History of England* was written to provide a Whig alternative to the Tory history of David Hume.

Political bias is most apparent in textbooks because of their importance for socializing the young into the group and because their authors usually assume that children miss subtleties. Textbook history must reflect myths; it also plays a role in shaping the myths by which a people lives. States recognize this function of history and therefore endeavor to exercise some control over what appears in textbooks. Control is most obvious in totalitarian states, but, even in democratic countries, legislatures have been known to review school texts to verify that they present the country's past "correctly." What is taught must conform to the dominant group's views.

Selectivity is the chief device employed to propagate a particular viewpoint. No fact used is necessarily inaccurate, but the facts add up to a distorted total picture. A quotation from the Nazi text *Der Weg zum Reich* about the Battle of Waterloo is an example:

Napoleon had thrown himself immediately on the English commander-in-chief Wellington at Waterloo, in the hope of a speedy decision. Wellington, however, trusting in the promise of Prussian assistance, stood his ground. By forced marches the Prussians succeeded in reaching the battlefield and attacked the French on the flank. Their arrival decided the issue. Napoleon was defeated, followed immediately by Gneisenau, and his army completely liquidated.[1]

The British view Waterloo differently.

Prejudice in one's own favor is the source of such bias, and the instances are legion. Catholic and Protestant interpretations of the Massacre of St. Bartholomew differ sharply. A Russian account of the partition of Poland reads: "Austria wished to conquer, Prussia to annex," while Russia strove to "recover."[2] Both Northerners and Southerners regarded the American Civil War as a war of principle, but disagreed completely on which principle was at stake.

Although political bias rarely assumes such crude form in professional history, political considerations influence scholarship and, therefore, scholarly historical periodicals. To a certain extent, they should. Historians may write about the past but they live in and write for the present. At their best, they lead a "double life, responsive on the one side to the questions and issues of [their] own age, faithful on the other side to the integrity of an age gone by."[3] Unless their efforts are informed by values, they degenerate into antiquarianism, or the study of the past for its own sake. They can expect to be read only if their audience finds something that speaks to its condition.

Historians' definition of professionalism imposes limits on the play of prejudice. However differently they individually perceive the truth, they all ultimately aspire to Ranke's dictum: to write history "as it really happened." Nineteenth-century Western historians hoped to achieve complete objectivity, but findings in psychology and sociology have demonstrated that historians, like other individuals, cannot escape their own cultural conditioning, an important part of which is political. Recognizing that impossibility, non-Marxist historians strive to be as politically neutral as possible.

The degree of political involvement of a scholarly historical periodical depends upon the philosophical assumptions of those writing for it. Marxist historians, for example, argue that to determine what "really happened" requires a specific political commitment, and their periodicals express that commitment. Among periodicals, three major schools of practice, named for the areas where they dominate, are apparent, Anglo-American, Continental, and Russian, respectively reflecting little, some, and considerable direct political involvement.

To call the collection of traditions that characterize Anglo-American practices a "school" is somewhat misleading because their essence is variety. In contrast to the historical professions of Continental Europe and Soviet Russia, no coherent philosophical system forms an intellectual basis. Instead, general agreement prevails on ground rules that are essentially the same as those of the political arena. This position was established during a period when most Englishmen and most Americans agreed on fundamental values, regardless of their party allegiance.

The most conspicuous and significant characteristic of the Anglo-American school is its ideal of scholarly impartiality. Scholars advocated neutrality while at the same time holding definite convictions on progress and on the value of democracy. Historians were educated to believe that they should not let present political issues color their interpretation of past events. Although the consensus that supported this view has disappeared as deep cleavages have occurred within the intellectual community, nothing has replaced impartiality as the official doctrine of English and American historiography.

Because they were differentiating themselves from the great reviews, almost all of which had explicit political allegiances, the first scholarly historical periodicals in Britain and the United States found it necessary to state this doctrine clearly. The introduction to the *EHR* asked the rhetorical question "How will the *Historical Review* avoid the suspicion of partisanship in such political or ecclesiastical questions as are still burning questions, because they touch issues presently contested?" and then proceeded to answer it: "It will avoid this danger by refusing contributions which argue such questions with reference to present controversy." In case any doubt remained, the editorial offered further clarification:

> Some topics it will be safer to eschew altogether. In others fairness may be shown by allowing both sides an equal hearing. But our main reliance will be on the scientific spirit which we shall expect from contributors likely to address us. An article on the character and career of Sir Robert Peel will be welcome, so long as it does not advocate or deprecate the policy of protective tar-

iffs. . . . Recognising the value of the light which history may shed on practical problems, we shall not hesitate to let that light be reflected from our pages, whenever we can be sure that it is dry light, free from any tinge of partisanship.[4]

The *AHR* printed a similar statement: "This review, therefore, must by the auspices under which it begins display the largest catholicity possible, and an impartiality willing always to hear the other side. It can in no sense be an organ of any school, locality, or clique. Controversial it certainly must be, but we trust always within the limits of courtesy."[5] These statements assume that the rules for scholarship are fundamentally the same concepts of fair play that govern the playing fields of Eton. They assume that a truth exists on which only two positions are possible, analogous to those of the two major political parties in each country. Once the journal has aired those two positions, the truth will have been stated, whether or not it is recognized. How to deal with a situation in which only one side of the argument is available is not considered.

In fulfilling the goal of political objectivity, the *AHR,* like the *EHR,* has avoided articles on currently controversial topics. Contemporary politics are usually present not in scholarly articles but in the news section, where the association's activities are reported. Because the AHA has been involved in the great issues of its times, accounts of its affairs in stressful periods are likely to touch on political issues. During World War I, J. Franklin Jameson gave the National Board for Historical Service, a group of historians organized for the war effort, more publicity in the *AHR* than it could otherwise have acquired.[6] Max Farrand's 1940 presidential address called upon American scholarship to do its duty in that time of urgent danger and encouraged historians to take the lead. The United States alone possessed the resources "to realize the hopes and to maintain the scholarly ideals that have been our heritage."[7] In 1968 the debate in the association as to whether, in view of the recent Soviet invasion of Czechoslovakia, it should participate in the Moscow Congress of Historians was reported. R. R. Palmer's 1970 presidential address mentioned the business-meeting discussion the previous year on condemning American policy in Vietnam.[8]

Historiographically more significant are the articles and statements with clear political implications that are occasionally found in the journals. One presenting a definite political view of contemporary significance, "The Rise of the Junkers in Brandenburg-Prussia, 1410–1653," by Hans Rosenberg, was published in the *AHR* in 1943 and 1944.[9] It contained such statements as:

> Men of action, of vitality, and of physical courage, who valued the tools of might and combined tenacity with adaptability, political acumen with brutality and cruelty, wherever individual or corporate interests were involved, the Junkers in the centuries to come remained inspired by the lust for power rather than by the passion for virtue, wisdom, or beauty. Arrogant and self-centered, they were ready to gamble for high stakes.

Even the Junkers' achievements were couched in derogatory language:

> They made their peace with liberalism and nationalism, capitalism and socialism alike, making all serviceable to the ultimate end of retaining power, directly or indirectly. . . . They outwitted the Hohenzollerns in 1918. They outwitted the Allied Powers in 1918 and 1919. They outwitted the Social Democrats and the Weimar Republic.

Incidental value-laden statements also appear occasionally in other articles, such as "Roosevelt and Hitler, the one essentially benign, the other malevolent."[10]

A number of articles in the *AHR* look very kindly upon the British, including one by Robert Schuyler in which he argued that most nineteenth-century English statesmen viewed Colonial independence with equanimity.[11] Sidney Fay's 1920 article on the origins of World War I declared the Germans bore the main responsibility for the war, although he did clear them of charges of deliberately plotting its beginning.[12]

It would be misleading to give such examples undue prominence. Their importance lies not in their existence, for American historians would be expected to hold an American point of view. Their significance is their place in the total picture of the *AHR*. It is a place that is small.

Such examples of even a mild nationalistic spirit are infrequent. They are more than balanced by many examples that can be described as almost antinationalistic. In his scholarly "Europe, Spanish America, and the Monroe Doctrine,"[13] Dexter Perkins demythologized the Monroe Doctrine. He argued that Monroe did not scare off the great powers of Europe; the United States in 1821 did not have much power to wield; and the doctrine in fact exerted little influence. The *AHR* also publishes opponents of traditional American values. The historians of the New Left are present in numbers that exceed tokenism. They publish articles,[14] have their books reviewed no more unfavorably than those of other historians, and themselves review others. Similarly, feminist historians contribute. A Marxist historian, Eugene Genovese, has even served on the board of editors.

Journals founded more recently share the same ideal of neutrality, but only those that deal with events that are currently divisive usually feel obliged to state their position. The *Russian Review* declared:

> The review is not committed to any partisan interpretation of Russian history or of the Russian Revolution. It offers its hospitality to authors of quite divergent viewpoints, provided that they possess the quality of competent knowledge of the subject which they propose to discuss. Completely aloof objectivity is not easy to attain in dealing with a country which twenty-four years ago experienced one of the most gigantic social upheavals in history. It seems probable that more is to be gained by giving contributors full freedom of expression and letting divergent viewpoints balance each other than by attempting to enforce any kind of unreal uniformity of judgment.[15]

Civil War History sought to explore the period of the American Civil War "on a non-partisan, scholarly basis."[16]

The experience of the *SEER* is especially illuminating. Because it focused on an area marked by sharp political differences and constant political change, its editors were forced to confront the issue of the journal's political involvement. Their response in various contexts helps to define the Anglo-American tradition.

The *SEER* began without a formal policy on political involvement. As successor to *The New Europe*, it was intended to perpetuate that journal's political traditions, but it later became clear that political commitment of that kind was incompatible with an essentially scholarly purpose. Even before the first issue appeared, some of the difficulties were apparent. Harold Williams, the third editor during the planning stage, wrote to Seton-Watson about a proposed article: "I have objected to an article on co-operation which is now a very confused subject, mixed up with politics, and would need a lot of explanation. And we don't know what the political position will be by the time the number comes out."[17]

Foreign contributors who came from cultures where impartiality was not a part of the scholarly tradition frequently caused difficulties. Pares complained, for example, "Most Poles seem incapable of understanding that purely controversial statements without any foundation and entirely inaccurate are of all places most unsuitable in a foreign Slavonic review conducted by University men."[18] In such circumstances, the Englishmen often found themselves doing considerable editing. Pares cut a good deal from the Polish article to which he was referring.

In 1931 Pares and Seton-Watson decided to state more plainly the position of the school and of the *SEER*. In an unsigned article, "The Crisis of Democracy and the Slavonic World,"[19] they declared, "From the first it has been our endeavour not to make of this *Review* a platform for this or that party programme, and, in fact, there are few shades of opinion which have not found expression in it." Although they were clearly advocating an equal-time form of scholarly impartiality, they went on to state in unmistakable language their own and by implication the school's and the *SEER*'s fundamental opposition to Bolshevism. The editorial referred to the Bolshevists' "rejection of all those ideas of personal and public liberty which our western civilisation had since the age of enlightenment come to regard as its crowning expression." Deploring terrorism, the authors argued:

> Bolshevism, as installed in Russia today, has repeatedly, for purely tactical reasons, violated the teachings of Marx and Lenin themselves, and above all that its application rests at one and the same time upon a reckless disregard for the spiritual facts of human nature and upon an acceptance of all and every means of justifying a high theoretic end.

The factors behind the timing of this editorial are somewhat more complex than the assertion with which Pares and Seton-Watson began: that the tenth year of the *SEER*'s existence was an appropriate time for stocktaking. General convenience was probably a not inconsequential stimulus. This editorial gave Pares a statement to which he could point when faced with such criticism as that by Constantine

Skirmunt, the Polish foreign minister, of the article "Galicia and the Polish-Ukrainian Problem," by Basil Paneyko, a Ukrainian.[20] Pares could describe the journal's editorial position as "the standards of judgment which we believe are generally adopted in our own country."[21]

Another factor was the pressure of events. In the issue immediately preceding that in which the editorial appeared, trials of Soviet scholars were reported.[22] The editorial declared, "Nowhere is this blunt denial of freedom more in evidence than in the academic world; and it is that fact above all else that has rendered our protest inevitable." Among other things, "The Crisis of Democracy" is a passionate affirmation of the Anglo-American concept of academic freedom.

The Mirsky affair probably provided further incentive. When D. S. Mirsky, a lecturer in Russian literature at the School of Slavonic and East European Studies, became a member of the Communist party, his action "brought to a head a problem which has long been latent." The Soviet exploitation of the opportunity provided by Mirsky exacerbated the situation. Mirsky was invited to Russia; Pares, who had been trying to gain admission for years, was not.[23] In the March 1931 issue, an article by Mirsky appeared that was loaded with such politically pregnant statements as this one:

> That the immediate effect of the October Revolution on literature should not have been greater than it was, is due to the cultural state of the upper classes it eliminated. The squires had long since ceased to exist culturally, and their cultural sterility (since about the time of the conversion of Tolstoy) is in striking agreement with the hopelessly antiquated character of the Tsarist polity.[24]

The following August, in a memorandum on the Mirsky affair, Seton-Watson raised a fundamental question that carried further the issues he and Pares had posed in their March editorial: could members of the staff all write freely on opposite sides of so fundamental a controversy as Russian communism—especially fundamental to the school—and on the desirability (or the reverse) of applying it to England or Western Europe? Would this be compatible with close and cordial cooperation among them?[25]

The *SEER* did not curtail its policy of free expression. Three years later, Pares answered a letter from Stafford C. Talbot, director of the

British Russian Gazette and Trade Outlook, which criticized the School of Slavonic and East European Studies for failing to be a training institute in Russian economic conditions and for being polemical. Pares replied that an active Communist (Mirsky) was on the staff. He also restated the *SEER*'s policy in a way that clarified some of the difficulties it was experiencing and the fundamental incompatibility of the Anglo-American and Soviet positions:

> I have also more than once invited communists to contribute to our Slavonic Review. I was assured, however, by a member of the Soviet Embassy in London, that this could not be regarded as satisfactory to them if we also printed other views than theirs. I am afraid that such a monopoly is hardly possible in work associated with a University, and I imagine that you will find that the University to which we both belonged would hardly be likely to take any other view.[26]

Over the years, the problem has diminished. As the *SEER* has moved away from contemporary issues, politics have been less obtrusive. That it publishes little Sovietica has helped make workable a policy of official impartiality.

The Continental European attitude toward the political involvement of scholarly historical periodicals differs significantly from the Anglo-American. From the beginning, European journals have shown a definite political orientation and have considered it right and proper to do so. Democratic representation is achieved because different journals express different points of view. In France, the *Revue historique* was Protestant and republican, the *Revue des questions historiques* Catholic and monarchical. Two Spanish journals that contributed to the growth of historical scholarship were the Augustinian *La Ciudad de Dios* and the Jesuit *Razón y Fé*. Italian historians who favored the Entente powers founded the *Nuova Rivista Storica* in 1917 to provide an alternative to the leading *Rivista Storica Italiana*, a typical bourgeois liberal journal, heavily influenced by German thought.

The considerable variation from the Anglo-American practice results from the different societal roles of European intellectuals, more specifically of historians. During the late nineteenth century, when the early scholarly historical periodicals were being founded, deeper cleavages divided the French, Germans, Italians, and Spanish, to mention only some of the major nationalities, than those dividing

Englishmen and Americans. Many fundamental questions on the nature of the state, the form of government, and the values of society had not been determined. Widespread consensus like that in the two English-speaking countries did not exist, and European historians recognized a responsibility to elucidate contemporary issues with historical background. They saw an opportunity to shape national consciousness and thereby to influence events directly.

The administrative organization of European scholarly historical periodicals contributed to the difference in method of political involvement. The contrast between the essentially one-man foundations of the *HZ* and *RH* and those of the *AHR* and *EHR* with their efforts to involve all the leaders of the profession is typical. European editors were relatively independent and could unify editorial policy, which did not need to represent a committee compromise. The *HZ* had no editorial board until 1896, the *RH* none until 1925. Editors tended to be senior professors. A European professorship is a position of great prestige and some consequence, and this status strengthened their position as editor.

The early years of the *RH* illustrate how a Continental scholarly historical periodical manifests its political convictions. Begun in the aftermath of 1870, its founder Gabriel Monod hoped it would "provide our country the moral unity and vigor it needs, enabling it both to become familiar with its historical traditions and to comprehend the transformations it has undergone."[27] Although the disproportionate attention to the eighteenth century may be one manifestation of his intentions, the "Bulletin" was "the place where the philosophy and practice of the Revue is condensed, its conscience in a sense, moral and political conscience rather than intellectual or scientific."[28] In the "Bulletin," Monod revealed editorial direction. In addition to reporting regularly on French scholarship, he urged the reform of higher education and mourned the death of Thiers.[29]

The French Revolution was at the heart of French politics in the nineteenth century, and the *RH* treatment of it illuminates the journal's political orientation. On the centenary of 1789, Monod reminded those who regretted the downfall of the *ancien régime* that they were forgetting that the *ancien régime* had ruined itself by excessive monarchical centralization; that it was an incoherent mixture of anarchy and despotism; and that all its machinery was rusty, strained, and corrupt.[30] At the same time, Monod deplored the form the revolution had taken. As men lost their sense of justice, they came to identify their party with the good of the nation and approved all violence and crimes that served their interests.[31]

Monod never allowed his political views to dominate his scholarship. In 1877 he reviewed favorably *Histoire des assemblées politiques en France de 1783 à 1876*, by E. Pierre, a royalist, praising Pierre for his fairness and impartiality.[32] There is no special pleading of the kind that appears in the *RQH*. In the *RQH* review of a book by François Guizot, the prominent historian and politician, in which he coupled enthusiasm for a royal restoration with distaste for actual royal governments, the reviewer argued that Guizot did not recognize adequately the difficulties of all kinds that came from both the Right and Left.[33]

Under Monod's editorship, the *RH* treated the sensitive topic of Germany with equal judiciousness. He remained personally sympathetic to Germany and throughout his career hoped for international peace based on a Franco-German rapprochement. Several 1890 reviews reveal his attitudes. He reproached A. A. Debidour, author of *Histoire diplomatique de l'Europe depuis 1815*, for an unjustified hostility to the Triple Alliance and especially toward Germany. Monod expressed his doubts about the alliance advocated by Chaudordy in *La France en 1889*, which later came into being as the Triple Entente. Lévy-Bruhl's thesis of two Germanies, with Prussia representing the evil side, he contended was contradicted by the facts, but he condemned the Prussian annexation of Alsace-Lorraine and Schleswig-Holstein.[34]

After Monod's death in 1912 and the outbreak of the First World War, the *RH* became more anti-German. Although it was not officially mobilized, it did serve the national interests during the war.[35] Christian Pfister, the codirector during that period and an exile from Alsace since the age of thirteen, frequently commented in the *RH* on the lost provinces. He argued that Alsace and Lorraine were spiritually and psychologically French. They shared nothing in common with Germany, and the German claim on historical grounds was a tissue of lies.[36] The German historians were portrayed as propagandists who had used their scholarship insidiously to achieve a scholarly hegemony.[37] The Allies benefited from a positive press. Great Britain, for example, was presented as the mother of a form of democracy. The *RH* became an advocate for the oppressed nationalities: Belgians, Poles, and various Slavs.[38]

The political orientation of the *HZ* is somewhat more obvious than that of the *RH*, but it too allowed politics to dominate scholarship on only a few specific issues. In his foreword, Sybel had made clear that the *HZ*'s guiding principles were those of National Liberalism: a unified Germany, dominated by Prussia and practicing economic as well as social individualism. He identified the country's enemies as feudalism, radicalism, and Ultramontanism.[39]

The application of these principles is apparent primarily in *HZ*'s attitude toward Catholic historians and its stand on the policies of Frederick the Great, especially the origins of the Seven Years' War. The journal published no articles by Catholic historians who were pan-German in their outlook. In reviews, their books were criticized pitilessly, often unfairly. The *HZ* treated the question of Frederick's vindication, which had obvious implications for the contemporary problem of Prussia's relationship to Austria, as a patriotic duty.[40]

The *HZ* during World War I, in contrast to the *RH*, shows little evidence of the influence of rabid nationalism. An article entitled "Das erste Auftreten Russlands und der russischen Gefahr in der europäischen Politik" is actually a calm, scholarly analysis of Russian diplomacy in the sixteenth century and does not mention any evil, dangerous, and uncivilized hordes that might be anticipated.[41] The review of two catalogs of English parliamentary papers, 1807–1900 and 1901–1910, elicits only the justified response from its German reviewer that dependence on these alone would result in a one-sided picture of prewar diplomatic history.[42]

For the *HZ*, the year 1935 marked a distinct break with its established traditions. In the spring, Friedrich Meinecke resigned as editor, and the new management made an effort to replace the journal's definite but comparatively unobtrusive stance of Wilhelmian liberalism with a pervasive, aggressive Nazism. The change is the difference between a philosophy and an ideology, between autocracy and totalitarianism.

The Nazi approach to history cannot really be dignified with the term "philosophy." It was not a unified doctrine[43] but a collection of heterogeneous, sometimes inconsistent, statements on selected issues. More than anything else, Nazi history was an attempt to apply retrospectively the slogans of the National Socialist party. Conversely, it also served as a program for the future.

The principal characteristics of Nazi history were strong emphasis on the state, assertion of the unity of all Germans, glorification of military power and the cult of the hero, rejection of decadent Western democratic ideas,[44] and, of course, warnings about the Jewish danger. These ideas were repeated endlessly and applied with only slight variations in many historical situations, from Spartacus to Adolf Hitler.[45] The historian ceased to be an impartial observer[46] and became a political activist.

In addition to these intellectual features, Nazi history had an active dimension. In 1935 the Reichsinstitut für Geschichte des neuen Deutschlands was founded. Headed by Walter Frank, it coordinated existing historical projects in Germany, such as the Historische Reichskommission, and engaged directly in historical research and writing. Frank, who functioned as the official historian of the Third Reich, involved himself in all phases of historical activity and used his opportunity in typical Nazi style to redress old grievances.

As one of the leading ornaments of the German historical profession, the *HZ* immediately attracted attention. Only four months after the Nazi takeover of January 1933, Meinecke was receiving clear hints that the journal was in danger. By the beginning of 1934, the publisher, Wilhelm Oldenbourg, himself under pressure, was urging him to make the *HZ* conform more closely to the new political order. Meinecke's reply set forth the position to which he continued to adhere throughout the ensuing negotiations: "to remain true to ourselves in the maintenance of a rigorous scholarly striving toward pure, unbiased knowledge."[47]

Oldenbourg discussed the problems of the *HZ* with several historians, the most important of whom were Albert Brackmann, coeditor for medieval history, and Gunther Franz, one of the younger generation. Oldenbourg discovered that a certain amount of dissatisfaction with Meinecke's editorial policies existed, especially among the younger historians, and that a Nazi historical journal would probably soon be founded to compete with the *HZ*.

Oldenbourg hoped that Meinecke would resign of his own volition, but before that took place in February 1935 the two men made various proposals and counterproposals. During the course of these negotiations, it quickly became apparent that the question was not whether Meinecke would leave, but when and what the future arrangements for the *HZ* would be. Meinecke made some concessions, such as refusing to accept contributions from Jews or other "political undesirables." He warned Hedwig Hintze, the wife of Otto Hintze, his longtime friend and colleague who was also on the editorial board, that, though he was willing to print an article by her that he had already accepted, it would need to appear anonymously. Nor would he be able to accept any future contributions. She was a "particularly burdened political personality."[48] Otto Hintze resigned from the editorial board, accusing Meinecke of trying to strike 1789 from world history and to ensure that in fifty years no one in Germany would know what the word "Marxism" meant.[49]

Meinecke was not always so accommodating to the demands that were made of him. He supported Hermann Oncken, another old friend and longtime colleague, on such enterprises as the Historische Reichskommission and in Oncken's public disagreement with Frank. Oncken had given a lecture at the Prussian Academy of Sciences on changes in the structure of history during revolutionary periods. Frank seized the opportunity to attack Oncken as a scholar and a man in the *Völkischer Beobachter*. In his review of Frank's essay, "Kämpfende Wissenschaft," Meinecke backed Oncken and also offered to publish his lecture in the *HZ*.[50]

In February 1935 the crisis came to a head. Oldenbourg reminded Meinecke that he was a businessman and that his instinct for self-preservation required him to satisfy external demands. If the *HZ* wished to survive in the new Reich, a party member must be editor. He proposed as coeditor Helmut Berve, who would act as a political censor and have the right to object to any material he did not judge satisfactory. Oldenbourg would then take any differences of opinion to the appropriate party authority.[51] Meinecke had already stated he was unwilling to allow Berve the right of acceptance or rejection outside his area of expertise[52] and refused to agree. He resigned, stating that he could not allow partisan political motives to enter into editorial direction.[53]

Although Meinecke described the chasm between the pre- and post-1935 *HZ* as "unüberbrückbar," unbridgeable, the changes were in fact superficial, grafted on a largely unaffected body, and were partial rather than pervasive. Karl Alexander von Müller, a Bavarian historian and Frank's former teacher, became editor. The first issue under his direction contained a message that charted a new path for German historians. Germans were at a turning point in history; the German *Volk*, inspired by a great leader, were to construct a new Reich. German historiography was being shaken to its roots. Then, using Nazi code words, he exhorted German historians to fulfill their calling:

> For us, as for few generations, comes the consciousness that we have something to say in the decisions of the present, and in determining the future of our whole folk. Out of that which is becoming, we will search for and illumine that which has been, and revivify its bones with our blood; out of the real past we will recognize and strengthen the forces of a living present. The writing of history has always been given wings by deeds, and like its closest sister, the art of poetry, it is capable once again of making deeds. From the fullest participation in the life of our times, we hope, our science will also win new life; out of our science, we hope, will once again stream new springs of courage and strength for our folk.[54]

That same number carried a speech of Frank in which he tried to establish that a truly professional history dedicated to the service of the Nazi party was possible. His presentation is a masterpiece of sophistry and paradoxes. Typical is his statement that professional history must be scientific; science may not be used in the service of conquerors, but science itself may become the conqueror.[55] Frank would be a frequent contributor during the *HZ*'s Nazi period.

Two other items were also part of the effort to reorient the journal: an article by Hölzle on the concepts of "race" and "folk" in the English Revolution and a review section on the Jewish question. Hölzle sought a common ideological basis for all revolutions and found it in race and *Volk*. The review section on the Jewish question was a bibliographical essay and represented a departure for the *HZ*, which had always left research on Jewish topics to Jewish periodicals. The section was intended to be a regular feature, but proved to be highly occasional.[56]

Only these few items can properly be labeled Nazi. The remaining contents of the volume are indistinguishable from what the *HZ* printed under Meinecke. He had in fact intended to publish one of the articles, by Heinrich von Srbik on the Schönbrunn Conference of 1864, but the new managers had used a certain amount of chicanery to postpone it.[57] Their interest in this particular article indicates that they did not want the *HZ* to lose its traditional strengths. The strategy called for a few overtly Nazi pieces, like an article by von Richthofen in volume 154 (1936)[58] that attempted to provide arguments for the Central and Eastern European countries to unite against the Russians; one about Jewish influence on German civil and church law in volume 155 (1937),[59] and a eulogy for a Nazi hero-historian (Kleo Pleyer, volume 166, 1942).[60] It also required a mass of material that was not overtly Nazi. This remained the pattern of the *HZ* until its suspension in 1943.

Because the *HZ* was such an important institution, still the dominant scholarly historical periodical in many of the smaller European countries of Scandinavia and Central Europe, the changes aroused criticism. Foreigners recognized that the *HZ* had been coordinated with Nazi objectives. Some saw it as no more than an organ for Frank's Reichsinstitut. Even its new prose style was compared unfavorably to Meinecke's.[61]

Although the Nazis did succeed in gaining control of the *HZ*, they failed to fulfill their long-term objectives. The periodical was not transformed. Because it was only partially Nazified, it could not serve as an effective weapon to redirect the German historical profession. It did not become the profession's single voice as had been intended when the *Preussische Jahrbücher* was eliminated and the *Historische Vierteljahresschrift* encouraged to cease publication.

Many of the reasons for the failure are the same as those responsible for the failure of other Nazi projects. Time was limited. Only four years after Meinecke's resignation, the country was at war. During the twelve years it controlled the country, Nazism did not have time to become deeply rooted and to raise up a new generation in its own image. Those people who were most directly concerned with the new model *HZ* did not follow through on their initial enthusiasm. Although Frank became a member of the editorial board, he devoted most of his energies to the Reichsinstitut. Nazism did not succeed in making much of an impact on the well-entrenched traditions of the German historical profession. The majority of historians did not change their research interests, philosophy, or methods, but continued to produce the same kind of articles and book reviews they always had.

Wartime difficulties and the German defeat brought about a suspension of the *HZ* from 1943 until 1949. When it resumed, it had a new editor, Ludwig Dehio, an archivist and historian of the modern period. Walter Kienast, who had been a coeditor under Meinecke but who had also been a Nazi party member and served under von Müller, was the new coeditor. The first volume after the suspension was silent on the Nazi period of the *HZ;* and, reflecting a certain embarrassment, Dehio, in his introductory message, harked back to the *HZ's* days of glory under Sybel[62] and Meinecke. Dehio also spoke of restored freedom of thought. His printing of an article on Meinecke's book about the German catastrophe symbolized the journal's redirection.

The resurrected *HZ* had to do some reeducation. Kienast wrote to Meinecke that colleagues needed to be reminded of principles that had once been self-evident but even before the Nazi period had been disregarded. He spoke of frequent letters from publishers requesting favorable reviews.[63] The new editors printed a set of directions for contributors,[64] which stressed the elimination of any political slant and insisted on maximum objectivity.

The post-World War II *HZ* remains the *HZ,* but with a difference. Its underlying editorial philosophy is no longer historicism nor does it have a clearly definable political orientation. Like so many German institutions of the postwar period, it has come to resemble its British and American counterparts and is now politically pluralistic in the same way.[65] During the thirty years since 1949, articles have appeared in the *HZ* on the old topics of German historiography, the medieval empire, and Frederick the Great, as well as on recent events, but they are no longer habitually interpreted in the light of present political issues.

The third type of political involvement, in which a scholarly historical periodical serves the ends of a political regime, is best illustrated by Soviet periodicals. In a totalitarian society, scholarly historical periodicals, like all other institutions, are strictly controlled and regulated. The Nazis had hoped to achieve this "ideal," but their efforts in regard to the *HZ* were abortive. The third type of political involvement employs direct state intervention in the publication of journals that extends to subject matter, interpretations, and even acceptable bibliographic citations. It is part of a larger effort to exercise control over the historical profession as a whole. Nikita Khrushchev summarized the official Soviet attitude in 1956: "Historians are dangerous people. They are capable of upsetting everything. They must be directed."[66]

The Marxist-Leninist conception of history is the dogma of the

Soviet historical profession and therefore of Soviet scholarly historical periodicals. Unlike Nazi views on history, it is a complex and multifaceted system of ideas.[67] Marx articulated the basic premise: the forces of history are determined by the conditions of material production. The rise, expansion, and decline of different modes of production decide the social structure. Marx's and Engels's assertion of the significance of revolution and the mission of the working class provided the context in which historical scholarship was to function. Using this analysis, Marx gave history a foundation that Marxists describe as "scientific" and apply universally. Lenin elaborated on this thesis:

> [He] developed materialist epistemology and dialectical-materialist historicism, defended scientific tenets proving the existence of objective historical laws and the knowability of historical phenomena, and elaborated principles of party-mindedness (partiinost') in historical science and the class approach to the evaluation of historical events.[68]

The application of these basic principles has produced a scholarship that focuses on economic relations. Lenin is considered to have "resolved such basic problems as the periodization of Russian history and of the Russian revolutionary movement, the specific features of feudalism in Russia, the origin of capitalism, socioeconomic and political development in Russia in the reform period, and the domestic and foreign policies of tsarism."[69]

Professional historical scholarship in Soviet Russia has passed through several distinct phases. During the immediate postrevolutionary period, it examined such problems as bourgeois revolutions and the national liberation movements. The next period was dominated by M. N. Pokrovsky and the beginnings of the institutionalization of the profession through such organizations as his Society of Marxist Historians. Since World War II, Soviet historians have been steadily expanding their interests. During the 1950s they began to work more intensively on the history of Marxism and Leninism; on the formation and development of the world socialist system; and on the history of African, Latin American, and Asian countries. Domestic history concentrated on the history of Soviet society. During the 1960s historians carried these trends further; they devoted more attention to specific local and regional manifestations of their principal themes of feudalism, capitalism, and imperialism. In addition, they began to take greater interest in intellectual history and in the history of culture and wrote more frequently about historiography and methodological and conceptual problems.[70]

The different phases represent different interpretations of the basic Marxist-Leninist dogma. These interpretations have been closely related to political imperatives because historical scholarship "has become ever more closely bound up with the concerns of governing."[71] In practice, Lenin's concept of *partiinost'* has meant for historical scholarship "unconditional and enthusiastic submission to the interests and demands of the Communist Party."[72] Even so bland a work as the Soviet encyclopedia, which seeks to state no more than the general consensus, by implication acknowledged that fact when it pointed out that under Stalin historical scholarship had suffered from dogmatism, oversimplification, and subjective interpretations.[73]

Important social functions of history and historical scholarship are recognized. An official work like the Soviet encyclopedia demonstrates this recognition by the prominent place it assigns to history and to various aspects of historical scholarship and publication.[74] The formal, acknowledged functions are that the subject is the repository of tradition and legend, and it is an instrument of instruction. The informal, unacknowledged, but very real, functions include the following: to legitimate the system, rationalize politics, indicate the political climate, permit ideological and theoretical discussion, and serve as a political weapon.[75] Party history occupies a special place. It is not a branch of the discipline like an analogue in a Western country, but is in a sense Soviet history itself. Because the Communist party has been the agent of government and the only significant social, intellectual, and cultural institution, its history "both contains and is contained by the record of all the years after 1917."[76]

The political function added to the professional function of Soviet scholarly historical periodicals has resulted in a universe very different from that typical of Western countries. An elaborate system of state and party controls censors all material before publication and directs the management of journals.[77] The journals are born, change direction, and die in response to political imperatives rather than to internally generated scholarly concerns. Scholarly historical periodicals can themselves become an arena for political battle, a part of rather than a reporter of or an influence on history in the manner of European and American journals.

In the evolution of Russian scholarly historical periodicals, the Revolution of 1917 marked a sharp break with the past. There had been historical journals, most of them publications of societies or predominantly amateur groups, but a few showed more scholarly aims. A relatively undeveloped historical profession did not require an extensive publication network. *Russkaia starina* (Russian antiquity), published between 1870 and 1918, was the country's leading historical periodical in the opinion of most Western Europeans.[78] It published a few articles and many original documents and, like the *HZ*, hoped through its activity to contribute to a growing national spirit. The rhetoric of the introduction is reminiscent of Sybel's: "At the present time, Russian society . . . is rapidly beginning to develop along the path of national consciousness. The study of native history—mainly of most recent times, based not on individual views or views of other writers, but on original historical documents—can all the more facilitate this development."[79] *Russkaia starina* remains more than a historiographical curiosity—it is one of the few czarist historical periodicals to be described in the *Great Soviet Encyclopedia*—because of the space it gave to popular disturbances. It is especially extensive on the Decembrists.[80]

Czarist historical periodicals usually had a distinct political cast. *Russkaia starina* drew contributors from different social and political groups, but *Istoricheskii viestnik* (Historical messenger), whose orientation was conservative and monarchical, is more typical.[81] *Starina i novizna* (Antiquity and modernity), another monarchist periodical, focused on the life and reign of Alexander III to a degree that approached glorification.[82] *Byloe* (The past), which specialized in the history of the revolutionary and social movement, published only twenty-two issues in the two years after its initial foundation, 1906 to 1907, but was revived for another nine years in 1917. One of its editors was so repugnant to the czarist government that his name could not appear on the journal's masthead. *Byloe* drew most of its contributors from participants in *Narodnichestvo*, the Russian populist movement of the 1870s.[83]

A prerevolutionary journal that particularly suffered was *Kievskaia starina* (Kievan antiquity). It modeled itself on *Russkaia starina* but took as its scope the Ukraine and Russia, to which most of its difficulties can be traced. The government appreciated the role of history in fostering national consciousness, and the journal was under constant suspicion of fostering Ukrainian separatism. A statement from its first editor denying such a goal did nothing to quell official misgivings. The conditions of censorship required the periodical to confine itself to publishing older material, but it was probably suppressed in 1906.[84]

Few historical journals survived the Revolution of 1917 and the widespread disruption in its aftermath. When they again began to appear, they were quite different in character from their czarist predecessors. Most obvious is the emphasis on new areas of study that reflected the interests of the new regime and, especially, on collecting revolutionary materials. *Proletarskaia revoliutsiia* (Proletarian revolution) and *Katorga i ssylka* (Hard labor and exile) were founded in 1921. The first published source materials on the revolution.[85] The second, the publication of the All-Union Society of Former Political Prisoners and Exiles, printed articles, documentary materials, and news items relating to former political prisoners.[86] *Krasnaia letopis'* (Red annals), begun in 1922, was similar to *Proletarskaia revoliutsiia,* although it emphasized Petrograd slightly.[87] *Krasnyia arkhiv* (Red archives) was also founded in 1922 "to disclose the secrets of imperial politics and diplomacy."[88] *Letopis' revoliutsii* (Annals of the revolution) covered the revolution in the Ukraine.[89]

The preface to the first volume of *Proletarskaia revoliutsiia* explained the purpose of these collecting journals. The editor began by stating that before 1905 it was nearly impossible to publish anything in Russia on the history of revolution and pointing out the paucity of source materials. Commenting on the relative value of different sources, he emphasized the crucial role of selection:

The hands from which documents appeared in historical journals were, of course, almost entirely bourgeois. . . . The bourgeoisie fervently seized, described and transmitted all the gossip on those having power, naively imagining that it was they, Aleksandr, Nikolai, and their courtiers and ministers who "made history." In reality, it was made more often by department chiefs and gendarmes of the Okhranka [tsarist secret police]. . . . Further the bourgeoisie were drunk with stories about exploits of revolutionary terrorists. . . . The terrorist was a revolutionary idol for the bourgeoisie. . . . At the instigation of their readers, our historical journals from 1906 to 1908 went downhill . . . full of savory stories of *provocateurs*. . . . The main hero of the Russian revolution, the working class, was almost completely absent. . . . As much as the bourgeois reader loved the terrorist, he hated the revolutionary worker.[90]

The editor promised to publish various kinds of source materials, including those from White Guard and secret police archives. He hoped that the journal would become the base for future historians of the proletarian revolution.

Journals of broader scope illustrate more clearly than the source journals the process during the 1920s of adaptation within the historical profession to the new society. Many older historians continued to publish, usually beginning their accommodation with articles in nonparty journals on revolutionary events and episodes in the workers' movement. *Annaly* (Annals), an academic historical journal founded in 1922, published in its second volume articles by historians of the older generation on the social evolution and feudalization of Byzantium, Nicholas I and the revolutionary movement in France, and on the French Revolution. Traditional articles still dominated, but they were decreasing steadily. *Russkoe proshloe* (The Russian past) carried the process further. Articles "of current importance" outnumbered those of general academic interest, and it published not only older authors but also those whose scholarly interests were new. *Russkoe proshloe*'s attitude toward the past is characteristic of Soviet historiography during the 1920s and 1930s. It scorned everything that did not relate to revolution and generally condemned the past.[91]

Among the journals of the 1920s and 1930s, that of the Society of Marxist Historians, *Istorik-Marksist* (*IM*, Marxist historian) stands out. The statutes of the society enumerated its purposes and those of the journal: the unification of all Marxists engaged in scientific work in the field of history; the scientific resolution of problems of history and Marxist methodology; correcting the distortion of history by bourgeois scholarship; the critical illumination of current historical literature from the Marxist point of view; the proffering of assistance of members of the society in obtaining scientific literature, access to archives, research travel grants, and the like; and the propagation and popularization of the Marxist method as well as familiarization of the broad masses with Marxist achievements in the field of history.[92] M. N. Pokrovsky, founder of the society as well as of the journal and the top Soviet historian until his downfall in the 1930s, left no doubt about the society's priorities among professional and political goals in his inaugural address: "To correct this sin of the old Russian historiography [it had not portrayed the rural Russian as sufficiently conscious or as political] is the foremost task of the coming generation of Marxist historians."[93]

In format and structure, *IM* is typical of journals published by historical societies. Articles dominate. The first issue contained "The Paris Commune and the French Bank," by O. L. Vainshtein; "Class Struggle in June–July 1793," by Ts. Fridiland; "The Thermidor Reaction," by K. P. Dobroliubskii; "About the Little Bokharans," by Faizulla-Khodzhaer; "The Society of United Slavs," by M. V. Nechkina; and "The 1905 Revolution in the East," by M. P. Pavlovich. A documents section printed material from the Decembrist archives of V. L. Davydov; a proceedings section included reports presented at the Society of Marxist Historians; a news note treated the All-Russian Methodological Conference of Teachers of History in Soviet Party Schools; and a bibliographical section surveyed the literature and listed historical journals and offered book reviews.

What distinguished *IM* from other Soviet historical journals and from journals of other historical associations was its method of informing historians of subjects with which they should concern themselves and interpretations they should make. These were new departures in the world of scholarly historical periodicals.

Typical of *IM's* modus operandi was its treatment of the dispute between S. N. Dziubinsky and L. P. Mamet. Dziubinsky argued that the teaching of social science in the labor schools should proceed from contemporary events alone; Mamet, that the social science programs should include entire sections devoted to history. Among other things, Mamet charged Dziubinsky with failure to understand the tasks of the Soviet school and of social science and with petty bourgeois distortion of the Marxist position. *IM* published both articles; this was still during the period one scholar has labeled as "coexistence," but the periodical made its position clear. Dziubinsky's name included only his first initial and surname; Mamet's, not only his full first name but also the significant t. (for *tovarishch*, comrade). The journal also preceded Dziubinsky's article with the announcement that it did not agree with his argument and supported Mamet's answer to him.[94]

A dispute between E. V. Tarle, a historian of the older generation, and Pokrovsky was more important. In this quarrel, it is difficult to separate political, professional,and personal motivations. Tarle's *Europe in the Age of Imperialism* had gained him international distinction. Relying upon his sources to be truthful, he reached certain conclusions that diverged from the party line: denying any aggravation of the class struggle during the years preceding World War I, holding Germany primarily responsible for the war, and arguing that the Treaty of Brest-Litovsk stimulated further consolidation of the Entente. Pokrovsky in his 1928 article "New Currents in Russian Historical Literature" pointed out Tarle's "mistake." Tarle then erred by replying to Pokrovsky, an act of impertinence that undoubtedly contributed to his banishment in 1931. Tarle argued scientifically. Pokrovsky was then editor in chief of *IM*; its answer to Tarle's reply argued politically. The controversy clarifies party Marxist history as opposed to Marxist history. The nonparty Marxist historian looks for an objective historical order, but the party Marxist recognizes a natural order of things only when such an order fulfills a party purpose.[95]

The Tarle and Dziubinsky-Mamet episodes taught readers by example, but *IM* could also be more direct. An article by its editor in 1939 warned historians of a number of serious mistakes they were making as they attempted to conform to the new emphasis on Russian patriotism and isolationism. They were incorrectly treating the question of the "lesser evil" as they reinterpreted czarist conquests; they held a mistaken concept of just and unjust wars; and they had reduced Soviet patriotism to blustering.[96]

Although *IM* played a significant role in the struggle with bourgeois historigraphy and in the consolidation of Marxist conceptions in Soviet historical science,[97] it ceased publication in 1941. Its position as the leading Soviet scholarly historical periodical has been filled by *Voprosy istorii* (*VI*, Problems of history). The Soviet encyclopedia states that *VI* was founded in 1926 as *IM*, but in fact its genealogy is somewhat more complicated. *VI* is the replacement for *Istoricheskii zhurnal* (Historical journal), which was in turn the successor of *Bor'ba klassov* (Class struggle), another Pokrovsky-founded journal. *Bor'ba klassov* had been intended for the masses, but *Istoricheskii zhurnal* was predominantly scholarly. Because *Istoricheskii zhurnal*'s editorial staff was judged not to be "ensuring the conduct of the journal at the appropriate scientific level,"[98] it was later terminated. *VI*'s focus was stated clearly. The introduction recognized the incompatibility of professional and popular purposes: "The broad inclusion of historical problems must not turn the journal into an organ of popular science. . . . The task of the popularization of science is a highly important task, but for its solution there exist—and should exist—specialized organs. Voprosy istorii is a research organ—not a popularizing one."[99] *VI*'s contents confirm its scholarly character. Its sections are: "Articles," "Publications," "Memoirs," "Documentary Sketches," "Historical Scholarship in the USSR," "Historical Scholarship Abroad," and "Facts, Events, and People."

The introduction of *VI* also made clear that political involvement was inseparable from Soviet historical scholarship. *VI* "must be the fighting organ of Marxist-Leninist historical science. The task of the journal is the struggle for the principle of dialectical materialism and for its application to the study of the phenomena of the historical life of peoples."[100] The editors hoped that *VI* would be a means of expanding scholarly contacts with foreign countries and would influence historical thought abroad.

VI's career was unremarkable until 1956, when it became the focus of an effort to realign Soviet historiography to the changing political environment that followed the death of Stalin. At a conference of readers in January, the editor and assistant editor made speeches praising articles on long-forbidden topics recently published by *VI* and rejecting past policies. E. N. Burdzhalov, the assistant editor, criticized much Soviet historical work on the 1905 and 1917 revolutions as "oversimplification, time-serving, vulgarization,"[101] and other speakers denigrated the cult of personality surrounding certain military men.

On February 25 Nikita Khrushchev made his famous "secret" speech on the cult of personality at the Twentieth Party Congress. It reinforced and sanctioned tendencies in historical scholarship already apparent at the *VI* readers' conference. During 1956 *VI* published articles that broke sharply with earlier patterns, emphasizing such themes as the reentry of Soviet historiography into the world and coupling it to more interest in historical work being done abroad. The journal displayed considerable concern for the reevaluation of prerevolutionary and early Soviet historians; it was no longer enough to dismiss the discredited Pokrovsky slightingly.[102]

VI was clearly in the grip of revisionist historians. Their program was set forth in the editorial of number 3, of 1956. Underlying all specifics was a plea for truth in scholarship. The program points were made in relation to party history. Stalin's *Short Course,* for instance, had badly distorted and oversimplified. Areas requiring study were identified. But the cry for truth stood out. "The task of historians is to explain and not to hush up facts" might be said to be the theme of this editorial.[103]

The articles in number 4, the April issue, can be regarded as the applied version of the editorial in number 3. Two articles deal with the Stalin cult; there is a devastating critique of the historiography of the Communist party. In another article, Burdzhalov challenges the long-held position that Lenin encountered no opposition within the party on his return to Russia in 1917. Finally, the editing practices used on old Bolsheviks' memoirs were indicted; misedited versions falsified history.[104]

The new trend of *VI* was not allowed to continue unchecked. The fluid political situation was beginning to crystallize, and the party leadership was realizing the dangers of an unchecked assault on the cult of personality. An editorial in the July *Kommunist* complained about lack of proper party spirit on the part of *VI;* for example, it underplayed the differences between Bolsheviks and Mensheviks on major questions during 1905. *Kommunist* criticized *VI* for an article arguing against the official position that czarist Russia was becoming a semicolony, dependent on the West. This editorial was followed by an even sharper attack in *Partiinaia zhizn* on Burdzhalov's presentation of Bolshevik tactics in 1917. *Pravda* published a letter on November 20 accusing *VI* of revising indisputable truths, and in December *Partiinaia zhizn* printed another sharp editorial criticizing *VI.*[105]

Shortly thereafter, *VI*'s editorial board was reorganized. A decree from the Central Committee informed the editor officially of the serious shortcomings she had allowed the journal to develop. Burdzhalov was dismissed, and N. I. Matiushkin was appointed as first deputy editor in chief. The journal was transferred from the Academy of Sciences Institute of History to the Academy's Division of Historical Sciences.[106] Today, it is published jointly by that division and the Ministry of Higher and Specialized Education.[107]

The attack on the *VI* had been in terms of its treatment of Russian and especially Communist party history; another approach to a solution was the establishment of *Voprosy istorii KPSS* (*VI KPSS*, Problems of the history of the CPSU). The new journal broke *VI*'s monopoly on party history and established a division of labor. *VI* was no longer to treat "narrowly specialized topics," but was to focus on broad problems.[108] The circulation statistics—*VI* has 32,000, *VI KPSS* 70,000—indicate the relative importance of the two roles. *VI KPSS* is a publication of the Institute of Marxism-Leninism of the Central Committee of the CPSU, an administrative arrangement that links historical research directly to current politics. The statement "The journal fights against those who falsify CPSU history," which appears in the Soviet encyclopedia, recognizes its essentially political function.[109]

Since the events of 1956 and 1957, relative calm, both historiographically and politically, has prevailed in the USSR. Some distance has begun to separate the two worlds, and political events are no longer automatically reflected in historical scholarship.[110] Most of the criticism of *VI* and *VI KPSS* has been on scholarly grounds. In November 1963 the party journal *Partiinaia zhizn*, which had figured so prominently in the *VI* campaign, published a resolution of the Central Committee which charged that *VI KPSS* had not achieved the goals decreed by the Twenty-second Party Congress. The Central Committee then gave the editors specific directions to publish "scholarly articles, collections and documents relating to the pre-October period of the Party's activities, with the aim of liquidating the mistakes and distortions of historical truth promulgated by the cult of personality of Stalin" and "to inform readers concerning the state of scholarly research work in the Institutes of Party History under the central committees of the communist parties of the union republics."[111]

The three patterns of political involvement—Anglo-American, Continental European, and Soviet—are the classics, but, like all classical definitions, they are subject to modification. In England and America since World War II, there has been an admixture of the Continental type of journal. Scholarly historical periodicals have been founded to give expression to a particular political view, usually leftist. Some examples are *Past and Present, History Workshop, Marxist Perspectives*, and the *Radical History Review*. The larger, and especially the general, journals still adhere to the older tradition of catholicity.

Continental periodicals, on the other hand, have been moving away from strict division along party lines. Many of the more important European periodicals, especially the general journals, display the same openness to diverse points of view that is typical of the English and American. Even in Russia, although nothing has altered the basic pattern of subordination of historical research to the state and state-defined ideologies, some evidence points to new influences at work, and many former truths are less absolute.

Ultimately, the relation of a periodical to politics is part of a larger pattern and reflects both the rules established in the historical profession and the standards of society as a whole. It is no accident that in England and America journals with ideological themes have recently been founded; during these years, political conditions have changed, and disagreements have begun to be argued in ideological terms. Similarly, in Western Europe the postwar period was one of great American influence when many institutions were remodeled on the American, or to a lesser extent, the British, pattern. In Eastern Europe, East German history is being sovietized. Politics is an inescapable aspect of historical periodicals because it is an integral aspect of history. The particular form it takes derives from the norms of a society as a whole.

EIGHT 🐦 BIBLIOGRAPHICAL
CONTROL AND USE OF SCHOLARLY
HISTORICAL PERIODICALS

The use and bibliographical control of scholarly historical periodicals are closely interrelated. The ways in which historians use this literature influence the form and range of the bibliographical aids that are developed. The diversified array of bibliographies, guides, indexing, and abstracting services can in turn affect the frequency and ease with which the literature is used.

Few studies have been made of the ways in which historians use their periodical literature in contrast to the substantial attention given to this subject in the natural sciences and in medicine. To supplement what little data are available, a questionnaire was sent to 767 historians listed in the *Directory of American Scholars*.[1] The response rate was close to 50 percent. The primary purpose of the survey was to determine how the professional used scholarly periodicals and the bibliographical apparatus that provides access to their content. It also sought information on attitudes toward them and included questions on other aspects of their information-seeking habits. An analysis of the completed questionnaires and a comparison of the results with those of similar surveys in other disciplines has been published as *The Information Needs of Historians*.[2]

The Bibliographical Control of Scholarly Historical Periodicals

Bibliographical control is probably best defined as the development and maintenance of a system for the adequate recording of all forms of published and unpublished material that add to human knowledge.[3] In other words, this control involves the ability to retrieve information through the preparation and use of lists of the various units in which it is recorded. When they list books, they are usually called bibliographies. The term index usually indicates a list of the subunits of larger composite works, such as articles in periodicals or single essays in collected volumes, but the two terms are sometimes used interchangeably.

Although bibliographical efforts can be traced back to classical antiquity, total bibliographical control has never been achieved. The fundamental problem has always been that of quantity; the task was too large for the means available. The invention of printing gave it a new dimension and each technical improvement in the printing press, the appearance of each new format in which information was made available, only exacerbated it. The coming of the "information age" and advanced technology have had revolutionary implications. Technology may make possible a more complete and more versatile bibliographical record, but it has also multiplied the different media in which the graphic record is preserved, which in turn creates new bibliographical problems.

After the rapidly increasing volume of printing forced bibliographers to abandon the dream of a single universal bibliography, two different approaches to bibliographical control emerged. The first attempts to enumerate large aggregates, like all books published in Germany or the holdings of a major library like the British Museum. This approach is usually favored by librarians who prefer indexes and bibliographies that provide access to as much of their collections as possible. These bibliographies divide the universe of recorded knowledge primarily on the basis of the physical nature of the unit, book, periodical, manuscript, film, or other format, and are usually arranged by author. Scholars, on the other hand, prefer directly targeted sources that inform them only about items in which they are likely to be interested and do not obscure those with irrelevant entries.[4] Bibliographies that divide recorded knowledge on the basis of subject serve this need better. Because the subject is the unifying feature, such bibliographies usually include material in a variety of formats.

The format bibliographies, the major general and national bibliographies, have listed historical materials as completely as they have listed those in any other field, but subject coverage in history is relatively less satisfactory than that available in many disciplines. The sciences, especially medicine, have made some progress toward complete coverage of their literatures; history has only made a beginning.

The problem is almost overwhelming because the volume of material to be covered is so vast, the miscellany of formats so diverse, the publications that might be relevant so dispersed, and the funding available so small.

A concerted total approach to history's bibliographical problems has never been made, perhaps because as a field it is really a multi-faceted federation of subdisciplines that share only an agreement on method. The most successful efforts in the field have been limited to specialized topics and to highly selective bibliographies. For most major subfields, the very useful *Guide to Reference Books*[5] lists selectively bibliographies, dictionaries, encyclopedias, and other reference sources.

Historians have been aware of their bibliographical problem for almost a century. The book reviews that have been a standard section of scholarly historical periodicals from the beginning constitute a highly important but narrowly limited bibliographical contribution. The *HZ*'s efforts and those of other journals to supplement book reviews led to various experiments with systematic bibliography. The American Historical Association organized a committee on bibliography in 1898 and supported, sometimes even initiated, such major bibliographic efforts as *Writings on American History* and the *Guide to Historical Literature*. In 1967 a conference of the Joint Committee on Bibliographical Services to History was held.[6] Recently, an association for historical bibliography has been organized. Except for the Joint Committee, none of these groups has attempted to address historical bibliography as a theoretical problem; they have instead devoted their energies to particular parts of the problem.[7] This approach is not unreasonable; historians' bibliographical needs are so large that every contribution helps and only partial solutions may at this time be economically feasible.

Subject bibliographies, limited in scope, have proliferated. Many of them cover both monographic and periodical literature, but few are planned as continuing publications to keep the bibliographical information up to date. The specificity of their subjects ranges from topics such as the United States[8] to pioneer Jews in the California Mother Lode.[9] In addition to those published in book form, many bibliographies of this type have appeared in journals.

To publish a bibliography limited in scope and covering only publications that have appeared within a clearly defined period is much less difficult than to maintain continuing coverage on a current basis, even for a subfield of history. If successful, bibliographies of this kind serve a double purpose: they provide current information, and their cumulation provides a retrospective record.

Currency of bibliographical information is of concern to historians. Of 339 who responded to a question on its importance for their current research, 40.75 percent considered it very important, 47.8 percent moderately important, and only 11.5 percent not very important. Historians prefer to use indexes and bibliographies that appear regularly, that are reasonably up-to-date, and that focus on their general areas of research, such as the *Handbook of Latin American Studies* and the *Bibliography of Asian Studies*. The desire for current information is confirmed by a preference for such items as the American Historical Association's *Recently Published Articles*. Not one British historian referred to *Writings on British History*, now twenty years in arrears. A few American historians cited *Writings on American History*, but one qualified his mention of it by the statement "now that it is up to date."

Specialized continuing bibliographies that include periodical articles usually take as their scope a particular geographical area, although several cover a chronological period, such as the *Archiv für Reformationsgeschichte*, founded in 1972. They may appear in many different forms. Most usual is the separately published annual. It can be published as soon as all materials for a particular year have been accumulated and indexed and thus appears relatively quickly. In this category fall *Writings on American History* and the *Handbook of Latin American Studies*. *Writings on British History* began as an annual, but was interrupted by World War II and has never caught up. The war years were covered in one volume, 1940–45, and what has been published since usually cumulates several years in one volume. The major alternative to the annual specialized bibliography is a supplement to a periodical, like the *Bibliography of Asian Studies*, published as part of the *Journal of Asian Studies*.

History as a field rather than its subfields is a relative latecomer to the world of indexing and current bibliography, perhaps because the specialized bibliographies and lists of current articles in periodicals seemed adequate. One exception is the *Jahresberichte der Geschichtswissenschaft*, published since 1880. The Historical Association did not start its annual *Bibliography of Historical Literature* until 1947; in France the history section of the *Bulletin Signalétique* was initiated in 1961.

The only American effort at comprehensive coverage was the short-lived *Social Science Abstracts*, from 1929 to 1933. Although these bibliographies purport to cover "history" in general, they usually emphasize the writings of the country in which they are published and are far less international and general than their titles indicate.

Fortunately, coverage provided by the more general periodical indexes supplements these scattered and uncoordinated efforts. Indexes like the *Social Sciences Index*, the *Humanities Index*, and the *British Humanities Index* include history among the disciplines they cover. They try to identify the leading journals in the different areas and then index them completely, a different modus operandi from that of the subject bibliographies, which select only those articles directly related to their subject but attempt to locate them wherever they appear. Many historical periodicals, especially those published outside the United States, are not indexed in any source of either type giving current coverage. Some are indexed in several.

The various sources listing articles in scholarly historical periodicals are too disorganized to deserve to be called a system, but they seem to satisfy most historians. Many view incomplete coverage as an advantage rather than a disadvantage because the present haphazard bibliographical arrangements give access to most important published research without overloading historians with the less significant. The combination of different types of indexes, abstracts, and annual bibliographies offers most English-speaking historians the means to find out the most significant research that has appeared in their fields within a reasonable period of time—if they choose to take advantage of it.

The Use of Scholarly Historical Periodicals by Historians

The use of scholarly historical periodicals cannot be fully understood without recognizing the generally low esteem in which most historians hold periodical literature. Since history first emerged as a scholarly discipline, the monograph has been the dominant form of publication, and the article has never successfully challenged its preeminence. One historian clearly expressed this long-standing tradition when he responded in the questionnaire, "I write books (10) not articles." Articles have been perceived as a way of getting started.

As Dexter Perkins commented in his autobiography, after two of his articles were published in the *American Historical Review* he began to receive recognition in a small way in the scholarly community.[10] Arthur Schlesinger singled out for special mention five of his own articles that he felt suggested fresh avenues for scholarly inquiry,[11] but such pride is unusual.

Despite the lack of prestige of periodicals, historians nonetheless subscribe to them. Those who responded to the questionnaire subscribed to approximately six each. The *AHR* was the single most commonly received journal, but others covered a wide range. Few were foreign. Even historians concentrating in areas like German history, where much important work is published in the journals of that country, rarely subscribed to anything other than American journals.

Judged most useful are those journals that are specialized but not too highly specialized. Twenty of twenty-six Colonial American specialists selected the *William and Mary Quarterly* as the periodical most useful to them; twelve out of twenty Latin American, the *Hispanic American Historical Review*; nine of twelve Far Eastern, the *Journal of Asian Studies*; and four of five African, the *Journal of African History*.

The choices in other fields are not so clear, an indication of a less-tightly-knit network of communications. Four medieval scholars rated *Speculum* as the most useful journal, but fourteen others chose different ones. Among the five Middle East specialists, four different journals were named as most useful; and no two ancient historians chose the same one. More Western European specialists listed the *AHR* as the most valuable journal than any other.

The most influential factor in these choices appears to be the book reviews. When asked if they read articles, book reviews, and news notes in the journals to which they subscribed thoroughly, partially, or not at all, more than half of the historians (57.0 percent) replied that they read the book reviews thoroughly; fewer (43.9 percent), the news notes; and still fewer (35.2 percent), the articles. Only a small number named journals without substantial book review sections as their most useful periodical. Specialists in areas where journals exist but consist mainly of articles usually preferred a more general journal that did publish numerous book reviews.

Most historians feel that the present periodical system is satisfactory. The number of those responding to the questionnaire who felt that periodicals were too numerous (35.5 percent) was more or less balanced by the number of those who believed that more were needed

(26.8 percent). The most common arguments echo those presented in so many proposals for new scholarly historical periodicals: a subject field is not adequately covered and too many poor articles are accepted to fill the pages of existing journals. Although many people in the profession would like to see improvements in the quality of periodicals—some kind of rationalization in the overall pattern and less humanly fallible editors—they propose no drastic suggestions and recognize the difficulties in the way of altering the present system. Doubtless speaking for many, one historian commented that the availability of numerous journals in which to publish benefited both the profession and the individual.

The findings of citation studies[12] provide complementary evidence on the importance of periodical literature to historians and the characteristics of the periodicals they use. Although periodical use appears to be increasing,[13] this category remains a relatively small proportion of the total materials consulted. The historians publishing in seven English historical periodicals cited books 34.1 percent, periodicals 21.5 percent, and manuscripts 10.9 percent.[14] American historians writing in 1948 used monographs 27.6 percent, articles 10.3 percent, and manuscripts 12.7 percent.[15] Some historians view articles as so unimportant that they omit them altogether from the bibliographies in their books.

All citation studies show that the range of dates, the subject areas, and the individual titles of periodicals cited by historians are widely dispersed. Even after the periodicals that might be considered as primary source material have been subtracted, historians still are more likely to use older articles than scholars in most other disciplines. Titles are even more widely scattered than dates. In 1981 the fifteen titles most frequently cited in the *AHR* accounted for only 5.9 percent of its citations. That year, the *AHR* included citations from 2,362 other journals besides. Only narrowly defined areas of history show less spread. In the 1981 *Economic History Review,* the top fifteen titles accounted for almost double the *AHR*'s figure, or 11.1 percent of the total number of citations. The most frequently cited journal, the *Economic History Review,* was alone responsible for 5.1 percent. A high percentage of self-citation is common in journals which, like the *Economic History Review,* the *Arkansas Historical Quarterly,* and the *Journal of Negro History,* have been the leaders in their fields since their founding and have enjoyed near-monopolies in them.

Few cited articles are in foreign languages. The study of English historical periodicals, for example, found that only 7.7 percent of all references were in a foreign language, a figure that included articles in medieval history in which non-English research is of considerable significance. Only historians with determinedly broad vision overcome the apparent barrier.

Historians' perspectives on research influence in other ways the kind of periodical they use. Both Fernand Braudel in *The Mediterranean and the Mediterranean World in the Age of Philip II* and William McNeill in *The Rise of the West* most frequently cited interdisciplinary journals. McNeill also referred to many scholarly articles in fields other than history as did Carl Degler in his comparative study of slavery in the United States and Brazil and the authors of *Time on the Cross*, another analysis of slavery. A writer of traditional political or diplomatic history will ordinarily use general or geographically specialized periodicals because they publish primarily the traditional type of articles.

Historians can only cite articles or other material of which they are aware, and they undoubtedly often overlook relevant items. Their bibliographical methods as they are revealed in responses to the questionnaires can best be described as "unsystematic." Apparently, few of them undertake any kind of comprehensive search. The most frequently used source for relevant references for research as well as for keeping up with current publication is bibliographical references in books and journal articles. For research, the second and third most popular methods are specialized bibliographies and book reviews; for keeping up with current publication, book reviews rank second and specialized bibliographies third. Abstracts and indexes were a poor fifth in both cases. Nonbibliographical sources included discussion or correspondence with acquaintances for research references and searching library shelves for current information. Some historians mentioned publishers' advertisements as important to their personal information systems and a few cited conferences.

The answers to a question on the use of indexes and abstracts confirmed their minor role for bibliographical needs. This question was the one most frequently unanswered. Many respondents indicated that they do not use these publications or judged the question to be inapplicable to them.

The single most popular index among historians is the *Readers' Guide to Periodical Literature;* for many, it is the only index they use. Dependence upon an index that is so general in scope, popular in coverage, and intended for small public and school libraries may explain the poor showing of indexes and abstracts as a source of citations. The *Readers' Guide* is probably the only index known to many historians. One scholar of the American frontier claimed it is the only source related to the needs of his specialty. Its heavy use is a tribute to the success of generations of teachers and librarians in how-to-use-the-library instruction, but it is intended to serve only as a prototype. Other similar indexes covering more scholarly periodicals are more suitable for the needs of advanced students and scholars.

Among the respondents, the second most popular index or abstract is *Historical Abstracts*, the only index or abstract among those listed in the questionnaire that includes the word "history" in its title. Many historians whose specialty it does not include, for example American historians, checked it.

Historians are not very critical of the indexes and abstracts they use, and the validity of their opinions is in some ways questionable. They rate the *Internationale Bibliographie der Zeitschriften Literatur* (IBZ), the *British Humanities Index,* and the *Social Sciences Citation Index* (SSCI) as the most difficult to employ, but for the most part they are unable to give reasons. The *SSCI* is complex in structure and tedious to use because complete citations are not given in either of the sections that are designed to provide subject access. It is only surprising that more people do not consider it difficult. The *IBZ* is German, but cross-references in English and in French to the German entries are given for the subject headings. Particularly hard to explain is why 17.4 percent of the users of *America: History and Life* find it difficult in contrast to 11.5 percent of those who consult *Historical Abstracts*. The two series are published in an identical format by the same company. There is a similar inconsistency of reaction to the three H. W. Wilson indexes listed in the questionnaire. Only 6.0 percent of those using the *Readers' Guide* and 5.8 percent of those using the *Social Sciences Index* find them difficult, but twice as many place the *Humanities Index* in this category. The *Humanities Index* features the same dictionary arrangement and even typography as the *Readers' Guide.*

An inescapable conclusion from the results of this survey is that historians do not take full advantage of the coverage offered to them by indexes, the best means of locating recent periodical articles. Prominent among the many possible reasons for this neglect is the fairly common belief that they do not contain relevant material. This

may be true for a few historians, but many probably do not understand the function of indexes and abstracts. They undoubtedly couple
their lack of understanding to a conviction that their personal information systems are adequate, that somehow they will discover anything significant from the sources on which they depend. Further-
more, a thorough literature search on almost any topic takes a
considerable amount of time. Thoroughness may be important for
primary sources, but not necessarily for secondary.

Three groups of historians are exceptional in their heavy use of
indexes. It is significant that for each group the dependence is upon a
specialized index. Latin American historians rely heavily on the *Handbook of Latin American Studies,* which is comprehensive but relatively
current; art historians, the *Art Index* and *Répertoire internationale de la
littérature de l'art;* and historians of science, the *Isis* bibliographies.
American historians may possibly constitute a fourth group. Their
identification with a bibliographical source is not so complete, but
almost half of the respondents checked *America: History and Life.*

Editors of scholarly historical periodicals, themselves historians
and scholars, have indirectly contributed to the underuse of indexing
and abstracting services. They have seen their primary audience as
the individual scholar and have for the most part shown little interest
in the indexing of their journals in bibliographical tools. They have
sought library subscriptions, but seem never to have understood that
such indexing is important in librarians' priorities. If a journal is covered by an index, the demand for it is automatic.

Although bibliographical control over scholarly publications in history and especially over periodical literature needs considerable improvement, it is unlikely that any major changes in overall structure
will occur in the near future. The lack of available money and disin-
terest that frustrated action on the proposals of the conference of the
Joint Committee on Bibliographical Services to History would almost
certainly hamper other bibliographical experiments. During the 1970s
neither the American Historical Association nor any other organization attempted to develop any information system that was reasonably comprehensive, let alone the Total Information System called for
by the conference. New bibliographical enterprises tended to be
efforts by commercial firms whose focus was limited and whose publications were directed toward an obvious market, such as *Reviews in
American History* or *The Middle East: Abstracts and Index.*

The absence of any marked dissatisfaction contributed to the failure of the profession in the United States to explore the dramatic possibilities technology has made possible. The technical capacity now exists to provide bibliographical control over all historical materials in one comprehensive service. Intellectual advances have not kept pace with the mechanical, but experiments in such areas as machine-readable indexing of manuscripts are highly promising.

To facilitate better use of new opportunities, as well as to resolve long-standing problems and achieve true bibliographical control, historical bibliography needs to be transformed from its present series of ad hoc arrangements into a system. The system with the greatest potential for success would probably be one that would achieve control through different self-contained units, organized to correspond to areas of interest rather than in one unified whole. This approach would improve existing components and eliminate the many gaps, but it would not alter the underlying concept. An additional bonus for historical writers would be the enlargement of the readership of individual scholarly works. Such a system would be analogous to history: a federation of somewhat overlapping subfields rather than a seamless unity.

This type of system would not have the intellectual neatness of an all-encompassing one in which each item is listed and listed only once, but it offers advantages beyond the all-important one of historians' preferences. To be forced to work in smaller units is not, bibliographically speaking, necessarily a bad thing. The larger a bibliography becomes, the more subjects and the more formats it includes, the more unwieldy and less precise it becomes—a fact that is true whether it is in paper or machine-readable format.

Many constituent parts of a bibliographical system already exist. What is missing is any kind of planning on a broad scale. Historians need to address their bibliographical problem systematically and in concert with editors, publishers and librarians, as the Joint Committee attempted to do. The technological revolution has intensified the problem. Only after historians act will a critical element in their research be significantly improved.

NINE ❧ SCHOLARLY HISTORICAL PERIODICALS ❧ RETROSPECT AND PROSPECT

During the last century and a quarter, scholarly historical periodicals have become an integral part of the institutional framework of the profession. They have helped shape its direction, and in turn their own character has been formed by the needs and values of historians. Without these journals, the world of professional historical scholarship would be vastly different from what it is today.

Although each scholarly historical periodical is unique, the elements studied in this book—the circumstances of founding, the nature of articles and contributors, the character of book reviews and other material, and the management practices—often exhibit common patterns. These depend to some degree on time and place, but they also show similarities and consistency that are not dependent upon circumstances. The profession's nature has imposed some likenesses, and scholarly historical periodicals have developed characteristic procedures and traditions.

Until recently, the founding of a new periodical followed a fairly set course. A group of scholars specializing in the same field would become convinced they needed a better place to publish their articles than those already available. Sometimes their arguments would stress quantity: existing journals did not give enough space to their interests. Sometimes they would stress quality: they could not write as they wished or they sought a medium they could be sure their colleagues would read.

Usually one individual, who often went on to become the first editor, would take the lead in organizing. Like all first editors, this person could then count on many opportunities for hard work and self-sacrifice. The survival of many scholarly historical periodicals through their first uncertain years is a tribute to one dedicated individual.

In recent years, more periodicals have been begun on a trial basis;

their founders' attitude is "if it succeeds, there must be a place for it." These journals are more likely to emphasize that they hope to encourage the growth of their particular subfield of history rather than that they seek to provide publication space for those already working in it. Conditions have been sufficiently favorable for many of these experiments to succeed.

During preliminary discussions, planners have tended to concentrate on the article component, which continues to absorb most editorial attention. Except for a few recently founded reviewing and abstracting journals, all scholarly historical periodicals have published articles and some have published nothing else. The article format, a scholarly investigation of a limited problem, was quickly established; and the principal alternative formats, the long review-essay and the reflective hortatory essay, have almost completely disappeared.

Articles have been the heart of a periodical because through them it defined the field of study it claimed as its own: the link in the network of communication for which it made itself responsible. The choices it made, the articles it included and those it excluded, set the limits for its audience.

Articles have also been important because they have been the means by which a journal established its, and by extension the profession's, standards. The use of editorial boards and outside referees to help judge articles enhanced the collaborative nature of the periodicals. Because individuals have been chosen to serve in these capacities on the basis of the high quality of their own contributions, publication conferred an imprimatur. Even when editors single-handedly made the decisions, they were in a sense acting as representatives of the profession and their decisions carried similar force.

The characteristics of contributors have been remarkably uniform. Almost all have been professional scholars, holding doctorates and teaching in universities. Some minor fluctuations have occurred in age distribution, and changes in the percentage of teachers have paralleled expansions and contractions in academic employment, but the basic pattern was established quickly and has remained constant.

The homogeneity of contributors has been one manifestation of the principle underlying the publication of scholarly historical periodicals: they were created and written by professional historians for their colleagues. The primary purpose of articles has been to advance the discipline's knowledge base. Some of the early scholarly historical periodicals hoped that their aims would not be incompatible with appeal to educated individuals who were interested in the subject, but this hope proved to be a chimera. Editors were forced to choose between their hope of attracting laymen and serving the needs of their scholarly clientele; invariably, they chose the latter group. The decision was one indication of the increasing isolation of the profession. History may still retain its traditional humanistic role as a subject necessary for informed civic behavior and cultural advancement but few professional historians have written for the responsible man of good breeding as they did in the nineteenth century.

The nonarticle material in the periodicals has reinforced their professional and academic character. For scholars, the book reviews have been at least as important as the articles. The reviews have enabled individuals to follow research in their fields. There, their own work has been judged. News sections have reported research in progress and provided other useful information. Items about colleagues have strengthened professional ties.

Editors have obviously occupied key positions in determining the direction and quality of the periodicals. Ultimately, and perhaps unfairly, because they could not publish what had not been written, they have been held responsible for the character of their journals. The editors of the earliest journals were particularly influential because their journals became the models for the entire profession.

On most scholarly historical periodicals, editorial boards now share the responsibility, although the nature of their participation varies widely from journal to journal. On some, they seem to exist purely for cosmetic effect; on others, they share in policy decisions and routinely assist the editor in selecting and rejecting articles. But, however inactive they may be, their very existence serves as a check on the authority of the editor.

The spread of editorial boards to the extent that they are now almost de rigueur is one indication of increasingly formalized procedures. This pattern has been closely related to the more frequent use of outside specialists to help evaluate articles, a practice particularly common on American and Canadian journals. These changes have resulted in broader involvement of historians, which enhances the claim of the periodicals to represent the profession.

Formalization of management procedures has not paralleled the formalization of the editorial process. Scholarly historical periodicals have been relatively small operations in both personnel and monetary terms and have not required elaborate administrative structures. New journals and the less well-established ones have tended to operate very informally, and even for the leading journals most aspects of management remain casual. The process of selecting an editor, for example, has remained largely a matter of informal consultation, and the final decision has been made by the editorial board or the governing board of the sponsoring organization. Only the largest journals, which have a substantial impact on large areas of the historical world, are exceptions to this rule. The *AHR* and the *JAH*, with their specially appointed search committees, are such exceptions.

Because scholarly historical periodicals almost invariably have been in a financially precarious position, they have practically always required a sponsor. Yet, through subscriptions and advertising, those periodicals studied in this book contributed the largest share to their own maintenance. Few were truly self-supporting. The more broadly based journals, especially those devoted to the history of their own country or those providing some essential service like book reviews, were least likely to require subsidies. Most, however, required assistance in some form, whether it was in the form of cash or services.

Where a periodical obtained its financial support varied and was related to nationality, the year, and chance. Leading European periodicals, like the *HZ* and *EHR*, have always been published by commercial publishers; and, after an initial period when assistance was required, have been self-supporting. The state-subsidized Russian scholarly historical periodicals and some European journals have also received governmental aid. Support for the American periodicals has come largely from universities, which appear to be increasing their share of responsibility, and to a lesser extent from private voluntary associations. The private benefactor was an important factor during earlier years in all capitalist countries.

When viewed as a whole, the predominant characteristic of the universe of scholarly historical periodicals has been a fundamental lack of order. This absence was apparent by 1900 and has intensified during the twentieth century. The periodicals are organized on a national basis. With the possible exception of the *Annales*, none can claim to be international and even that journal appears so only by comparison. To some extent, this parochialism is a matter of language and some crossing of national boundaries can be observed within a language community as, for example, on the *HZ* or the *EHR*, but it goes beyond that. There is no international language for historians as there is for scientists because the focus of historians is national. In each country, interest in its own heritage has been the most notable stimulus for the advancement of historical scholarship. The majority, or at least the plurality, of American historians study American history; German historians, German. The periodicals reflect that fact by the primacy the general, leading scholarly historical periodical of each country gives to the national history.

The lack of international coordination is repeated on the national level. No central authority exists in any Western country to control, guide, or advise on the establishment of a new scholarly historical periodical. Foundations may exercise some influence, but they rarely coordinate their activities. Nor does any organization provide a structure to ensure that the different periodicals maintain contact with each other once they are founded. All relationships are informal, and the strength of these bonds has not been sufficient to impose any observable degree of order.

Lack of organization does not preclude an informal division of labor among the periodicals, but the spheres of activity of the different types of periodicals and of individual periodicals often overlap. The overlap is most apparent in a field like Colonial American history. A scholar may submit an article dealing with Colonial Virginia to several highly respected periodicals with a reasonable hope of acceptance. Bibliography, on the other hand, is an obvious gap. Some journals, such as the *Journal of Asian Studies,* provide an excellent annual current bibliography in the area of their concentration, but many ignore it completely to the disadvantage of the historians in their fields.

A number of serious disadvantages result from the lack of integration. The availability of many avenues of publications limits the ability of the periodicals to enforce the profession's standards. The large numbers of journals blur the lines of communication. Unless one of them succeeds in establishing itself as the leader in its field, the scholars interested in that field have no intellectual focus. They find it more difficult to discover who their colleagues are. This absence of a clear rallying point is particularly serious in view of the lack of other bonds in the historical profession, like the summer schools, specialized conferences, and team research projects that are characteristic of the natural sciences and which link scholars in a subject area.

Not all consequences of the loose structure are harmful. It has enabled the discipline to accommodate change readily. An individual scholar who has espoused a new methodology or a new topical area could conceivably found a scholarly historical periodical devoted to his or her enthusiasm with only minimal financial and collegial support. Because it is not necessary to convince the intellectual establishment, entrenched in positions of authority on the larger, more significant journals, of the value of something new, the field encompasses greater variety. The corollary of that variety is vitality. This flexibility has been necessary because scholarly historical periodicals tend to establish their personalities early and remain true to them. Many can be seen as living monuments to a trend in historical scholarship that has passed.

The loose structure has helped the periodicals to fulfill some of the needs of the profession. Their abundance has facilitated publication for scholars, who must publish to survive in the academic world. The existence of a periodical devoted to one particular type of history—geographical, topical, or methodological—has defined that subfield and has clarified its relationship to other subfields. Individual periodicals have improved communication with specific subfields.

To some extent, organizational disorder is the result of the intellectual character of history. National orientation is only one force increasing disunion. Lack of agreement on the historical problems worth solving and the appropriate means to be used also significantly deepens organizational discontinuities.

The intellectual trends that have dominated the development of scholarly historical periodicals and given them their direction have been specialization and the reaction against it. The first is by far the more powerful. The nature of specialization is such that it has reinforced other centrifugal forces. Well entrenched by the turn of the century, it is still dominant; most new journals are elaborations on the basic theme. So many journals now exist that a few have begun to take already claimed areas of scholarship for their subject.

The reaction against specialization has never assumed quite the large-scale proportions that specialization itself has, although it is a persistent current in historical thinking. Journals that devote themselves to history as a whole or to some aspect that will contribute to integration of the discipline, such as theory, are rare. Somewhat more common are interdisciplinary journals, which are the more usual form the reaction against specialization has taken. The growing numbers of this type of scholarly historical periodical reflect a conviction within the profession that specialization has approached its limits.

The organizational structure of the periodicals has influenced how they fulfill their purposes. They knit historians together, but only in small segments, not into an articulated whole. Their focus on a particular group has enhanced fragmentation within the profession. The survival of individual periodicals has provided groups of historians with a common goal, and they have created a network of communication informing historians about current publication and research activity, but both these accomplishments have been limited to subfields of history. The worth of these results depends upon the individual historian's viewpoint and values.

Another purpose modified by organizational structure has been the setting of standards. Articles accepted by leading journals serve as models; those rejected, as examples of the unacceptable. Because, however, so many articles rejected by one journal are published elsewhere, the entire process is altered. It is possible to claim that standards and values appropriate for one journal are not appropriate for another. It can also be argued that history as a whole should have absolute standards and that it is the mission of all scholarly historical periodicals to enforce those standards. Again, the response must depend on the individual historian's views.

The third major purpose of scholarly historical periodicals, to expand the knowledge base, is also affected by their structure. Their unrestrained proliferation has provided many places to publish. Research that would not otherwise be disseminated has been made available to all who are interested. In rare cases, the periodicals have even had considerable impact in shaping the direction of historical scholarship. The example of the *Annales* shows that a scholarly historical periodical can provide the same kind of intellectual leadership a single brilliant historian can.

Since their beginning, scholarly historical periodicals have fulfilled the hopes of their founders and served the basic needs of the profession with some, if not total, success. Now new forces are emerging that may well profoundly affect their future. Each of the separate worlds to which they belong—scholarship, history, and publishing—is changing rapidly and the periodicals will inevitably be influenced by the changes. The potential exists for a vastly different scholarly historical periodical in the near future.

Intellectually, the future of the scholarly historical periodicals will be decided by what happens within the discipline. Western historians are looking for new theories and a new synthesis as their enthusiastic reception of the ideas of the *Annales* group and frequent calls for new ideas indicate. The shape of a new synthesis is not yet apparent, and indeed the debate has only begun. Studies in theory and historiography appear infrequently. All that can be said with assurance about a vigorous system is that a new definition of purpose must lie at its center and that this definition will change the configuration of scholarly historical periodicals. At a minimum, new journals will be founded to propagate the new faith. Some older ones that represent the profession as a whole, like the *AHR*, will be converted if the system is widely enough accepted.

The increasingly social scientific orientation of historical research contains considerable potential for changing the character of scholarly historical periodicals. Because a larger proportion of the literature of the social sciences is in article format, as history becomes more social scientific, the scholarly historical periodical will become more prominent. The social sciences emphasize currency, a need the periodical is admirably adapted to serve. These factors strengthen the position of the periodicals and improve their prospects for survival and significance. Intensified interest in the methodology and concepts of the social sciences has also increased the interdisciplinary involvement of history and benefited interdisciplinary periodicals.

More worldly considerations will help shape the new scholarly historical periodical. One of the determinants will be trends in the academic world. The totally academic character of these journals ties their fortunes inseparably to those of higher education, where, by general agreement, many difficulties lie ahead. Universities will have less money for subsidies. The growth rate of scholarly historical periodicals will decline and some existing ones will probably cease publication. At the same time, this contraction will probably be accompanied by a reduction in pressures to publish. Faculties are contracting, especially in the lower ranks, where such pressures are the heaviest, and universities are depending more on part-time teachers, who are not expected to publish. Entire programs will probably be phased out.

Another presently emerging trend that may entail long-term consequences for scholarly historical periodicals is the reviving interest in the humanities and in educational basics. Although many historians view their field as one of the social sciences, traditionally its educational role has been similar to that of other fields in the humanities in that it is regarded as a fundamental part of an individual's education. Changing curricula and requiring more courses in these areas eventually will help declining enrollments in history and in the long run, by strengthening its position as a whole, strengthen the role of scholarly historical periodicals.

This discussion of future possibilities assumes that these periodicals will retain their current form, but the present communication revolution makes this assumption questionable and presents the possibility that change may be drastic as present constraints are removed. Information, both factual and bibliographical, has been available on-line for some time. Now books, such as the *Encyclopaedia Britannica*, are publishing in machine as well as print format. The *Harvard Business Review,* an established, scholarly periodical, is doing the same. The paperless society the information experts have been predicting has become more than a possibility.

Scholarly historical periodicals will not remain apart from this revolution, although they will not be involved until relatively late because the priorities and profits of information technology lie elsewhere. But, when these journals are published in machine-readable form, a number of possibilities present themselves. Machine communication has the potential to improve greatly accessibility for scholars who at present depend on inadequate research facilities. Further, such a radically new format invites changes in content and approach. Its economics make feasible publication of a much larger proportion of the articles submitted to the existing journals. And these are only two of the more obvious possibilities. Information technology holds out the promise of a world that is transformed beyond recognition or imagination.

What will emerge from these interacting forces is unclear, but the scholarly historical periodical can be expected to continue in some form. Inertia and the conservative habits of the academic world will help protect it, but it also fulfills basic needs of the historical profession. The scholarly historical periodical is indispensable to the expansion of history's knowledge base, to the evaluation of its research, and to the dissemination of information—processes that are integral to the profession's continuation. Only when historians cease to carry on these activities will scholarly historical periodicals disappear. Their features may change, but the idea of the scholarly periodical, if not its outlines, will survive.

NOTES

Chapter 1: Introduction

1. *Ulrich's International Periodicals Directory, 18th ed., 1979–1980* (New York and London: R. R. Bowker, 1979).

2. These figures differ significantly from those obtained by Machlup and Leeson in their six-year sample of eighty-six journals; they based their average circulation of 7,580 for historical journals on five of them. Fritz Machlup and Kenneth Leeson, *Information through the Printed Word*, vol. 2: *Journals* (New York: Praeger, 1978), p. 192.

3. *Scholarly Communication: The Report of the National Enquiry* (Baltimore and London: The Johns Hopkins University Press, 1979), p. 4.

4. "NISP: Noisy Signal in Psychology," *Trans-Action* 7(May 1970): 10.

5. "Bibliographical Services in the Social Sciences," *Library Quarterly* 20(April 1950): 79–99.

6. Elizabeth H. Thompson, *A.L.A. Glossary of Library Terms* (Chicago: American Library Association, 1943), p. 99.

7. Dorothy B. Hokkanen, "U.S. Book Title Output: A One Hundred-Year Overview," in *The Bowker Annual of Library and Book Trade Information, 26th Edition, 1981* (New York and London: R. R. Bowker, 1981), Table 3: Book Title Output by Subject, 1970–1979, p. 328.

8. *International Encyclopedia of the Social Sciences*, s.v. "History: Intellectual History," by Crane Brinton.

9. Appearing too late to be considered in this discussion of the role of periodicals in general and scholarly historical periodicals in particular was Charles B. Osburn, "The Place of the Journal in the Scholarly Communications System," *Library Resources and Technical Services* 28(October–December 1984): 315–24.

Chapter 2: The *Historische Zeitschrift*

1. David Knowles, "The 'Monumenta Germaniae Historica,'" in *Great Historical Enterprises* (London: Thomas Nelson, 1963), pp. 65–97.

2. G. P. Gooch, *History and Historians in the Nineteenth Century* (Boston: Beacon Press, 1959), p. 75.

3. Georg G. Iggers, *The German Conception of History: The National Tradition of Historical Thought from Herder to the Present* (Middletown, Conn.: Wesleyan University Press, 1968), pp. 3–4.

4. The discussion of the historicist position in the following pages relies

heavily on Iggers, *The German Conception of History,* but the following sources were also used: Gooch, *History and Historians;* Heinz-Otto Sieburg, *Deutschland und Frankreich in der Geschichtsschreibung des 19. Jahrhunderts,* vol. 2: *1848–1871,* Veröffentlichungen des Instituts für europäische Geschichte, Band 17 (Wiesbaden: Franz Steiner, 1958), pp. 165–223; and Heinrich von Srbik, *Geist und Geschichte vom deutschen Humanismus bis zur Gegenwart,* 2 vols. (Munich: F. Bruckmann; Salzburg: Otto Müller, 1950–1951).

5. These views were fairly widespread. Thomas Mann expressed them eloquently in *Betrachtungen eines Unpolitischen* (Frankfurt am Main: S. Fischer, 1956), pp. 22–23, 239–43.

6. Quoted in Sieburg, *Deutschland und Frankreich,* p. 192.

7. "Chronologisches Verzeichnis," in Heinrich von Sybel, *Vorträge und Abhandlungen,* introduction by C. Varrentrapp (Munich and Leipzig: R. Oldenbourg, 1897), pp. 157–61.

8. Gooch, *History and Historians,* p. 104.

9. Iggers, *The German Conception of History,* pp. 70–71.

10. [Foreword], *Historisch-Politische Zeitschrift* 1(1832): 1–3.

11. Srbik, *Geist und Geschichte,* vol. 1, p. 250.

12. Ibid., p. 363.

13. Gooch, *History and Historians,* p. 120.

14. *Encyclopaedia Britannica,* 11th ed., s.v. "Sybel."

15. Sybel to Johann Gustav Droysen, 6 Dezember 1853, in Johann Gustav Droysen, *Briefwechsel,* ed. Rudolf Hubner, Deutsche Geschichtsquellen des 19. Jahrhunderts, Band 26 (Berlin and Leipzig: Deutsch Verlags-Anstalt Stuttgart, 1929), vol. 2, pp. 197–98.

16. "Exposé Heinrich von Sybels für König Max II. von Bayern," printed in Theodor Schieder, "Die deutsche Geschichtswissenschaft im Spiegel der Historische Zeitschrift," *HZ* 189(1959): 72–74.

17. Sybel to Georg Waitz, Mai 1857, quoted in Sybel, *Vorträge und Abhandlungen,* p. 85.

18. Quoted in Walter A. Ricklinger, "Heinrich von Sybel und die Historische Zeitschrift" (Ph.D. diss., Universität München, 1936), pp. 28–29.

19. *Encyclopaedia Britannica,* 11th ed., s.v. "Maximilian II, King of Bavaria."

20. Bundesarchiv, Koblenz, Nachlass Sybel, undated list.

21. Schieder, "Die deutsche Geschichtswissenschaft," p. 11.

22. "Oldenbourg, Rudolf," *Allgemeine Deutsche Biographie* (Leipzig: Duncker and Humblot, 1906), vol. 25, pp. 703–4.

23. "Hofrat v. Pfistermeister an Heinrich von Sybel," in Schieder, "Die deutsche Geschichtswissenschaft," pp. 74–75.

24. Heinrich von Sybel, "Vorwort," *HZ* 1(1859): iii.

25. *Kleindeutsch* was the solution to the problem of German unification that would have excluded Austria from the new nation. In such a state, the influence of Prussia would inevitably have been paramount.

26. Schieder, "Die deutsche Geschichtswissenschaft," p. 6.

27. Antoine Guilland, *Modern Germany and Her Historians* (London: Jarrold, 1915), pp. 1–40; Richard Whiteing, "Prussianized History," *English Review* 20(May 1915): 156–67.

28. See index volumes covering vols. 1–56 and 57–96.

29. John Higham, review of *The Past before Us: Contemporary Historical Writing in the United States,* ed. Michael Kammen, in *AHR* 86(October 1981): 807.

30. Sybel to Johann Gustav Droysen, 29 April 1861, in Droysen, *Briefwechsel,* vol. 2, p. 754.

31. Karl Zangemeister, *Theodor Mommsen als Schriftsteller* (Berlin: Weidmannsche Buchhandlung, 1905); Ernest Steindorff, *Bibliographische Übersicht über Georg Waitz' Werke* (Göttingen: Dieterich'sche Verlags-Buchhandlung, 1886).

32. Sybel to Rudolf Oldenbourg, 17 Februar 1866, quoted in Schieder, "Die deutsche Geschichtswissenschaft," p. 7; Ricklinger, "Heinrich von Sybel," pp. 33–34.

33. LeRoy Harold Linder, *The Rise of Current Complete National Bibliography* (New York: Scarecrow Press, 1959), pp. 88–95.

34. Srbik, *Geist und Geschichte,* vol. 1, p. 363.

35. Heinrich von Sybel to Johann Gustav Droysen, 19 September 1856, in Droysen, *Briefwechsel,* vol. 2, p. 457.

36. Schieder, "Die deutsche Geschichtswissenschaft," p. 20.

37. Ibid., p. 18.

38. Ibid., pp. 18–19.

39. Karl Lamprecht to Friedrich Ratzel, 9 August 1895, printed ibid., p. 82.

40. Rudolf A. Oldenbourg to Karl Lamprecht, 18 August 1895, printed ibid., pp. 83–84.

41. For example, J. C. B. Mohr (Paul Siebeck), Tübingen, Archives, Ludwig Quidde to Paul Siebeck, 30 Juni 1888.

42. Sybel to Max Lehmann, B. i. Marz 1893, printed in Schieder, "Die deutsche Geschichtswissenschaft," pp. 75–76; Friedrich Meinecke, *Erlebtes, 1862–1919* (Stuttgart: K. F. Koehler, 1964), p. 121.

43. Friedrich Meinecke to Verlag Oldenbourg, 2/8 1895, printed in Schieder, "Die deutsche Geschichtswissenschaft," pp. 79–80.

44. Karl Lamprecht to Friedrich Ratzel, 9 August 1895, printed ibid., pp. 81–82.

45. Friedrich Meinecke to R. A. Oldenbourg, 21 August 1895, printed ibid., pp. 88–90.

46. Rudolf Oldenbourg to Karl Lamprecht, 18 August 1895, printed ibid., pp. 83–84; R. A. Oldenbourg to Friedrich Meinecke, 19 August 1895, printed ibid., pp. 85–86.

47. Friedrich Meinecke to R. A. Oldenbourg, 20.8.1895, printed ibid., pp. 87–88.

48. Friedrich Meinecke to Heinrich von Treitschke, 10.9.1895, printed ibid., pp. 95–96.

49. Heinrich von Treitschke to R. A. Oldenbourg, 2/10.95, printed ibid., p. 99.

50. Iggers, *The German Conception of History,* pp. 195–228.

51. Ibid., p. 197.

52. Schieder, "Die deutsche Geschichtswissenschaft," p. 64.

53. Meinecke, *Erlebtes,* p. 121.

54. Hans Mommsen, "Haupttendenzen nach 1945 und in der Ära des Kalten Krieges," in *Geschichtswissenschaft in Deutschland,* ed. Bernd Faulenbach (Munich: C. H. Beck, 1974), pp. 112–20.

Chapter 3: The Spread of Scholarly Historical Periodicals

1. G. Monod and G. Fagniez, "Avant-propos," *RH* 1(janvier–juin 1876): 1.

2. Gabriel Monod, *De la possibilité d'une réforme de l'enseignment superieur* (Paris: Ernest Leroux, 1876), p. 43, quoted in William R. Keylor, *Academy and Community: The Foundation of the French Historical Profession* (Cambridge, Mass.: Harvard University Press), p. 41.

3. "Prefatory Note," *EHR* 1(January 1886): 2.

4. William M. Sloane, "History and Democracy," *AHR* 1(October 1895): 11.

5. Library of Congress, American Historical Association, Box 376, AHR Miscellany, Papers Relating to the Establishment of the AHR.

6. This account of the French historical profession relies heavily on Keylor, *Academy and Community,* chapters 1–3.

7. Paul Frédéricq, *The Study of History in Germany and France,* trans. Henrietta Leonard, Johns Hopkins University Studies in Historical and Political Science, 8th series, nos. 5 and 6 (Baltimore: Publication Agency of the Johns Hopkins University, 1890).

8. Keylor, *Academy and Community,* p. 74.

9. Keylor, *Academy and Community,* pp. 32–33; Charles-Olivier Carbonell, *Histoire et historiens* (n.p.: Privat, 1976), pp. 325–99; content analysis of the *RQH* (see chapter 1).

10. Keylor, *Academy and Community,* pp. 30–31, 51.

11. C. H. K. Marten, *On the Teaching of History and Other Addresses* (Oxford: Basil Blackwell, 1938), p. 7.

12. Marten, *On the Teaching of History;* C. H. Firth, *Modern History in Oxford, 1841–1918* (Oxford: Basil Blackwell, 1920); Paul Frédéricq, *The Study of History in England and Scotland,* trans. Henrietta Leonard, Johns Hopkins Studies in History and Political Science, 5th series, no. 10 (Baltimore: Johns Hopkins, 1887); James Westfall Thompson, *A History of Historical Writing* (Gloucester, Mass.: Peter Smith, 1967), vol. 2, pp. 309–32.

13. Ian Jack, *English Literature, 1815–1832* (Oxford: Clarendon Press, 1963), p. 10.

14. For example, review of *The Personal Government of Charles I,* by

Samuel R. Gardiner, *Westminster Review* 109, n.s. 53(January 1878): 276; review of *A History of England in the Eighteenth Century,* vols. 1 and 2, by William H. Lecky, *Quarterly Review* 145(April 1878): 498–534; review of *Die Osmanen und die Spanische Monarchie,* by Leopold von Ranke, *Westminster Review* 109, n.s. 53(April 1878): 541.

15. [J. E. E. D. Acton], "The Massacre of St. Bartholomew," *North British Review* 51(October 1869): 30–70.

16. Jürgen Herbst, *The German Historical School in American Scholarship: A Study in the Transfer of Culture* (Ithaca, N.Y.: Cornell University Press, 1965); John Higham, Leonard Krieger, and Felix Gilbert, *History* (Englewood Cliffs, N.J.: Prentice-Hall, 1965).

17. George B. Adams, "The Origins of the Feudal System," *Andover Review* 7(April 1887, May 1887): 366–75; 505–18.

18. George B. Adams, "Petrarch and the Beginning of Modern Science," *Yale Review* 1(August 1892): 46–61.

19. Harry Pratt Judson, "Is Our Republic a Failure?" *American Journal of Sociology* 1(July 1895): 28–40.

20. Albert Bushnell Hart, "The Rise of American Cities," *Quarterly Journal of Economics* 4(January 1908): 129–57.

21. George Burton Adams, "The United States and the Anglo-Saxon Future," *Atlantic Monthly,* July 1896, pp. 35–46; E[phraim] E[merton], "Labor Day in Europe," *Nation,* May 29, 1890, pp. 429–30; Albert Bushnell Hart, "Causses and Gorges of the Cévennes," *Nation,* July 5, 1894, pp. 6–8; John Bach McMaster, "The Political Depravity of the Fathers," *Atlantic Monthly,* May 1895, pp. 626–33; Moses Coit Tyler, "The Declaration of Independence in the Light of Modern Criticism," *North American Review* 163(July 1896): 1–16.

22. John Franklin Jameson, "Montauk and the Common Lands of Easthampton," *Magazine of American History* 9(April 1883): 225–39; "The Origin and Development of the Municipal Government of New York City," *Magazine of American History* 8(May 1882, September 1882): 315–30, 598–611.

23. Higham, Krieger, and Gilbert, *History,* p. 99.

24. Iggers, *The German Conception of History,* 63–65.

25. Higham, Krieger, and Gilbert, *History,* p. 99.

26. Ibid., pp. 8–14, 26.

27. Charles-Olivier Carbonell, "La naissance de la Revue historique," *RH* 225(avril–juin 1976): 340–41; Keylor, *Academy and Community,* pp. 36–37; Christian Pfister, "Gabriel Monod," *RH* 110(1912): i–vi.

28. Monod and Fagniez, "Avant-propos," p. 1; Carbonell, "La naissance," p. 331.

29. Cambridge University, Acton Papers, Bryce to Acton, July 8, 1885.

30. Information taken from biographical articles in *Dictionary of National Biography.*

31. Information taken from biographical articles in *Dictionary of American Biography.*

32. Monod and Fagniez, "Avant-propos," p. 2.

33. Cambridge University, Acton Papers, Mandell Creighton to Lord Acton, July 24, 1888.

34. "Report of the Managing Editor for 1964," *AHR* 70(April 1965): 964.

35. "Historical News: American Historical Association, Final Report of the Committee of Ten on Reorganization and Policy, December 29, 1939," *AHR* 46(October 1940): 246.

36. Library of Congress, American Historical Association Collection, Box 257, Editorial Correspondence "F" 1901, Andrew C. McLaughlin to Fred Morrow Fling, November 16, 1901.

37. Quoted in J. Franklin Jameson, "The American Historical Review, 1895–1920," *AHR* 26(October 1920): 8.

38. "The Year's Business, 1954," *AHR* 60(April 1955): 758.

39. "Editor's Note," *AHR* 61(October 1955): 263–64.

40. "Articles for the *AHR:* An Editorial," *AHR* 75(October 1970): 1577.

41. Ibid.

42. Ibid., p. 1578.

43. Ibid., pp. 1578–79.

44. Cambridge University, Acton Papers, Mandell Creighton to Lord Acton, April 29, 1886.

45. J. L. Strachan-Davidson, "The Growth of Plebeian Privilege at Rome," *EHR* 1(April 1886): 209–17.

46. William Henry Simcox, "Alfred's Year of Battles," *EHR* 1(April 1886): 218–34.

47. James Gairdner, "The Death of Amy Robsart," *EHR* 1(April 1886): 235–59.

48. E. Blanche Hamilton, "Paris under the Last Valois Kings," *EHR* 1(April 1886): 260–76.

49. W. Cunningham, "The Repression of the Woollen Manufacture in Ireland," *EHR* 1(April 1886): 277–94.

50. J. Theodore Bent, "King Theodore of Corsica," *EHR* 1(April 1886): 295–307.

51. Jameson, "The American Historical Review," p. 8.

52. "Your Business," *AHR* 48(April 1943): 467.

53. Cambridge University, Acton Papers, Mandell Creighton to Lord Acton, July 17, 1885.

54. "The American Historical Review," *AHR* 47(April 1942): 707–8; "The American Historical Review," *AHR* 48(April 1943): 468; "Carrying On," *AHR* 49(April 1944): 579; "The Year's Business, 1947," *AHR* 53(April 1948): 679; "The Year's Business, 1949," *AHR* 55(April 1950): 758; "The Year's Business, 1951," *AHR* 57(April 1952): 826; "The Year's Business, 1955," *AHR* 61(April 1956): 802; "Report of the Managing Editor, 1964," *AHR* 70(April 1965): 964.

55. "Carrying On," *AHR* 49(April 1944): 580.

56. This summary is based on an analysis by the Library of Congress. American Historical Association, Boxes 570–579.

57. Library of Congress, J. Franklin Jameson Collection, Box 53, File 78, J. Franklin Jameson to Lynn Thorndike, July 22, 1921.

58. Library of Congress, American Historical Association Collection, Box 498, File 1958 B, David H. Burton to Boyd C. Shafer, August 12, 1958.

59. Clyve Jones, Michael Chapman, and Pamela Carr Woods, "The Characteristics of the Literature Used by Historians," *Journal of Librarianship* 4(July 1972): 143; Arthur Monroe McAnally, "Characteristics of Materials Used in Research in United States History" (Ph.D. diss., University of Chicago, 1951), p. 135.

60. *SSCI Journal Citation Reports,* vol. 6 of *Social Sciences Citation Index, 1978 Annual,* comp. and ed. Eugene Garfield (Philadelphia: Institute for Scientific Information, 1979), p. 421.

61. "Articles for the *AHR,*" p. 1580.

62. Library of Congress, American Historical Association Collection, Box 522, Thank You Replies to Questionnaire, Boyd C. Shafer to Jerome Blum, March 19, 1959.

63. Ibid., Box 378, Board of Editors, Minutes, 1935, Memorandum in pencil.

64. Ibid., Box 257, Editorial Correspondence "C" 1901, Mrs. H. Caldwell to Andrew C. McLaughlin, August 7, 1901.

65. F. N. T., review of *Constitutional Studies: State and Federal,* by James Schouler, *AHR* 3(January 1898): 379–82. The reviewer made such statements as "Like other books by Mr. Schouler, this is badly written," and said that he had probably never exhaustively studied state constitutions.

66. Yale University, Library, George Burton Adams Papers, Box 1, File 1, A. B. Hart to George B. Adams, January 23, 1898.

67. Library of Congress, American Historical Association Collection, Box 499, 1958 "P," Boyd C. Shafer to R. R. Palmer, September 8, 1958; Box 522, Thank You Replies to Questionnaire, Boyd C. Shafer to Fritz Stern, March 18, 1959.

68. Yale University, Library, George Burton Adams Papers, Box 7/33, Circular, January 10, 1905.

69. Library of Congress, American Historical Association Collection, Box 571, Helen P. Kaltenborn to American Historical Association, November 5, 1969.

70. Yale University, Library, George Burton Adams Papers, Box 10/60, J. Franklin Jameson to George B. Adams, April 30, 1918; "Report of the Managing Editor for 1964," p. 964.

71. J. Franklin Jameson, "The Present State of Historical Writing in America," *Proceedings* of the American Antiquarian Society, n.s. 20 (October 1910): 516.

72. "The Year's Business, 1957," *AHR* 63(April 1958): 837.

73. Library of Congress, American Historical Association Collection, Box 499, 1958 "L," Boyd C. Shafer to Richard Lowitt, October 2, 1958.

74. "Reviewing in the *AHR,*" *AHR* 75(December 1970): 1889.

75. "News from the AHR," *AHA Newsletter* 17(December 1979): 3.

76. "The Year's Business, 1954," *AHR* 60(April 1955): 758.

77. "Report of the Managing Editor for 1968," *AHR* 74(April 1969): 1461.

78. *Unesco Statistical Yearbook, 1977* (Paris: United Nations Educational, Scientific, and Cultural Organization, 1978), pp. 813–34; *Unesco Statistical Yearbook, 1976* (Paris: United Nations Educational, Scientific, and Cultural Organization, 1977), pp. 821–39; *Unesco Statistical Yearbook, 1974* (Paris: United Nations Educational, Scientific, and Cultural Organization, 1975), pp. 702–10; *Unesco Statistical Yearbook, 1969* (Paris: United Nations Educational, Scientific, and Cultural Organization, 1970), pp. 538–45; "News from the *AHR*," p. 3.

79. Louise Creighton, *Life and Letters of Mandell Creighton* (London: Longmans, Green, 1904), vol. 1, p. 334, Mandell Creighton to C. J. Longman, June 20, 1885.

80. Cambridge University, Acton Papers, Mandell Creighton to Lord Acton, December 13, 1888.

81. Library of Congress, American Historical Association Collection, Box 257, Editorial Correspondence "J" 1901, printed Instructions to Book Reviewers.

82. "Prefatory Note," *EHR* 1(January 1886): 5.

83. Monod and Fagniez, "Avant-propos," p. 4; Monod, "Introduction," p. 38.

84. Alice Gérard, "Histoire et politique: La Revue historique face à l'histoire contemporaine (1885–1898)," *RH* 255(avril–juin 1976): 354–55.

85. Cambridge University, Acton Papers, Creighton to Acton, December 23, 1885. The article cannot be identified.

86. Ibid., Creighton to Acton, January 24, 1887.

87. Between 1867 and 1876, J. R. Green, author of *A Short History of the English People*, had tried to found a historical periodical. It would have been published by Macmillan, but foundered when the two were unable to decide how popular and how scholarly it should be and when Green's health deteriorated. He was supported by most of the historians who eventually founded the *EHR*. *Letters of John Richard Green*, ed. Leslie Stephen (London, New York: Macmillan, 1901), passim.

88. Creighton, *Life and Letters of Mandell Creighton*, vol. 1, p. 336.

89. Sloane, "History and Democracy," p. 21.

90. Library of Congress, American Historical Association Collection, Box 257, American Historical Review, Editorial Correspondence "F" 1901, Andrew McLaughlin to Fred Morrow Fling, November 5, 1901.

91. Ibid.

92. Library of Congress, American Historical Association Collection, Box 378, Board of Editors, Minutes, November 26, 1910.

93. Ibid., December 1, 1911.

94. G. Monod, "Introduction: Du progres des études historiques en France depuis le xvie siecle," *RH* 1(janvier–juin 1876): 36.

95. Carbonell, *Histoire et historiens*, pp. 441–50.

96. "Prefatory Note," *EHR*, p. 4.

97. Sloane, "History and Democracy," p. 21.

98. The most important articles on the gentry were those of R. H. Tawney, H. R. Trevor-Roper, Lawrence Stone, J. R. Cooper, and J. H. Hexter. All except Hexter's appeared in the *Economic History Review*. His was published in *Encounter*. The disagreement over the origins of World War II was precipitated by A. J. P. Taylor's 1961 book, *The Origins of World War II*. Most of the controversy took place in the correspondence columns of the *TLS*, though an important review by Trevor-Roper was published in *Encounter*.

99. "The Master of the Mediterranean," *Time*, May 23, 1977, pp. 77–78.

100. Jacques Revel, "The *Annales:* Continuities and Discontinuities," *Review* 1(Winter–Spring 1978): 11–12.

101. Interview with Jacques Revel, June 29, 1977.

102. Revel, "The *Annales*," pp. 11–12.

103. Ibid., p. 13; "À nos lecteurs," *Annales d'histoire economique et sociale* 1(janvier 1929): 1–2.

104. Lucien Febvre, "À nos lecteurs, à nos amis," *Annales: Economies, Sociétés, Civilisations* 1(janvier–mars 1946): 2.

105. Revel, "The *Annales*," p. 18.

106. "On Publication Policy," *Review* (Winter–Spring 1978): inside cover.

107. J. H. Hexter, "Fernand Braudel and the *Monde Braudellien . . .*," *Journal of Modern History* 44(December 1972): 485–86.

108. E. J. Hobsbawm to Margaret Stieg, April 20, 1977; "Introduction," *Past and Present* 1(February 1952): i–iv.

109. E. J. Hobsbawm to Margaret Stieg, April 20, 1977.

110. Quentin Skinner, review of *Crisis in Europe, 1560–1660*, ed. Trevor Aston, *EHR* 81(October 1966): 791.

111. Fernand Braudel, "Personal Testimony," *Journal of Modern History* 44(December 1972): 461.

112. Creighton, *Life and Letters of Mandell Creighton*, vol. 1, p. 70, Mandell Creighton to R. L. Poole, February 15, 1891.

113. Cambridge University, Acton Papers, James Bryce to Lord Acton, July 2, 1891.

114. Ibid., James Bryce to Lord Acton, December 25, 1886; James Bryce to Lord Acton, July 2, 1891.

115. Ibid., Mandell Creighton to Lord Acton, July 24, 1888.

116. George T. Blakey, *Historians on the Home Front: American Propagandists for the Great War* ([Lexington, Ky.]: University Press of Kentucky, 1970), p. 19.

117. Library of Congress, American Historical Association Collection, Box 378, Board of Editors, Minutes, December 27–30, 1927.

118. Dexter Perkins, *Yield of the Years* (Boston: Little Brown, 1969), pp. 66–67.

119. Library of Congress, American Historical Association Collection, Box 376, Papers Relating to Establishment of AHR 1895, Memorandum of

an Agreement between the Board of Editors and the Managing Editor, May 23, 1895.

120. Yale University, Library, George Burton Adams Papers, Box 3/13, Conference on an Historical Journal, April 6, 1895.

121. Library of Congress, American Historical Association Collection, Box 258, Editorial Correspondence, "A" 1902, Andrew C. McLaughlin to George B. Adams, March 1, 1902. McLaughlin inquired whether or not he should arrange for Charles Haskins to write an extended note on the congress of historians he would be attending in Rome.

122. Ibid., Box 257, Editorial Correspondence, "A" 1901, George B. Adams to Andrew C. McLaughlin, July 23, 1901. This letter concerned whether or not Goldwin Smith should be paid for an article he had submitted.

123. Ibid., Box 378, Board of Editors, Minutes, October 22–23, 1897.

124. Denys Hay, "Goronwy Edwards," *EHR* 91(October 1976): 722.

125. Library of Congress, American Historical Association Collection, Box 370, AHR Bancroft Controversy, Correspondence c. 1915, "An Historical Statement Concerning the American Historical Review" (pamphlet).

126. Ibid., Box 282, Editorial Correspondence, "A" 1915, J. Franklin Jameson to George B. Adams, October 12, 1915; Frederic Bancroft, *Why the American Historical Association Needs Thorough Reorganization* (Washington, D.C.: National Capital Press, 1915). Letters that appeared in the *Nation* included those of Ulrich B. Phillips, September 16, 1915, pp. 355–56; Frederic Bancroft, September 16, 1915, pp. 356–57; John Latané, September 16, 1915, p. 357; Albert Bushnell Hart, September 30, 1915, pp. 411–13; Ulrich B. Phillips, October 21, 1915, p. 495; Frederic L. Paxson, October 21, 1915, p. 495; S. B. Fay, January 6, 1916, pp. 21–23; John H. Latané, February 10, 1916, pp. 170–71. A more complete account of the controversy is given in Ray Allen Billington, "Tempest in Clio's Teapot: The American Historical Association Rebellion of 1915," *AHR* 78(April 1973): 348–69.

127. Library of Congress, American Historical Association Collection, Box 370, AHR Bancroft Controversy, Correspondence c. 1915, clipping from Boston *Herald,* September 20, 1915.

128. Ibid., *The American Historical Association.*

129. Ibid., Frederic Bancroft to Clarence W. Bowen, January 26, 1915.

130. Library of Congress, J. Franklin Jameson Collection, Box 47, File 39, Clarence W. Alvord to J. Franklin Jameson, November 15, 1914.

131. Library of Congress, American Historical Association Collection, Box 282, Editorial Correspondence, "A" 1915, Clarence W. Alvord to J. Franklin Jameson, November 10, 1915.

132. Ibid., Box 376, Papers Relating to the Establishment of the AHR, Albert Bushnell Hart to H. Morse Stephens, April 12, 1895.

133. Ibid., Box 370, AHR Bancroft Controversy, Correspondence c. 1915, Frederic Bancroft to Clarence Bowen.

134. Guy Stanton Ford to Harvey O'Higgins, May 31, 1918, 3-A2, Tray 2, CPI Records, quoted in Blakey, *Historians on the Home Front,* pp. 54–55.

135. Library of Congress, American Historical Association Collection, Box 370, AHR Bancroft Controversy, Correspondence c. 1915, Frederic Bancroft to Clarence Bowen, November 8, 1915.

136. Ibid., Box 282, Editorial Correspondence, "A" 1915, J. Franklin Jameson to George B. Adams, October 12, 1915.

137. Ibid., Box 378, Board of Editors, Minutes, June 2, 1917.

138. Ibid., Box 282, AHR Editorial Correspondence, "A" 1915, J. Franklin Jameson to Clarence W. Alvord, November 16, 1915.

139. Reading University Library, Longmans Papers, Pt. 1, Item 162, Impression Box 23, pp. 27, 56, 85, 107, 137, 150, 187, 198, 225, 253, 271, 297.

140. Cambridge University, Acton Papers, Mandell Creighton to Lord Acton, January 24, 1887.

141. Reading University Library, Longmans Papers, Pt. 1, Item 162, Impression Book 25, p. 50.

142. Ibid., Pt. 1, Item 162, Impression Book 23, pp. 56, 271.

143. Creighton, *Life and Letters of Mandell Creighton*, vol. 1, p. 343, Mandell Creighton to R. L. Poole, October 17, 1889.

144. Yale University, Library, George Burton Adams Papers, Box 1/1, A. B. Hart to George B. Adams, January 7, 1896.

145. Library of Congress, American Historical Association Collection, Box 375, File Treasurers' Reports, 1895–1920, American Historical Review, Comparative Financial Statement, to June 30, 1926.

146. Ibid., Box 376, AHR Miscellany, Papers Relating to Establishment of AHR, 1897 Subscription List.

147. Library of Congress, J. Franklin Jameson Collection, J. Franklin Jameson to Victor Clark, December 17, 1928.

148. Ibid., H. E. Bourne to J. Franklin Jameson, February 25, 1929.

149. Library of Congress, American Historical Association Collection, Box 378, Board of Editors, Minutes, December 29, 1930.

150. Library of Congress, J. Franklin Jameson Collection, J. Franklin Jameson to William K. Boyd, March 21, 1929.

151. "Historical News: American Historical Association Report of the Executive Secretary for 1934," *AHR* 40(April 1935): 581.

152. "AHR Moves to Indiana," *AHA Newsletter* 13(November 1975): 1.

153. This includes only income from libraries and other institutions. An individual can obtain the *AHR* only by becoming a member of the AHA.

154. "The *AHR* and the AHA: An Editorial," *AHR* 77(October 1972): 967–76.

155. Library of Congress, American Historical Association Collection, Box 376, AHR Miscellany, Papers Relating to the Establishment of the AHR, Preliminary Call.

156. Ibid., Box 378, Board of Editors, Minutes, May 5, 1934; Box 375, File Treasurers' Reports, 1895–1920, American Historical Review, Comparative Financial Statement, to June 30, 1926.

157. Ibid., Box 378, Board of Editors, Minutes, December 27, 1917, December 30, 1919.

158. "The *AHR* and the AHA," p. 976.
159. "The Year's Business, 1959," *AHR* 65(April 1960): 756.
160. Cambridge University, Acton Papers, Mandell Creighton to Lord Acton, May 7, 1888.
161. Jameson, "The American Historical Review," p. 17.
162. Flexner, *Universities*, p. 221.
163. A. Ducellier, "Les études historiques en Republique populaire d'Albanie (1945–1966)," *RH* 237(janvier–mars 1967): 127–28.

Chapter 4: Geographical Specialization

1. Abstract of Stefan Kieniewicz, "Czasopiśmiennictwo Historyczne," *Kwartalnik Historyczny* 84(1977): 385–90, in *Historical Abstracts* 25, 25A–45: 4.
2. Interview with Georg Siebeck, June 6, 1977; Hans Widmann, *Tübingen als Verlagsstadt*, Contuberium, Beiträge zur Geschichte der Eberhard-Karls-Universität Tübingen, Band 1 (Tübingen: J. C. B. Mohr (Paul Siebeck), 1971), pp. 177–81.
3. University of Illinois, Illinois Historical Survey Library, Illinois Historical Survey Library Archives, Part III. I, Clarence W. Alvord Administration, Folder 54.c, Clarence W. Alvord to Thomas M. Owen, January 28, 1908; Summary by Alvord of Objections to Proposed Publication Series, undated.
4. Ibid., Box II-2, Folder 54.f, Clarence W. Alvord to Logan Esarey, October 21, 1912. This letter was also sent to a number of other American historians.
5. Walter B. Posey, "The Southern Historical Association: Its Founding and First Year," *JSH* 43(February 1977): 71.
6. This account draws on "Historical News and Notices," *JSH* 1(1935): 107; Posey, "The Southern Historical Association"; Thomas D. Clark, "Wendell Holmes Stephenson, 1899–1970: Master Editor and Teacher," *JSH* 36(August 1970): 335–49; Edwin A. Davis to Walter B. Posey, September 18, 1975; and a memoir of "Hokum Kollege" by Davis. Copies of the last two items were sent to the author by Professor Davis, who is not certain that Stephenson made the first suggestion of a journal at the "Hokum Kollege" meeting.
7. Posey, "The Southern Historical Association," p. 62.
8. Prestige and leadership are intangible but nonetheless real qualities. The movement of faculty provides a significant clue to their location. Historians would achieve eminence in their field while working in places like Königsberg, Illinois, and LSU and then be invited to universities like Berlin, Harvard, and Yale. Flexner recounts an anecdote about the University of Greifswald told by Willamovitz in his memoirs that is informative about the hierarchy of prestige. Flexner, *Universities*, p. 322.
9. L. Quidde, "Zur Einführung," *DZG* 1(1889): 1.
10. "News and Comments," *MVHR* 1(June 1914): 157–58.

11. Yale University, Library, George Burton Adams Papers, Box 10/60, George B. Adams to J. Franklin Jameson, February 13, 1916.

12. Library of Congress, Bernadotte Schmitt Papers, Container 3, Folder 10/26-5/27, list of publications with application for Guggenheim Fellowship.

13. Quidde, "Zur Einführung," p. 2.

14. University of Illinois, Illinois Historical Survey Library, Illinois Historical Survey Library Archives, Part III. I, Clarence W. Alvord Administration, Folder 54.j, Clarence W. Alvord to Louise P. Kellogg, September 22, 1914.

15. Posey, "The Southern Historical Association," p. 71.

16. Quidde, "Zur Einführung," pp. 1–2.

17. University of Illinois, Illinois Historical Survey Library, Illinois Historical Survey Library Archives, Part III. I, Clarence W. Alvord Administration, Folder 54.p, Clarence W. Alvord to Mitchell B. Garrett, January 27, 1915.

18. Ibid., Folder 54.p, Clarence W. Alvord to P. Hoekstra, November 23, 1915; Folder 54.t, Clarence W. Alvord to P. Hoekstra, January 21, 1916.

19. Nebraska State Historical Society, Organization of American Historians Papers, Series Three, Box 1, Paul W. Gates to Louis Pelzer, October 13, 1942.

20. Ibid., Series Four, Box 1, William C. Binkley to Ernest W. Dewey, March 2, 1955.

21. Duke University, Library, Wendell Stephenson Papers (Journal of Southern History), Wendell H. Stephenson to Thomas P. Abernethy, January 12, 1937; Wendell H. Stephenson to Ella Lonn, November 14, 1940.

22. David M. Potter, "An Appraisal of Fifteen Years of the Journal of Southern History, 1935–1949," *JSH* 16(February 1950): 28.

23. University of Illinois, Illinois Historical Survey Library, Illinois Historical Survey Library Archives, Part III. I, Clarence W. Alvord Administration, Folder 54.i, Clarence W. Alvord to K. C. Babcock, May 21, 1914, June 16, 1914; Folder 54.j, Clarence W. Alvord to Walter L. Fleming, June 24, 1914.

24. Ibid., Folder 54.q, Clarence W. Alvord to Clarence S. Paine, June 22, 1915.

25. In Quidde's five years of editing, there were 108 different contributors. Some 36 contributed more than once, E. Bernheim no fewer than five times, and several others four times.

26. University of Illinois, Illinois Historical Survey Library, Illinois Historical Survey Library Archives, Part III. I, Clarence W. Alvord Administration, Folder 54.r, C. H. Van Tyne to Clarence W. Alvord, February 10, 1915; Folder 54.j, Clarence W. Alvord to Katherine H. Dickerman, 8 July 1914, Clarence W. Alvord to Logan Esarey, July 2, 1914.

27. Ibid., Folder 54.u, Clarence W. Alvord, quoting an unnamed member of the board of editors, to John Mecklin, October 16, 1916.

28. Duke University, Library, Wendell Stephenson Papers (Journal of

Southern History), Wendell Stephenson to Horace Adams, October 24, 1940.

29. Ibid., Wendell Stephenson to Ruth Blackwelder, November 21, 1935.

30. Ibid., Fred Cole to Kenneth M. Stampp, July 11, 1942.

31. Nebraska State Historical Society, Organization of American Historians Papers, Series One, Box 103, Louis L. Pelzer to Francis Wiesenburge, October 4, 1941.

32. Carl Russell Fish, "Review of McMaster's History of the People of the United States," *MVHR* 1(June 1914): 31–43.

33. University of Illinois, Illinois Historical Survey Library, Illinois Historical Survey Library Archives, Part III. I, Clarence W. Alvord Administration, Folder 54.1, Clarence S. Paine to Clarence W. Alvord, July 6, 1914. Paine's informant was misinformed. The lead article was in fact by Barker on the United States and Mexico.

34. John W. Caughey, "Under Our Strange Device: A Review of the 'Review,'" *MVHR* 44(December 1957): 525.

35. University of Illinois, Illinois Historical Survey Library, Illinois Historical Survey Library Archives, Part III. I, Clarence W. Alvord Administration, Folder 54.m, Clarence W. Alvord to St. George L. Sioussat, April 7, 1914.

36. Caughey, "Under Our Strange Device," p. 525.

37. University of Illinois, Illinois Historical Survey Library, Illinois Historical Survey Library Archives, Part III. I, Clarence W. Alvord Administration, Folder 54.m, Justin H. Smith to Clarence W. Alvord, February 14, 1914.

38. Nebraska State Historical Society, Organization of American Historians Papers, Series One, Box 103, Milo M. Quaife to Louis Pelzer, October 3, 1941.

39. Duke University, Library, Wendell Stephenson Papers (Journal of Southern History), Ella Lonn to Wendell H. Stephenson, November 6, 1935.

40. J. C. B. Mohr (Paul Siebeck) Tübingen, Archives, contract between F. Liebermann on the one hand and L. Quidde and J. C. B. Mohr on the other, 10 August 1889.

41. Ibid., L. Quidde to Paul Siebeck, 8/12/91, 24 Januar 1892, 21 März 1892.

42. Ibid., L. Quidde to Paul Siebeck, 14 März 1891; Paul Siebeck to Gerhard Seeliger, 12 Juni 1896, Copir Buch 39; 23 Juli 1897, Copir Buch 44; Paul Siebeck to E. Marcks, Dezember 7, 1894, Copir Buch 34, p. 51.

43. Ibid., L. Quidde to Paul Siebeck, 5 September 1893.

44. University of Illinois, Illinois Historical Survey Library, Illinois Historical Survey Library Archives, Part III. I, Clarence W. Alvord Administration, Folder 54.m, Clarence W. Alvord to St. George Sioussat, September 1, 1914; Folder 54.o, Clarence W. Alvord to Lawrence J. Burpee, February 19, 1915.

45. Ibid., Folder 54.m, Clarence W. Alvord to Milo M. Quaife, July 2, 1914.

46. Quidde, "Zur Einführung," p. 7.

47. J. C. B. Mohr (Paul Siebeck) Tübingen, Archives, Ludwig Quidde to Paul Siebeck, 21 November 1889.

48. University of Missouri, Western Historical Manuscripts Collection, Clarence W. Alvord Papers, Clarence W. Alvord to the Editors of the Mississippi Valley Historical Review, March 31, 1914; University of Illinois, Illinois Historical Survey Library, Illinois Historical Survey Archives, Part III. I, Clarence W. Alvord Administration, Folder 54.m, Benjamin Shambaugh to Clarence W. Alvord, April 3, 1914.

49. Posey, "The Southern Historical Association," p. 72.

50. Duke University, Library, Wendell Stephenson Papers (Journal of Southern History), William C. Binkley to Wendell H. Stephenson, October 16, 1935.

51. Clark, "Wendell Holmes Stephenson," p. 343.

52. Ibid., p. 339.

53. James L. Sellers, "The Semicentennial of the Mississippi Valley Historical Association," *MVHR* 44(December 1957): 510–11.

54. For example, Nebraska State Historical Society, Organization of American Historians Papers, Series One, Box 104, John D. Hicks to Clarence S. Yoakum, September 6, 1940.

55. Ibid., John D. Hicks to Louis Pelzer, January 28, 1941.

56. Ibid., John D. Hicks to Carl Wittke, July 3, 1940.

57. Ibid., John D. Hicks to Clara S. Paine, July 15, 1940.

58. Ibid., Clara S. Paine to John D. Hicks, November 25, 1940.

59. Duke University, Library, Wendell Stephenson Papers (Journal of Southern History), Wendell H. Stephenson to William C. Binkley, November 15, 1940; William C. Binkley to Wendell H. Stephenson, November 20, 1940.

60. Ibid., Wendell H. Stephenson to Walter B. Posey, November 14, 1940. Stephenson also wrote to Lynch and Edwards.

61. Nebraska State Historical Society, Organization of American Historians Papers, Series One, Box 104, John D. Hicks to John Pomfret, December 17, 1940.

62. Ibid., John D. Hicks to Beverley W. Bond, Jr., January 3, 1941.

63. Ibid., Clara S. Paine to John D. Hicks, November 25, 1940.

64. J. C. B. Mohr (Paul Siebeck) Tübingen, Archives, Erich Marcks to Paul Siebeck, 21 Marz 1895.

65. Nebraska State Historical Society, Organization of American Historians Papers, Series One, Box 104, John D. Hicks to Louis Pelzer, January 28, 1941.

66. University of Missouri, Western Historical Manuscripts Collection, Clarence W. Alvord Papers, Clarence W. Alvord to Dunbar Rowland, October 7, 1915.

67. Ibid., C. H. Van Tyne to Clarence W. Alvord, September 28, 1915.

68. Ibid., Dunbar Rowland to Clarence W. Alvord, November 4, 1915; Clarence W. Alvord to Dunbar Rowland, November 22, 1915.

69. Ibid., Clarence W. Alvord to Clarence S. Paine, March 27, 1916.

70. Ibid., Meeting of the Board of Editors of the MVHR, December 29, 1913; Clarence W. Alvord to the Board of Editors of the MVHR, March 12, 1914.

71. Sellers, "The Semicentennial," p. 507.

72. Nebraska State Historical Society, Organization of American Historians Papers, Series One, Box 127, Report of Secretary-Treasurer, April 1, 1944, to March 31, 1946.

73. Ibid., Series One, Box 53, Milo M. Quaife to Solon J. Buck, May 3, 1929.

74. Duke University, Library, Wendell Stephenson Papers (Journal of Southern History), Binkley Folder: Memorandum to O. C. Carmichael, Chancellor, Vanderbilt University, June 17, 1942; Hodges Folder: [Stephenson] To the Members of the Budget Committee [1942].

75. J. C. B. Mohr (Paul Siebeck) Tübingen, Archives, contract between Ludwig Quidde and Paul Siebeck, signed by Siebeck 15 November 1888. At this time, the mark was worth approximately 24 cents.

76. Ibid., L. Quidde to Paul Siebeck, 30 Juni 1888, 7 Januar 1889.

77. Ibid., Zapf to Gerhard Seeliger, 7 September 1896, Copir Buch 40.

Chapter 5: Topical Specialization

1. Reed Whittemore, "Black Studies in Glass Houses," review of *Amistad I,* ed. John A. Williams and Charles F. Harris, *New Republic,* May 9, 1970, pp. 25–26.

2. "Editorial," *Journal of Mexican-American History* 1(Fall 1970).

3. "The Journal of Industrial Archaeology," *Journal of Industrial Archaeology* 1(May 1964): 1; interview with John Butt, July 14, 1977.

4. Interview with Clyde Walton, December 27, 1976.

5. Stephan Bauer, *VSWG* 18(1925): 337, quoted in Hermann Aubin, "Zum 50. Band der Vierteljahresschrift für Sozial- und Wirtschaftsgeschichte," *VSWG* 50(Juni 1963): 8.

6. J. C. B. Mohr (Paul Siebeck) Tübingen, Archives, Emil Szantó to Paul Siebeck, 9 Dezember 1891.

7. Aubin, "Zum 50. Band," pp. 5–6.

8. Ibid., p. 9.

9. John Tracy Ellis, "Peter Guilday, March 15, 1884–July 31, 1947," *CHR* 33(October 1947): 260.

10. Johns Hopkins University, Library, Arthur O. Lovejoy Collection, Letters of Philip P. Wiener, co-founder of *JHI,* with Arthur O. Lovejoy, Philip P. Wiener to Arthur O. Lovejoy, July 15, 1938.

11. "Vorwort," *ZSWG* 1(1893): i.

12. Aubin, "Zum 50. Band," p. 7.

13. Interview with Jack Simmons, July 11, 1977.

14. "The Catholic Historical Review," *The Catholic University Bulletin* 21(January 1915): 38.

15. Ibid.

16. [Lopez Ortiz, José], [Foreword], *Hispania Sacra* 1(1948): 6.

17. Solomon Grayzel, "An Adventure in Scholarship," *Historia Judaica* 23(April–October 1961): 16.

18. "Genesis," *Historical Methods Newsletter* 1(December 1967): 1.

19. Interview with Margaret Jean Hay, April 19, 1979.

20. Lloyd DeMause, "The History of Childhood: The Bases for Psychohistory," *History of Childhood Quarterly* 1(Summer 1973): 1.

21. J. C. B. Mohr (Paul Siebeck) Tübingen, Archives, Zeitschrift fur Sozial- und Wirtschaftsgeschichte Contract, signed June 18, 1892.

22. Ibid., Carl Grünberg to Paul Siebeck, 25 September 1893.

23. Aubin, "Zum 50. Band," pp. 4–9.

24. J. C. B. Mohr (Paul Siebeck) Tübingen, Archives, Carl Grünberg to Paul Siebeck, 15 September 1893; Charles M. Andrews, "Die Stadt in Neu-England, ihr Ursprung und ihre agrarische Grundlage," *ZSWG* 2(1894): 224–40. This article provoked considerable disagreement, although its exact nature cannot be determined with any degree of confidence. Only two facts are clear: Hartmann disliked it and led the fight against it; Siebeck was forced to act as the go-between for the feuding editors.

25. Aubin, "Zum 50. Band," p. 11.

26. Ibid., p. 13.

27. Ibid., p. 17.

28. Catholic University of America, Department of Archives and Manuscripts, Catholic Historical Review Archives, D2A-1, Peter Guilday to Dr. Browne, November 22, 1922.

29. Ibid., American Catholic Historical Association, D2-2, Peter Guilday to J. F. Jameson, February 21, 1921.

30. Ibid., Catholic Historical Review Archives, D2A-19, John Tracy Ellis to Sister M. Doris, August 9, 1941.

31. Camillus P. Maes, "Flemish Franciscan Missionaries in North America," *CHR* 1(1915): 13.

32. Library of Congress, J. Franklin Jameson Collection, Box 90, File 686, Peter Guilday to J. Franklin Jameson, December 10, 1927.

33. Duke University, Library, Wendell Stephenson Papers (Journal of Southern History), Wendell H. Stephenson to Jessie Parkhurst, July 19, 1937; Jessie Parkhurst, "The Role of the Black Mammy," *JNH* 23(July 1938): 349–69.

34. Interview with Clyde Walton, December 27, 1976.

35. Johns Hopkins University, Library, Arthur O. Lovejoy Collection, Letters of Philip P. Wiener, co-founder of *JHI*, with Arthur O. Lovejoy, Philip P. Wiener to Arthur O. Lovejoy, June 7, 1939.

36. Max Gruenewald, "An Appreciation," *Historia Judaica* 23(April–October 1961): 7.

37. Guido Kisch, "Historia Judaica, 1938–1961: An Historical Account and Reminiscences of the Retiring Editor," *Historia Judaica* 23(April–October 1961): 7.

38. Catholic University of America, Department of Archives and Manuscripts, Peter Guilday Papers, Correspondence No. 5, Peter Guilday to Austin Dowling, June 5, 1916.

39. Johns Hopkins University, Library, Arthur O. Lovejoy Collection, Letters of Philip P. Wiener, co-founder of *JHI*, with Arthur O. Lovejoy, Philip P. Wiener to Arthur O. Lovejoy, February 5, 1940.

40. Aubin, "Zum 50. Band," p. 19.

41. Ibid.

42. J. C. B. Mohr (Paul Siebeck) Tübingen, Archives, Carl Grünberg to Paul Siebeck, 4 October 1893.

43. Ibid.

44. Ibid., L. M. Hartmann to Paul Siebeck, 31 October 1893.

45. Ibid.

46. Ibid., L. M. Hartmann to Paul Siebeck, 12 Januar 1893, 31 October 1893.

47. Ibid., Paul Siebeck to L. M. Hartmann, 17 März 1894, Copir Buch 33; Paul Siebeck to Stephan Bauer, 9 April 1894, Copir Buch 33.

48. Ibid., S. Bauer to Paul Siebeck, 30 März 1894, 28 Mai 1901.

49. Catholic University of America, Department of Archives and Manuscripts, Catholic Historical Review Archives, File D2A-19, Leo Stock to John Tracy Ellis, July 18, 1941.

50. Ibid., File D2A-1, Wm. Arch. McLean to Rev. P. W. Browne, June 14, 1926.

51. Ibid., File D2-1, "The Origin of the A.C.H.A.," undated, unsigned memorandum by Guilday.

52. For example, see Johns Hopkins University, Library, Arthur O. Lovejoy Collection, Letters of Philip P. Wiener, co-founder of *JHI*, with Arthur O. Lovejoy, Philip P. Wiener to Arthur O. Lovejoy, February 27, 1952.

53. Ibid., Philip P. Wiener to Arthur O. Lovejoy, September 10, 1947, November 19, 1947, November 26, 1951, June 2, 1953; Arthur O. Lovejoy to Philip P. Wiener, May 30, 1953.

54. In 1894 the German mark was worth $0.238.

55. Kisch, "Historia Judaica," pp. 4, 13.

56. David Rogers, "Francis Dominic Allison, 1892–1966: A Tribute," *Recusant History* 9(January 1967): 3–4.

57. Library of Congress, Carter Woodson Collection, File 5/83, Cleveland H. Dodge to Carter Woodson, December 8, 1918; File 6/112, Charles Young to Carter Woodson, March 11, 1919; File 6/97N, Kodwo Nsaaku to Carter Woodson, July 21, 1923; File 5/77, John E. Bruce to Carter Woodson, June 13, 1921, February 8, 1921.

58. Johns Hopkins University, Library, Arthur O. Lovejoy Collection, Letters of Philip P. Wiener, co-founder of *JHI*, with Arthur O. Lovejoy, Philip P. Wiener to Arthur O. Lovejoy, December 1, 1939.

59. *Historia Judaica* 23(April–October 1961): verso of title page.

60. [Foreword], *Revue d'histoire moderne et contemporaine* 1(1954): 5.

61. J. C. B. Mohr (Paul Siebeck) Tübingen, Archives, Paul Siebeck to Stephan Bauer, 16 April 1894, Copir Buch 33.

62. Rogers, "Francis Dominic Allison," p. 3.

63. Johns Hopkins University, Library, Arthur O. Lovejoy Collection, Letters of Philip P. Wiener, co-founder of *JHI*, with Arthur O. Lovejoy, Philip P. Wiener to Arthur O. Lovejoy, November 21, 1955.

64. "How the Public Received the Journal," *JNH* 1(April 1916): 225–32.

65. Library of Congress, Carter Woodson Collection, File 5/69, Dada Adeshigbin to Editor, Journal of Negro History, January 10, 1917.

66. Catholic University of America, Department of Archives and Manuscripts, Catholic Historical Review Archives, D2A-1, Questionnaire, answered by John J. Cleary, March 29, 1926; Peter Guilday to John J. Cleary, March 31, 1926; Peter Guilday to Bishop [Shahan], January 11, 1926.

67. Higham, Review of *The Past Before Us*, p. 809.

68. Ibid.

69. Otto Pflanze, "New Editor Talks about *AHR*," *AHA Newsletter* 14(December 1976): 2.

70. Higham, Krieger, and Gilbert, *History*, p. 57; Higham, Review of *The Past Before Us*, p. 809.

71. Higham, Review of *The Past Before Us*, p. 809.

72. Pflanze, "New Editor Talks," p. 2.

Chapter 6: Interdisciplinary Scholarly Historical Periodicals

1. The term is included in neither of the older unabridged dictionaries of the English language, the *Oxford English Dictionary* (1888–1933) and *Webster's New International Dictionary of the English Language* (1934). It is included in both the *Supplement to the Oxford English Dictionary* (1972–) and *Webster's Third New International Dictionary of the English Language* (1961). In the *Supplement*, illustrative quotations are given, the earliest of which date from the 1930s.

2. *Webster's Seventh New Collegiate Dictionary* (Springfield, Mass.: G. and C. Merriam, 1963), p. 441.

3. *Interdisciplinarity: Problems of Teaching and Research in Universities* (Organization for Economic Cooperation and Development, 1972), pp. 25–26.

4. Georg G. Iggers, *New Directions in European Historiography* (Middletown, Conn.: Wesleyan University Press, 1975), p. 27.

5. Revel, "The *Annales*," p. 11.

6. Iggers, *New Directions*, pp. 51–52; Henri Berr, "Au bout du trente ans," *Revue de synthèse historique* 50(1930): 5–27.

7. Berr, "Au bout du trente ans," p. 14.

8. Iggers, *New Directions*, pp. 51–52.

9. Tamara Swora and James L. Morrison, "Interdisciplinarity and Higher Education," *Journal of General Education* 26(April 1974): 46–47.

10. Walther Fischer, "Zur Einführung," *Jahrbuch für Amerikastudien* 1(1956).

11. Interview with Michael Wolff, September 14, 1979.

12. "A Statement by the Editors," *Eighteenth-century Life* 1(September 1974): 1.

13. "Editorial: Declaration of Independence," *Business and Society* 1(Autumn 1960).

14. "Introduction," *Amistad I* (1970): viii.

15. Edward Kennard Rand, "Editor's Preface," *Speculum* 1(January 1926): 3.

16. "A New Journal," *Journal of European Studies* 1(1971): 1.

17. "Clio: A Prospectus," *Clio* 1(October 1971).

18. Interview with G. H. N. Seton-Watson, August 22, 1978; interview with Christopher Seton-Watson, August 26, 1978; "From the Editors," *Russian Review* 1(January 1912): 7–8; Samuel Harper, *The Russia I Believe In* (Chicago: University of Chicago Press, 1945), p. 67; Harry Hanak, "The New Europe, 1916–1920," *SEER* 39(June 1961): 369–99.

19. University of London, King's College, King's College Archives, Folder 86, School of Slavonic Studies (including addresses), R. W. Seton-Watson to Burrows, 8 September 1915.

20. "The Slavonic Review," *SEER* 1(June 1922): 1.

21. "Prefatory Note," *VS* 1(September 1957): 3.

22. To hire three junior faculty members in the same specialization at the same time is rare.

23. Interview with Michael Wolff, September 14, 1979.

24. Interview with Martha Vicinus, September 30–October 1, 1979.

25. Michael Wolff, "Retrospectives," *VS* 20(Supplement 1977): 7.

26. Ibid.; Indiana University, Victorian Studies Files, Progress Report, Philip Appleman, William A. Madden, Michael Wolff to President Wells and Members of the Administrative and Research Committees, 15 May 1957; Philip Appleman to Prof. James A. Work, June 1, 1956.

27. R. W. Seton-Watson, "Bernard Pares," *SEER* 28(November 1949): 29.

28. Bernard Pares, *A Wandering Student* ([Syracuse, N.Y.]: Syracuse University Press in cooperation with Howell, Soskin, 1948).

29. "The Slavonic Review," p. 1.

30. R. W. Seton-Watson Papers, Bernard Pares to R. W. Seton-Watson, August 26, 1921.

31. Ibid., "Notes on the Slavonic Review," undated carbon [1945?], almost certainly from R. W. Seton-Watson to Bernard Pares. The *SEER* was edited and published in the United States between 1941 and 1944.

32. Ibid., Bernard Pares to R. W. Seton-Watson, 23 March 1937.

33. Ibid., Bernard Pares to R. W. Seton-Watson, 12 December 1938.

34. "Editorial," *Soviet Studies* 1(June 1949): 1.

35. Indiana University, Victorian Studies Files, Brian Harrison to Michael [Wolff], 28 Feb. 67; Martha Vicinus to Park Honan, 11 March 1975.

36. Interview with Michael Wolff, September 14, 1979; interview with Martha Vicinus, September 30–October 1, 1979.

37. Indiana University, Victorian Studies Files, Walter F. Cannon to Michael [Wolff], [March 1967].

38. Ibid., Martha Vicinus to P. M. Ball, 17 January 1974.

39. R. W. Seton-Watson Papers, "Notes on the Slavonic Review."

40. Ibid.

41. R. W. Seton-Watson Papers, "Statement of Needs of School Prepared for Monday Lunch, Previous to July 15th, 1923."

42. Ibid., Bernard Pares to R. W. Seton-Watson, April 1, 1926.

43. Ibid., Bernard Pares to R. W. Seton-Watson, 18 August 1933.

44. E. M. Robson to Margaret F. Stieg, 9 March 1982.

45. E. M. Robson to Margaret F. Stieg, 25 February 1982.

46. Interview with Martha Vicinus, September 30–October 1, 1979.

47. Interview with Georgette Donchin, July 8, 1977.

48. Interview with Michael Wolff, September 14, 1979.

49. Interview with Donald Gray, October 1, 1979.

50. Interview with Michael Wolff, September 14, 1979; interview with Martha Vicinus, September 30–October 1, 1979.

51. Pares, *A Wandering Student*, p. 301.

52. E. M. Robson to Margaret F. Stieg, 9 March 1982.

53. In 1977 they published 1,520 books on history and 1,354 on the history and criticism of literature. Table 8.3: Number of Titles by Subject Group, *Unesco Statistical Yearbook, 1980* (Paris: United Nations Educational, Scientific, and Cultural Organization, 1980), p. 1024.

54. Interview with G. H. N. Seton-Watson, August 22, 1978.

55. Interview with Michael Wolff, September 14, 1979; interview with Martha Vicinus, September 30–October 1, 1979; Martha Vicinus, "Retrospectives," *VS* 20(Supplement 1977): 12.

56. Interview with Michael Wolff, September 14, 1979.

57. Interview with Georgette Donchin, July 8, 1977.

58. E. M. Robson to Margaret F. Stieg, 25 February 1982.

59. R. W. Seton-Watson Papers, Bernard Pares to R. W. Seton-Watson, 13 January 1933.

60. Indiana University, Victorian Studies Files, Philip Appleman to James A. Work, June 1, 1956.

61. Ibid., Martha Vicinus to Peter Stansky, 23 May 1975; Martha Vicinus to Michael Wolff, 19 May 1975.

62. Ibid., Martha Vicinus to Michael Wolff, 19 May 1975; Christopher Kent to Martha Vicinus, 30 June 1978.

63. R. W. Seton-Watson Papers. Bernard Pares to Baron _____, May 7, 1924.

64. Ibid., Bernard Pares to Seton on Subject of Conversation with Andrews, Coolidge, and Lord (1924); Bernard Pares to Baron _____, May 7, 1924; Bernard Pares to R. W. Seton-Watson, September 7, 1924.

65. Ibid., R. W. Seton-Watson to his wife, Marion, [Christmas Day, 1924]. The journal cannot be identified.

66. Interview with Michael Wolff, September 14, 1979.

67. Indiana University, Victorian Studies Files, H. J. Dyos to Martha Vicinus, 19 April 1971, 4 June 1971, 23 June 1971, 27 October 1971, 16 December 1971, 10 September 1972; Martha Vicinus to P. Collins and H. J. Dyos, 23 April 1971; Martha Vicinus to H. J. Dyos, 17 May 1971, 15 June 1971, 18 August 1971, 23 November 1971, 8 February 1972; Interdepartmental Communication, Martha Vicinus to Donald Gray, Patrick Brantlinger, 20 July 1971.

68. Ibid., Mimeographed List of New Editorial Board and Advisory Board Members (1970).

69. Interview with Michael Wolff, September 14, 1979; interview with Donald Gray, October 1, 1979.

70. Dorothy Galton, "Sir Bernard Pares and Slavonic Studies in London University, 1919–39," *SEER* 46(July 1968): 486.

71. W. J. Rose, "B. P.: III," *SEER* 28(November 1949): 37.

72. Galton, "Sir Bernard Pares," p. 486.

73. Harper, *The Russia I Believe In*, p. 67.

74. Pares, *A Wandering Student*, p. 288.

75. R. W. Seton-Watson Papers, Bernard Pares to R. W. Seton-Watson, 8 January 1935, June 20, 1933.

76. Rose, "B. P.: III," pp. 37–38.

77. R. W. Seton-Watson Papers, Bernard Pares to R. W. Seton-Watson, April 2, 1923.

78. E. M. Robson to Margaret F. Stieg, 25 February 1982.

79. R. W. Seton-Watson Papers, Bernard Pares to R. W. Seton-Watson, June 27, 1921, 8 January 1935, February 17, 1929, April 1, 1926.

80. Ibid., Bernard Pares to R. W. Seton-Watson, August 12, 1933.

81. Indiana University, Victorian Studies Files, Martha Vicinus to Michael Moore, 13 January 1978.

82. Ibid., Memorandum from Martha Vicinus to Members of the Editorial Board, 7 June 1973; Martha Vicinus to Paul Strohm, 24 February 1979; interview with Michael Wolff, September 14, 1979.

83. Ibid., Progress Report, Philip Appleman, William A. Madden, Michael Wolff to President Wells and Members of the Administrative and Research Committees, 15 May 1957; *Victorian Studies* to Research Committee, General and Financial Report, 1 March 1958; interview with Michael Wolff, September 14, 1979.

84. Ibid., *Victorian Studies*, Questionnaire: College Journal Evaluation, cover letter dated November 30, 1970; interview with Martha Vicinus, September 30–October 1, 1979. The figures are from an analysis of the subscription files.

85. R. W. Seton-Watson Papers, Bernard Pares to R. W. Seton-Watson, August 21st, 1922, October 25, 1922, September 8, 1923, August 19, [1925].

86. Ibid., Douglas Jenord to Bernard Pares, May 28, 1930; Bernard Pares to R. W. Seton-Watson, 8 January 1935.

87. Ibid., Bernard Pares to R. W. Seton-Watson, December 20, 1923, September 9, 1923; University of London, School of Slavonic and East European Studies, Bernard Pares Collection, General Correspondence, 1928–42, E. Sabline to Bernard Pares, 15 November 1933.

88. R. W. Seton-Watson Papers, Bernard Pares to R. W. Seton-Watson, 23 March 1937; University of London, School of Slavonic and East European Studies, Bernard Pares Collection, General Correspondence, 1928–42, George R. Noyes to Bernard Pares, February 24, 1940; Lucy Textor to Bernard Pares, November 27, 1941.

89. Indiana University, Victorian Studies Files, Martha Vicinus to Robert O'Neil, 8 December 1975, 1 March 1958; Ken Fielding to Michael Wolff, [1967]; Brian Harrison to Michael [Wolff], 28 Feb 67; interview with Michael Wolff, September 14, 1979.

90. Indiana University, Victorian Studies Files, Christopher Ricks to Michael Wolff, [1967].

Chapter 7: Politics and Scholarly Historical Periodicals

1. Quoted in E. H. Dance, *History the Betrayer: A Study in Bias* (London: Hutchinson, 1960), p. 56.

2. Ibid., p. 68.

3. John Higham, "Beyond Consensus: The Historian as Moral Critic," *AHR* 67(April 1962): 609.

4. "Prefatory Note" *EHR* 1(January 1886): 4–5.

5. Sloane, "History and Democracy," p. 21.

6. Blakey, *Historians on the Home Front*, p. 19.

7. Max Farrand, "The Quality of Distinction," *AHR* 46(April 1941): 511.

8. Richard R. Palmer. "The American Historical Association in 1970," *AHR* 76(February 1971): 1–3.

9. *AHR* 49(October 1943, January 1944): 1–22, 228–42.

10. John A. Garraty, "The New Deal, National Socialism, and the Great Depression," *AHR* 78(October 1973): 943.

11. Robert Livingston Schuyler, "The Recall of the Legions: A Phase of Decentralization of the British Empire," *AHR* 26(October 1920): 18–36.

12. Sidney B. Fay, "New Light on the Origins of the World War," *AHR* 25(July 1920): 616–39; 26(October 1920): 37–53.

13. *AHR* 27(January 1922): 207–18.

14. For example, Walter La Feber, "Roosevelt, Churchill, and Indochina, 1942–45," *AHR* 80(December 1975): 1277–95.

15. William Henry Chamberlin, "Foreword," *Russian Review* 1(November 1941): 1–2.

16. Clyde C. Walton, "Introduction," *Civil War History* 1(March 1955): 5.

17. R. W. Seton-Watson Papers, Harold Williams to R. W. Seton-Watson, August 23, 1921.

18. Ibid., Bernard Pares to R. W. Seton-Watson, 18 May 1929.

19. *SEER* 9(March 1931): 509–24.

20. Basil Paneyko, "Galicia and the Polish-Ukrainian Problem," *SEER* 9(March 1931): 567–87.

21. R. W. Seton-Watson Papers, Bernard Pares to R. W. Seton-Watson, May 10, 1930. The Paneyko article is an excellent illustration of their policy. He was a well-known Ukrainian journalist and politician. His article was accompanied by another that was written by a Polish professor with administrative experience in Austrian Galicia.

22. "Memorandum on the Russian Situation," *SEER* 8(December 1930): 497–503.

23. R. W. Seton-Watson Papers, R. W. Seton-Watson, Memorandum on the Mirsky affair, attached to letter of 25 August 1931 to Bernard Pares.

24. D. W. Mirsky, "Periods of Russian Literature," *SEER* 9(March 1931): 692.

25. R. W. Seton-Watson Papers, R. W. Seton-Watson, Memorandum on the Mirsky affair, attached to letter of 25 August 1931 to Bernard Pares.

26. University of London, School of Slavonic and East European Studies, Bernard Pares Collection, General Correspondence, 1928–42, Stafford C. Talbot to Bernard Pares, 3 September 1934; Bernard Pares to Stafford C. Talbot, 12 September 1934. Both Pares and Talbot were alumni of Cambridge University; Talbot had been at Caius College, Pares at Trinity.

27. Monod and Fagniez, "Avant-propos," p. 4.

28. Alice Gérard, "Histoire et politique: La *Revue historique* face à l'histoire contemporaine (1885–1898)," *RH* 255(avril–juin 1976): 355.

29. G. Monod, "Bulletin historique: France," *RH* 4(août 1877): 302; *RH* 5(decembre 1877): 361.

30. G. Monod, "Bulletin historique: France," *RH* 41(decembre 1889): 339.

31. G. Monod, "Bulletin historique: France," *RH* 17(decembre 1881): 368.

32. G. Monod, "Bulletin historique: France," *RH* 4(août 1877): 367.

33. Edmond deMolins, review of *L'histoire de France depuis 1789 jusqu'en 1848*, by F. Guizot, *RQH* 27(1880): 679–80.

34. Gérard, "Histoire et politique," pp. 387–88.

35. Michel Martin, "Histoire et actualité: La *Revue historique* pendant la première guerre mondiale," *RH* 255(avril–juin 1976): 434.

36. Ibid., pp. 438–41.

37. Ibid., pp. 435, 441.

38. Ibid., pp. 449–53.

39. H. von Sybel, "Vorwort," *HZ* 1(1859): iii.

40. Schieder, "Die deutsche Geschichtswissenschaft," p. 39.

41. Walter Platzhoff, *HZ* 115(1916): 64–77.

42. Adolf Hasenclever, review of *Catalogue of Parliamentary Papers 1807–1900*, ed. Hilda Vernon Jones, and *Catalogue of Parliamentary Papers 1901–1910*, ed. Hilda Vernon Jones, *HZ* 115(1916): 187.

43. Karl Ferdinand Werner, *Das NS-Geschichtsbild und die deutsche Geschichtswissenschaft* (Stuttgart: W. Kohlhammer, 1967), p. 24.

44. Karl Ferdinand Werner, "Die deutsche Historiographie unter Hitler," in *Geschichtswissenschaft in Deutschland*, ed. Bernd Faulenbach (Munich: Verlag C. H. Beck, 1974), p. 90.

45. Helmut Heiber, *Walter Frank und sein Reichsinstitut für Geschichte des neuen Deutschlands* (Stuttgart: Deutsche Verlags-Anstalt, 1966), p. 691.

46. Ibid., p. 693.

47. Friedrich Meinecke to Verlag Oldenbourg, 25 Januar 1934, quoted in Heiber, *Walter Frank und sein Reichsinstitut*, p. 280.

48. Hauptarchiv Berlin-Dahlem, Nachlass Meinecke, Rep 92, Nachtrag 23, handwritten letter on the back of a notice from Friedrichs Wilhelm Universität to Frau Hintze, 20 Mai 1933.

49. Ibid., Otto Hintze to Friedrich Meinecke, 21 Mai 1933.

50. Schieder, "Die deutsche Geschichtswissenschaft," p. 35.

51. Heiber, *Walter Frank und sein Reichsinstitut*, p. 289.

52. Hauptarchiv Berlin-Dahlem, Nachlass Meinecke, Rep 92, Nachtrag 23, Friedrich Meinecke to Helmut Berve, 19 Oktober 1934.

53. Heiber, *Walter Frank und sein Reichsinstitut*, p. 290.

54. "Von Müller: Editor's Note to the *Historische Zeitschrift* (1936)," in *The Varieties of History*, ed. Fritz Stern (Cleveland and New York: World, 1956), pp. 345–46.

55. Walter Frank, "Zunft und Nation," *HZ* 153(1936): 6–23.

56. Erwin Hölzle, "Volks- und Rassenbewusstsein in der Englischen Revolution," *HZ* 153(1936): 24–42; Wilhelm Grau, "Geschichte der Jüdenfrage, *HZ* 153(1936): 336–49.

57. Heiber, *Walter Frank und sein Reichsinstitut*, p. 301.

58. Bolko, Freiherr von Richthofen, "Völkergeschichte der Vorzeit Ostdeutschland und seiner Nachbarstaaten im ausländischen Licht," *HZ* 154(1936): 453–90.

59. Johannes Heckel, "Der Einbruch des jüdischen Geistes in das deutsche Staats- und Kirchenrecht durch Friedrich Julius Stahl," *HZ* 155(1937): 506–41.

60. Walter Frank, "Kleo Pleyer, Ein Kampf um das Reich," *HZ* 166(1942): 507–52.

61. Heiber, *Walter Frank und sein Reichsinstitut*, p. 307.

62. "Geleitwort zum Wiederscheinen der Historischen Zeitschrift," *HZ* 169(April 1949).

63. Hauptarchiv Berlin-Dahlem, Nachlass Meinecke, Nr. 18, Walter Kienast to Friedrich Meinecke, 13 Februar 1949.

64. W. Kienast, "An unsere Mitarbeiter," *HZ* 169(1949): 225–26.

65. Werner Conze, "Die deutsche Geschichtswissenschaft seit 1945: Bedingungen und Ergebnisse," *HZ* 225(August 1977): 12.

66. Quoted in Nancy Whittier Heer, *Politics and History in the Soviet Union* (Cambridge, Mass., and London: MIT Press, 1971), p. 11.

67. This discussion of Soviet historiography draws upon the *Great Soviet Encyclopedia*, translation of 3rd edition, s.v. "Historiography," by A. I. Danilov et al.; Heer, *Politics and History*, especially pp. 1–33; and Marin Pundeff, comp. and ed., *History in the USSR: Selected Readings* (Stanford, Calif.: Published for the Hoover Institution on War, Revolution, and Peace by the Chandler Publishing Company, 1967), pp. v–viii.

68. *Great Soviet Encyclopedia*, s.v. "Historiography," p. 92.

69. Ibid.

70. Ibid., pp. 93–95.

71. Heer, *Politics and History*, p. 13.

72. Pundeff, *History in the USSR*, p. vii.

73. *Great Soviet Encyclopedia*, s.v. "Historiography," p. 93.

74. A partial list of the separate relevant articles in the *Great Soviet Encyclopedia* includes those on historiography, history, historical sources, several historical organizations such as Istpart and Istprof, and specific historical journals.

75. Heer, *Politics and History*, pp. 13–33.

76. Ibid., p. 30.

77. Ibid., pp. 34–58.

78. It is one of two Russian periodicals for which the contents are listed in the first volume of the *English Historical Review*.

79. "Ob izdanii c l-go ianvaria 1870 goda ezhemesiachnago istoricheskago sbornika 'Russkaia Starina,'" *Russkaia starina* 1(1870, 3rd ed.): 1.

80. *Great Soviet Encyclopedia*, s.v. "Russkaia starina."

81. *Istoricheskii viestnik*'s conservatism and monarchism were particularly remarkable in the immediate aftermath of the Revolution of 1905 and during World War I. *Great Soviet Encyclopedia*, s.v. "Istoricheskii vestnik."

82. *Starina i novizna* 1(1897): vi.

83. S. A. Nikitin, *Istochnikovedenie istorii SSSR XIX v. (do nachala 90-kh godov)*, T. II (Moskva: Gosudarstvennoe sotsial' noekonomicheskoe izdatal'stvo, 1940), p. 174.

84. Ibid., p. 172.

85. P. Leneshinskii, "Ot Istparta," *Proletarskaia revoliutsiia* 1(1921): 3–9; *Great Soviet Encyclopedia*, s.v. "Proletarskaia Revoliutsiia."

86. *Great Soviet Encyclopedia*, s.v. "Katorga i ssylka."

87. "Ot Petrogradskogo biuro komissii po istorii oktiabr'skoi revoliutsii i rossiiskoi kommunisticheskoi partii," *Krasnaia letopis'* 1(1922): 5–7.

88. "Ot redaktsii," *Krasnyi arkhiv* 1(1922): 1.

89. "Ot Istparta," *Letopis' revoliutsii* 1(1922): 5–6.

90. Leneshinskii, "Ot Istparta," pp. 5–6.

91. Konstantin F. Shteppa, *Russian Historians and the Soviet State* (New Brunswick, N.J.: Rutgers University Press, 1962), pp. 25–26.

92. "Statutes of the Society of Marxist Historians," in Pundeff, *History in the USSR*, p. 76.

93. M. N. Pokrovskii, "Zadachi Obshchestva istorikov-marksistov," *Istorik-marksist* 1(1926): 7. This item is the same as that cited in note 92, but the message relating to the Mensheviks was not published in Pundeff's selection.

94. Shteppa, *Russian Historians*, pp. 31–32.

95. Ibid., pp. 58–62.

96. Ibid., p. 210.

97. *Great Soviet Encyclopedia*, s.v. "Istorik-Marksist."

98. Ibid., s.v. "Voprosy Istorii"; "Zadachi zhurnala 'Voprosy istorii,'" *VI* 1(1945): 3.

99. Ibid., p. 4.

100. Ibid.

101. Quoted in Heer, *Politics and History*, p. 70.

102. Heer, *Politics and History*, p. 73.

103. "XX Sezd KPSS i zadachi issledovaniia istorii partii," *VI* (no. 3, 1956): 7, quoted in Heer, *Politics and History*, p. 81.

104. Heer, *Politics and History*, pp. 84–85.

105. Ibid., pp. 87–91; Shteppa, *Russian Historians*, pp. 374–75.

106. "Decree of March 9, 1957, on *Voprosy istorii*," in Pundeff, *History in the USSR*, p. 234; Heer, *Politics and History*, p. 92.

107. *Great Soviet Encyclopedia*, s.v. "Voprosy Istorii."

108. Heer, *Politics and History*, p. 92.

109. *Great Soviet Encyclopedia*, s.v. "Voprosy Istorii KPSS."

110. Heer, *Politics and History*, p. 116.

111. *Spravochnik partiinogo rabotnika*, 4th ed. (1963), p. 454, quoted in Heer, *Politics and History*, p. 142.

Chapter 8: Bibliographical Control and Use of Scholarly Historical Periodicals

1. *Directory of American Scholars*, vol. 1: *History*, 7th ed. (New York and London: Bowker, 1978).

2. Margaret F. Stieg, "The Information of [*sic*] Needs of Historians," *College and Research Libraries* 42(November 1981): 549–60.

3. Donald Davinson, *Bibliographic Control* (London: Clive Bingley; Hamden, Conn.: Linnet Books, 1975), p. 7.

4. Verner W. Clapp, "Indexing and Abstracting Services for Serial Literature," *Library Trends* 2(April 1954): 517.

5. Eugene P. Sheehy, comp., *Guide to Reference Books*, 9th ed. (Chicago: American Library Association, 1976).

6. Organizations represented on the Joint Committee were the American Historical Association, the Organization of American Historians, the Southern Historical Association, the American Association for State and Local History, the Western History Association, the Agricultural History Society, the American Studies Association, the American Bibliographical Center, the Library of Congress, and the National Archives and Records Service.

7. The Association for Historical Bibliography is too new for its direction to be clear.

8. U. S. Library of Congress, General Reference and Bibliography Division, *A Guide to the Study of the United States* (Washington: Government Printing Office, 1960).

9. Sara G. Cogan, comp., *Pioneer Jews of the California Mother Lode, 1849–1880: An Annotated Bibliography* (Berkeley, Calif.: Western Jewish History Center, 1968).

10. Dexter Perkins, *Yield of the Years* (Boston: Little Brown, 1969), p. 62.

11. The distribution of these is interesting. Two were in the *Yale Review,* one in the *MVHR,* one in the *AHR,* and one in the *Proceedings* of the Massachusetts Historical Society. Clearly, not all were intended or written solely for other scholars. In time, they ranged over much of his career. Arthur M. Schlesinger, *In Retrospect: The History of a Historian* (New York: Harcourt, Brace and World, 1963), pp. 106–9.

12. Clyve Jones, Michael Chapman, and Pamela Carr Woods, "The Characteristics of the Literature Used by Historians," *Journal of Librarianship* 4(July 1972): 137–56; Arthur Monroe McAnally, "Characteristics of Materials Used in Research in United States History," (Ph.D. diss., University of Chicago, 1951); *SSCI Journal Citation Reports: A Bibliometric Analysis of Social Science Journals, Social Sciences Citation Index,* vol. 6 (Philadelphia: Institute for Scientific Information, annual). To supplement these studies, I also analyzed the periodicals used in six monographs: Thomas G. Barnes, *Somerset, 1625–1640: A County's Government during the "Personal Rule"* (Cambridge, Mass.: Harvard University Press, 1961); Fernand Braudel, *The Mediterranean and the Mediterranean World in the Age of Philip II,* vol. 2, trans. Sian Reynolds (London: Fontana/Collins, 1976); Gordon A. Craig, *The Germans* (New York: G. P. Putnam's Sons, 1982); Carl Degler, *Neither Black Nor White* (New York: Macmillan; London: Collier-Macmillan, 1971); Robert W. Fogel and Stanley L. Engerman, *Time on the Cross: The Economics of American Slavery,* vol. 2: *Evidence and Methods, A Supplement* (Boston: Little Brown, 1974); William H. McNeill, *The Rise of the West: A History of the Human Community* (New York and Toronto: New American Library; London: New English Library, 1963).

13. Jones, Chapman, and Woods, "The Characteristics of the Literature Used by Historians," p. 152.

14. Ibid., p. 141.

15. McAnally, "Characteristics of Material," p. 37.

BIBLIOGRAPHY

Interviews

John Butt (*Industrial Archaeology*), Glasgow, Scotland, July 14, 1977.
Georgette Donchin (*Slavonic and East European Review*), London, England, July 8, 1977.
Donald Gray (*Victorian Studies*), Bloomington, Indiana, October 1, 1977.
Margaret Jean Hay (*African Economic History Review*), Boston, Massachusetts, April 19, 1979.
Harro von Hirschheydt (*Baltische Hefte*), Hannover, Germany, June 14, 1977.
Kenneth Ponting (*Textile History*), Edington, Wilts., England, July 12, 1977.
Jacques Revel (*Annales*), Paris, France, June 29, 1977.
Christopher Seton-Watson (*Slavonic and East European Review*), London, England, August 26, 1978.
G. H. N. Seton-Watson (*Slavonic and East European Review*), London, England, August 22, 1978.
Jack Simmons (*Journal of Transport History*), Leicester, England, July 11, 1977.
Martha Vicinus (*Victorian Studies*), Bloomington, Indiana, September 30– October 1, 1979.
Clyde Walton (*Civil War History*), DeKalb, Illinois, December 27, 1976.
Michael Wolff (*Victorian Studies*), Amherst, Massachusetts, September 14, 1979.

Personal Letters

Patrick Brantlinger (*Victorian Studies*) to Margaret F. Stieg, March 18, 1982.
Edwin A. Davis (*Journal of Southern History*) to Walter B. Posey, September 18, 1975.
S. W. Higginbotham (*Journal of Southern History*) to Margaret F. Stieg, February 12, 1982.
E. J. Hobsbawm (*Past and Present*) to Margaret F. Stieg, April 20, 1977.
A. S. Macintyre (*English Historical Review*) to Margaret F. Stieg, 23 March 1982.
Lewis Perry (*Journal of American History*) to Margaret F. Stieg, March 19, 1982.
Elisabeth Robson (*Slavonic and East European Review*) to Margaret F. Stieg, 25 February 1982, 9 March 1982.
Theodor Schieder (*Historische Zeitschrift*) to Margaret F. Stieg, 15.3.1982.

Robert Trisco (*Catholic Historical Review*) to Margaret F. Stieg, February 13, 1982.

Manuscript Sources

FRANCE

Paris. Bibliothèque Nationale. Papers of G. Monod, first editor of the *Revue historique*.

GERMANY

Berlin. Geheimes Staatsarchiv. Papers of Friedrich Meinecke, long-time editor of the *Historische Zeitschrift*.

Koblenz. Bundesarchiv. Papers of Heinrich von Sybel, first editor of the *Historische Zeitschrift*.

Munich. Hausarchiv. Letters of Heinrich von Sybel, first editor of the *Historische Zeitschrift*.

Munich. Stadtbibliothek. Papers of Ludwig Quidde, first editor of the *Deutsche Zeitschrift für Geschichtswissenschaft*.

Tübingen. J. C. B. Mohr (Paul Siebeck) Firm. Archives. Records of the *Deutsche Zeitschrift für Geschichtswissenschaft* and the *Zeitschrift für Sozial- und Wirtschaftsgeschichte*.

GREAT BRITAIN

Cambridge. University Library. Acton Papers.

London. British Museum. Papers of Bernard Pares, first co-editor of the *Slavonic and East European Review*.

London. University of London. Kings College. Archives.

London. University of London. School of Slavonic and East European Studies. Papers of Bernard Pares, first co-editor of the *Slavonic and East European Review*.

London. Papers of R. W. Seton-Watson, first co-editor of *Slavonic and East European Review*, in possession of his sons, G. H. N. Seton-Watson and M. R. C. Seton-Watson.

Oxford. Jesus College. Papers of John Richard Green, nineteenth-century British historian.

Reading. Reading University. Library. Archives of Longmans publishing firm.

UNITED STATES

Baltimore, Maryland. Johns Hopkins University Library. Papers of Arthur O. Lovejoy, first editor in chief of the *Journal of the History of Ideas*.

Bloomington, Indiana. University of Indiana. Victorian Studies Files.

Champaign, Illinois. University of Illinois. Illinois Historical Survey Library. Papers of Clarence W. Alvord, first editor of the *Mississippi Valley Historical Review*.

Columbia, Missouri. University of Missouri. Western Historical Manu-
scripts Collection. Papers of Clarence W. Alvord, first editor of the
Mississippi Valley Historical Review.
Durham, North Carolina. Duke University. Library. Papers of Wendell H.
Stephenson, first editor of the *Journal of Southern History.*
Lincoln, Nebraska. Nebraska State Historical Society. Papers of the
Organization of American Historians.
New Haven, Connecticut. Yale University. Library. Papers of George
Burton Adams, nineteenth- and twentieth-century American historian.
Washington, D.C. Catholic University of America. Archives. Records of the
Catholic Historical Review; papers of Peter Guilday, first editor of the
Catholic Historical Review.
Washington, D.C. Library of Congress. Records of the American Historical
Association; papers of J. Franklin Jameson, first editor of the *American
Historical Review;* papers of Carter Woodson, first editor of the *Journal of
Negro History;* papers of Bernadotte Schmitt, first editor of the *Journal of
Modern History.*

Printed Sources

"The *AHR* and the AHA: An Editorial." *AHR* 77(October 1972): 967–76.
"*AHR* Moves to Indiana." *AHA Newsletter* 13(November 1975):1.
"À nos lecteurs." *Annales d'histoire économique et sociale.* 1(janvier 1929): 1–2.
"À nos lecteurs." *Revue des études juives* 1(1880): v–viii.
Achtert, Walter S. "Scholarly Journals in the Seventies." *Scholarly Publishing*
5(October 1973): 3–11.
Adams, George B. "A Note on a Point of Medieval History." *New Englander*
48(May 1888): 369–70.
———. "The Origins of the Feudal System." *Andover Review* 7(April 1887,
May 1887): 366–75, 505–18.
———. "Petrarch and the Beginning of Modern Science." *Yale Review*
1(August 1892): 146–61.
[Adams, George B.] Review of *The History of the Philosophy of History*, by
Robert Flint. *Nation*, June 14, 1894, p. 454.
A[dams], G[eorge] B. Review of *Social Evolution*, by Benjamin Kedd. *Yale
Review* 3(May 1894): 99–103.
Adams, George Burton. "The United States and the Anglo-Saxon Future."
Atlantic Monthly, July 1896, pp. 35–46.
Adams, Herbert B. *Historical Scholarship in the United States, 1876–1901: As
Revealed in the Correspondence of Herbert B. Adams.* Edited by W. S. Holt.
Johns Hopkins University Studies, 56, no. 4. Baltimore: The Johns
Hopkins Press, 1938.
Aiken, Henry D. "Interdisciplinary and Transdisciplinary Studies in the
Humanities: Problems and Possibilities." In Columbia University,
Seminar on General and Continuing Education in the Humanities,
Seminar Reports, May 15, 1974, pp. 1, 3–4.

"The Air Force Historical Foundation." *Airpower Historian* 11(October 1964): unnumbered.

Allgemeine deutsche Biographie, 56 vols. Leipzig: Duncker und Humblot, 1875–1912.

Altamira, Rafael. "La reforma de los estudios historicos en España." *Bulletin hispanique* 2(octobre–decembre 1900): 305–10.

Alvord, Clarence Walworth. "Planning the Publication Work of Historical Agencies." In American Historical Association, *Annual Review for the Year 1913,* vol. 1, pp. 217–24. Washington, D.C., 1915.

[Annual Report of the Editor of the American Historical Review]. Variously titled. *AHR* 40–74(April 1935–April 1969).

"Articles for the *AHR:* An Editorial." *AHR* 75(October 1970): 1577–80.

Aubin, Hermann. "Zum 50. Band der Vierteljahrschrift für Sozial- und Wirtschaftsgeschichte." *VSWG* 50(Juni 1963): 1–24.

Bancroft, Frederic. *Why the American Historical Association Needs Thorough Reorganization.* Washington, D.C.: National Capital Press, 1915.

Barbagallo, Corrado. "Conditions and Tendencies of Historical Writing in Italy Today." *Journal of Modern History* 1(June 1929): 236–44.

Barnes, Richard S. "German Influence on American Historical Studies, 1884–1914." Ph.D. diss., Yale University, 1953. Microfilm copy.

Barnes, Sherman B. "The Scientific Journal, 1665–1730." *Scientific Monthly* 38(March 1934): 257–60.

Barr, Diana. *Trends in Book Production and Prices.* London: National Central Library, 1972.

Bartošek, Karel. "Czechoslovakia: The State of Historiography." *Journal of Contemporary History* 2(January 1967): 143–55.

Bath University Library. Investigations into Information Requirements of the Social Sciences. *Research Report 1: Information Requirements of Researchers in the Social Sciences.* 2 vols. June 1971.

Battin, Patricia. "Libraries, Computers, and Scholarship." *Wilson Library Bulletin* 56(April 1982): 580–83.

Batts, M. S. "Citations in the Humanities: A Study of Citation Patterns in Literary Criticism in English, French and German." *IPLO Quarterly* 14(July 1972): 20–40.

Baumol, William J., and Yale M. Braunstein. "Empirical Study of Scale Economies and Production Complementarity: The Case of Journal Publication." *Journal of Political Economy* 85(October 1977): 1037–48.

Beale, Howard K. "The Professional Historian: His Theory and His Practice." *Pacific Historical Review* 22(August 1953): 227–55.

Bean, Walton E. "Revolt among Historians." *Sewanee Review* 47(July 1939): 330–41.

Beaucourt, G. du Fresne de. "Introduction." *RQH* 1(janvier–juin 1866): 5–10.

Behavioral and Social Sciences Survey, History Panel. *History as a Social Science.* Englewood Cliffs, N.J.: Prentice-Hall, 1971.

Bémont, Charles. "Notice nécrologique consacrée à Gustave Fagniez." *RH* 155(juillet–août 1927): 456–58.

Beneschevich, V. N., et al. "Ot redaktsii." *Russki istoricheskii zhurnal* 1(1917): 3–8.

Bent, J. Theodore. "King Theodore of Corsica." *EHR* 1(April 1886): 295–307.

Bergen, Dan. "Communication System of the Social Sciences." *College and Research Libraries* 28(July 1967): 239–52.

Bergquist, Charles W. "Recent United States Studies in Latin American History." *Latin American Research Review* 9(Spring 1974): 3–35.

Berr, Henri. "Au bout du trente ans." *Revue de synthèse historique* 50(1930): 5–27.

"Bibliographical Services in the Social Sciences." *Library Quarterly* 20(April 1950): 79–99.

Bibliography and the Historian: The Conference at Belmont of the Joint Committee on Bibliographical Services to History, May 1967. Edited by Dagmar Horna Perman. Santa Barbara, Calif., and Washington, D.C.: Clio, 1968.

Billington, Ray Allen. "Tempest in Clio's Teapot: The American Historical Association Rebellion of 1915." *AHR* 78(April 1973): 348–69.

Blakey, George T. *Historians on the Home Front: American Propagandists for the Great War.* [Lexington, Ky.]: University Press of Kentucky, 1970.

Boas, George. "To Philip Wiener." *JHI* 33(July–September 1972): 356–57.

Borsody, Stephen. "Bibliographical Article: Modern Hungarian Historiography." *Journal of Modern History* 24(December 1952): 398–405.

Bottle, R. T. "A User's Assessment of Current Awareness Services." *Journal of Documentation* 21(September 1965): 177–89.

The Bowker Annual of Library and Book Trade Information. 26th ed. New York and London: R. R. Bowker, 1981.

Braudel, Fernand. "Personal Testimony." *Journal of Modern History* 44(December 1972): 448–67.

Brentano, Lujo. "Die Volkswirthschaft und ihre konkreten Grundbedingungen." *ZSWG* 1(1893): 77–148.

Briggs, Harold. "An Appraisal of Historical Writings on the Great Plains Region since 1920." *MVHR* 34(June 1947): 83–100.

Broadus, Robert N. "The Literature of the Social Sciences." *International Social Science Journal* 23(1972): 236–43.

Brown, Harcourt. "History and the Learned Journal." *JHI* 33(July–September 1972): 365–78.

Butterfield, Herbert. "History of the Historical Association." *History Today* 6(January 1956): 63–67.

Calder, Angus. "Books: Playing the Dozens." *New Statesman,* 28 August 1970, p. 242.

Carbonell, Charles-Olivier. *Histoire et historiens.* N.p.: Privat, 1976.

⸻. "La naissance de la Revue historique." *RH* 255(avril–juin 1976): 331–51.

Carson, George Barr. "Changing Perspective in Soviet Historiography."
    South Atlantic Quarterly 47(April 1948): 186–95.
"The Catholic Historical Review." *Catholic University Bulletin* 21(January
    1915): 38–40.
Caughey, John W. "The Mosaic of Western History: Survey of Articles in
    Western Magazines." *MVHR* 33(March 1947): 595–606.
———. "Trends in Historical Criticism." *MVHR* 40(March 1954): 619–28.
———. "Under Our Strange Device: A Review of the 'Review.'" *MVHR*
    44(December 1957): 519–35.
"Le Centre Napoléon." *Presences napoléoniennes* 1(1–18 mai 1957): 1.
Le Centre National de la Recherche Scientifique. N.p., 1952.
Chamberlin, William Henry. "Foreword." *Russian Review* 1(November
    1941): 1–5.
Childe, V. G. "New Views on the Relations of the Aegean and the North
    Balkans." *Journal of Hellenic Studies* 50, pt. 2(1930): 255–62.
Clapp, Verner W. "Indexing and Abstracting Services for Serial Literature."
    Library Trends 2(April 1954): 509–21.
Clark, Thomas D. "Wendell Holmes Stephenson, 1899–1970: Master Editor
    and Teacher." *JSH* 36(August 1970): 335–49.
Clarkson, Jessie Dunsmore. "Escape to the Present." *AHR* 46(April 1941):
    523–59.
Cleverdon, C. W., et al. "Factors Determining the Performance of Indexing
    Systems." In *Studies in Indexing and Cataloguing*, pp. 1–424. Detroit:
    Management Information Service, 1970.
"Clio: A Prospectus." *Clio* 1(October 1971): unnumbered.
Coates, Willson H. "Editorial." *Journal of British Studies* 1(November 1961):
    unnumbered.
Coats, A. W. "The Role of Scholarly Journalism in the History of Econom-
    ics: An Essay." *Journal of Economic Literature* 13(March 1971): 29–44.
"Comment s'est formée notre societé." *La revolution de 1848* 1(1904): 1–2.
The Compact Edition of the Dictionary of National Biography. 2 vols. London:
    Oxford University Press, 1975.
Conference on Access to Knowledge and Information in the Social Sciences
    and Humanities, 1972. *Access to the Literature of the Social Sciences and
    Humanities.* New York: Queens College Press, 1974.
Conrad, Peter. "Grub Street and Dreaming Spires." *TLS*, March 22, 1974,
    pp. 285–86.
Contemporary History in Europe: Problems and Perspectives. New York and
    Washington, D.C.: Frederick A. Praeger, 1969.
Conze, Werner. "Deutsche Geschichtswissenschaft seit 1945: Bedingungen
    und Ergebnisse." *HZ* 225(August 1977): 1–28.
Crane, Diana. "The Gatekeepers of Science: Some Factors Affecting the
    Selection of Articles for Scientific Journals." *American Sociologist*
    2(November 1967): 195–201.
Creighton, Mandell. *Life and Letters of Mandell Creighton.* Edited by Louise
    Creighton. 2 vols. London: Longmans, Green, 1904.

"The Crisis of Democracy and the Slavonic World." *SEER* 9(March 1931): 509–24.

[Critical Article on the Review in a Polish Journal]. *AHR* 61(October 1955): 252–56.

Cunningham, W. "The Repression of the Woollen Manufacture in Ireland." *EHR* 1(April 1886): 277–94.

Dance, E. H. *History the Betrayer: A Study in Bias.* London: Hutchinson, 1960.

Davinson, Donald. *Bibliographic Control.* London: Clive Bingley; Hamden, Conn.: Linnet Books, 1975.

DeMause, Lloyd. "The History of Childhood: The Bases of Psychohistory." *History of Childhood Quarterly* 1(Summer 1973): 1–3.

deMolins, Edmond. Review of *L'histoire de France depuis 1789 jusqu'en 1848,* by F. Guizot. *RQH* 27(1880): 679–80.

deSolla Price, Derek. *Little Science, Big Science.* New York and London: Columbia University Press, 1965.

Droysen, Johann Gustav. *Briefwechsel.* Edited by Rudolf Hubner. Deutsche Geschichtsquellen des 19. Jahrhunderts, Bände 25–26. Berlin und Leipzig: Deutsche Verlags-Anstalt Stuttgart, 1929.

Ducellier, A. "Les études historiques en Republique populaire d'Albanie (1945–1966)." *RH* 237(janvier–mars 1967): 125–44.

Dunlap, Leslie Whittaker. *American Historical Societies, 1790–1860.* Madison, Wis.: Privately printed, 1944.

Eagly, Robert. "Economics Journals as a Communications Network." *Journal of Economic Literature* 13(September 1975): 878–88.

"Editorial." *Civil War Times* 1(1959): 8.

"Editorial." *Explorations in Entrepreneurial History* 1(1949): unnumbered.

"Editorial." *Journal of Mexican-American History* 1(Fall 1970): unnumbered.

"Editorial." *Soviet Studies.* 1(June 1949): 1–2.

"Editorial: Declaration of Independence." *Business and Society* 1(Autumn 1960): 3–4.

"Editorial Note." *Middle Eastern Studies.* 1(1964): 2.

"Editor's Foreword." *History of Education* 1(1972): 3.

"Editor's Note." *AHR* 66(October 1961): 263–64.

"Editor's Note." *American Journal of Ancient History* 2(1977): 1–2.

Ellegard, Alvar. *The Readership of the Periodical Press in Mid-Victorian Britain.* Acta Universitatis Gothoburgensis. Goteborgs universitatis arskrift, vol. 63, 1957: 3. Goteborg: [Distributed by Almqvist and Wiksell, Stockholm], 1957.

Ellis, Elmer. "The Profession of Historian." *MVHR* 38(June 1951): 3–20.

Ellis, John Tracy. "Peter Guilday, March 25, 1884–July 31, 1947." *CHR* 33(October 1947): 257–68.

E[merton], E[phraim]. "Labor Day in Europe." *Nation,* May 29, 1890, pp. 429–30.

Encyclopaedia Britannica, 11th edition. S.v. "Maximilian II, King of Bavaria"; "Sybel".

Engel, Josef. "Die deutschen Universitäten und die Geschichtsschreibung." *HZ* 189(Dezember 1959): 223–378.

Engel-Janosi, Friedrich. *Growth of German Historicism.* Johns Hopkins University Studies, 62, no. 2. Baltimore: The Johns Hopkins Press, 1944.

Enteen, George M. *The Soviet Scholar-Bureaucrat: M. N. Pokrovskii and the Society of Marxist Historians.* University Park, Pa., and London: Pennsylvania State University Press, 1978.

Farrand, Max. "The Quality of Distinction." *AHR* 46(April 1941): 509–22.

Faulenbach, Bernd, ed. *Geschichtswissenschaft in Deutschland.* Munich: C. H. Beck, 1974.

Fay, Sidney B. "New Light on the Origins of the World War." *AHR* 25(July 1920): 616–39; 26(October 1920): 37–53.

Febvre, Lucien. "À nos lecteurs, à nos amis." *Annales: Économies, Sociétés, Civilisations* 1(janvier–mars 1946): 1–8.

Ferris, Eleanor. "The Financial Relations of the Knights Templar to the English Crown." *AHR* 8(October 1902): 1–17.

Firth, C. H. *Modern History in Oxford, 1841–1918.* Oxford: Basil Blackwell, 1920.

Fischer, Walther. "Zur Einführung." *Jahrbuch für Amerikastudien* 1(1956): 5–7.

Fischer-Galati, Stephen. "Foreword." *East European Quarterly* 1(1967): unnumbered.

Fish, Carl Russell. "Review of McMaster's History of the People of the United States." *MVHR* 1(June 1914): 31–43.

Flexner, Abraham. *Universities: American, English, German.* New York, London, and Toronto: Oxford University Press, 1930.

Ford, Guy Stanton. "Carrying On." *AHR* 49(April 1944): 564–93.

"Foreword." *Biographical Studies* 1(1951): 2–3.

[Foreword]. *Historisch-Politische Zeitschrift* 1(1832): 1–8.

[Foreword]. *History of Medicine Quarterly* 1(1970): 1.

"Foreword." *History Today.* 1(1951): 9.

[Foreword]. *Revue d'histoire moderne et contemporaine* 1(1954): 5–7.

[Foreword]. *Starina i novizna* 1(1897): v–vii.

"The Founding of the Review." *HAHR* 1(February 1918): 8–23.

Francis, E. K. "History and the Social Sciences: Some Reflections on the Re-integration of Social Science." *Review of Politics* 13(July 1951): 354–74.

Frank, Walter. "Kleo Pleyer, Ein Kampf um das Reich." *HZ* 166(1942): 507–53.

Frédéricq, Paul. *The Study of History in England and Scotland.* Translated by Henrietta Leonard. Johns Hopkins University Studies in History and Political Science, 5th ser., no. 10. Baltimore: Publication Agency of the Johns Hopkins University, 1887.

————. *The Study of History in Germany and France.* Translated by Henrietta Leonard. Johns Hopkins University Studies in History and Political Science, 8th ser., nos. 5 and 6. Baltimore: Publication Agency of the Johns Hopkins University, 1890.

Fry, Bernard M., and Herbert S. White. "Economics and Interaction of the Publisher-Library Relationship in the Production and Use of Scholarly Research Journals." *Special Libraries* 68(March 1977): 109–14.

―――. *Publishers and Libraries: A Study of Scholarly and Research Journals.* Lexington, Mass., and Toronto: Lexington Books, 1976.

Gairdner, James. "The Death of Amy Robsart." *EHR* 1(April 1886): 235–59.

Galton, Dorothy. "Sir Bernard Pares and Slavonic Studies in London University, 1919–39." *SEER* 46(July 1968): 481–91.

Garfield, Eugene. *Essays of an Information Scientist.* 2 vols. Philadelphia: ISI Press, 1977.

―――, comp. and ed. *SSCI Journal Citation Reports.* Vol. 6, *Social Sciences Citation Index, 1978 Annual* (Philadelphia: Institute for Scientific Information, 1979); Vol. 6, *1981 Annual* (Philadelphia: Institute for Scientific Information, 1982).

Garraty, John A. "The New Deal, National Socialism, and the Great Depression." *AHR* 78(October 1973): 907–44.

Garvey, W. D., Nan Lin, and Carnot E. Nelson. "A Comparison of Scientific Communication Behavior of Social and Physical Scientists." *International Social Sciences Journal* 23(1972): 256–72.

Gay, Peter. "History as an Interdisciplinary Discipline." In Columbia University, Seminar on General and Continuing Education in the Humanities, *Seminar Reports,* March 27, 1974, pp. 1, 8.

"Genesis." *Historical Methods Newsletter* 1(December 1967): 1.

Gérard, Alice. "Histoire et politique: La Revue historique face à l'histoire contemporaine (1885–1898)." *RH* 255 (avril–juin 1976): 353–405.

German History: Some New German Views. London: George Allen and Unwin, 1954.

Goldberg, Aleksandr. "Information Needs of Social Scientists and Ways of Meeting Them." *International Social Sciences Journal* 23(1971): 273–84.

Gooch, G. P. *History and Historians in the Nineteenth Century.* Boston: Beacon Press, 1959.

Goossens, P. L. "Messieurs les professeurs." *Revue d'histoire écclesiastique* 1(1900): 3–4.

Gor'kii, M. "Narod dolzhen znat'svoiu istoriiu." *Bor'ba klassov* 2(1931): 8–31.

Gras, N. S. B. "The Rise and Development of Economic History." *Economic History Review* 1(January 1927): 12–34.

Grayzel, Solomon. "An Adventure in Scholarship." *Historia Judaica* 23(April–October 1961): 15–20.

Great Soviet Encyclopedia. Translation of 3rd edition. 28 vols. New York: Macmillan; London: Collier Macmillan, 1973–1981.

Green, John Richard. *The Letters of John Richard Green.* Edited by Leslie Stephen. London, New York: Macmillan, 1901.

Grigson, Geoffrey. "Friends of Promise: Four Editors Look Back at Outstanding Periodicals of Their Youth." *TLS,* June 16, 1978, p. 666.

Gruenewald, Max. "An Appreciation." *Historia Judaica* 23(April–October 1961): 21–22.

Guide to the Hispanic American Historical Review, 1918–1945. Edited by Ruth Lapham Butler. Durham, N.C.: Duke University Press, 1950.

Guilday, Peter, et al. *The Catholic Historical Review: General Index to Volumes I–XX.* Washington, D.C.: 1938.

Guilland, Antoine. *Modern Germany and Her Historians.* London: Jarrold, 1915.

Gusdorf, George. "Past, Present, and Future of Interdisciplinary Research." *International Social Sciences Journal* 29(1977): 580–98.

Haber, Samuel. "The Professions and Higher Education in America: A Historical View." In *Higher Education and the Labor Market,* edited by Margaret S. Gordon, pp. 237–80. New York: McGraw-Hill, 1974.

Hackett, Charles W. "Discussion of Lesley Byrd Simpson, 'Thirty Years of the *Hispanic American Historical Review*'; and Charles C. Griffin, 'Economic and Social Aspects of the Era of Spanish-American Independence.'" *HAHR* 29(May 1949): 213–28.

Halecki, Oskar. "Problems of Polish Historiography." *SEER* 21(March 1943): 223–39.

Hamilton, E. Blanche. "Paris under the Last Valois Kings." *EHR* 1(April 1886): 260–76.

Hammond, George P. "The Editor's Page." *The Historian* 1(1938): 4.

Hanak, Harry. "The New Europe, 1916–20." *SEER* 39(June 1961): 369–99.

Harper, Samuel N. "Communist View of Historical Studies." *Journal of Modern History* 1(March 1929): 77–84.

———. *The Russia I Believe In.* Chicago: University of Chicago Press, 1945.

Harrod, Leonard Montague. *The Librarians' Glossary.* 4th rev. ed. Boulder, Colo.: Westview Press, 1977.

Hart, Albert Bushnell. "Causses and Gorges of the Cévennes." *Nation,* July 5, 1894, pp. 6–8.

———. "The Colonial Shire." *Chautauquan* 14(December 1891): 274–78.

———. "The Rise of Modern Cities." *Quarterly Journal of Economics* 4(January 1890): 129–57.

Hasenclever, Adolf. Review of *Catalogue of Parliamentary Papers 1807–1900,* edited by Hilda Vernon Jones, and *Catalogue of Parliamentary Papers 1901–1910,* edited by Hilda Vernon Jones. *HZ* 115(1916): 187.

Haverfield, F. "An Inaugural Address Delivered before the First Annual General Meeting of the Society, 11th May, 1911." *Journal of Roman Studies* 1(1911): xi–xx.

Hay, Denys. "Goronwy Edwards." *EHR* 91(October 1976): 721–22.

Heckel, J. "Der Einbruch des jüdischen Geistes in das deutsche Staats- und Kirchenrecht durch Friedrich Julius Stahl." *HZ* 155(1937): 506–41.

Heer, Nancy Whittier. *Politics and History in the Soviet Union.* Cambridge, Mass., and London: MIT Press, 1971.

Heffter, Heinrich. "Von Primat der Aussenpolitik." *HZ* 171(1951): 1–20.

Heiber, Helmut. *Walter Frank und sein Reichsinstitut für Geschichte des neuen Deutschlands.* Stuttgart: Deutsche Verlags-Anstalt, 1966.

Heimpel, Hermann. "Über Organisationsformen historischer Forschung in Deutschland." *HZ* 189(Dezember 1959): 139–222.

Herbst, Jürgen. *The German Historical School in American Scholarship: A Study in the Transfer of Culture.* Ithaca, N.Y.: Cornell University Press, 1965.

Hexter, J. H. "Fernand Braudel and the Monde Braudellien . . ." *Journal of Modern History* 44(December 1972): 480–539.

Heynen, Walter. "Abschied." *Preussische Jahrbücher* 240(Juni 1935): 341–43.

Higham, John. "Beyond Consensus: The Historian as Moral Critic." *AHR* 67(April 1962): 609–25.

———. Review of *The Past before Us: Contemporary Historical Writing in the United States,* edited by Michael Kammen. *AHR* 86(October 1981): 807–9.

Higham, John, Leonard Krieger, and Felix Gilbert. *History.* Englewood Cliffs, N.J.: Prentice-Hall, 1965.

Himmelfarb, Gertrude. "The 'New' History." *Commentary* 59(January 1975): 72–78.

Histoire et historiens depuis cinquante ans. 2 vols. Paris: Librairie Felix Alcan, 1927.

"Historical News: American Historical Association, Final Report of the Committee of Ten on Reorganization and Policy, December 29, 1939." *AHR* 46(October 1940): 241–49.

"Historical News and Notices." *JSH* 1(February 1935): 107–8.

Hölzle, Erwin. "Volks- und Rassenbewusstsein in der englischen Revolution." *HZ* 153(1936): 24–42.

Hussey, Roland Dennis. "Pacific History in Latin American Periodicals." *Pacific Historical Review* 1(December 1932): 470–76.

Iggers, Georg G. *The German Conception of History: The National Tradition of Historical Thought from Herder to the Present.* Middletown, Conn.: Wesleyan University Press, 1968.

———. *New Directions in European Historiography.* Middletown, Conn.: Wesleyan University Press, 1975.

Interdisciplinarity: Problems of Teaching and Research in Universities. Organization for Economic Co-operation and Development, 1972.

"Interdisciplinary History." *Journal of Interdisciplinary History* 1(Autumn 1970): 3–5.

"Introduction." *Amistad* 1(1970): vii–ix.

"Introduction." *Past and Present* 1(February 1952): i–iv.

Istochnikovedenie istorii SSSR XIX-nachala XX V. Moskva: Izdatel'stvo moskovskogo universiteta, 1970.

Jack, Ian. *English Literature, 1815–1832.* Oxford History of English Literature, 10. Oxford: Clarendon Press, 1963.

Jackson, L. P. "First Twenty-five Years of the Journal of Negro History Digested." *JNH* 25(1940): 432–39.

Jameson, J. F. "The Present State of Historical Writing in America." *Proceedings* of the American Antiquarian Society, n.s. 20(October 1910): 408–19.

J[ameson], J. F[ranklin]. "The American Historical Review, 1895–1920." *AHR* 26(October 1920): 1–17.

Jameson, J. Franklin. "An Early Breton." *Chautauquan* 12(October 1890): 24–28.

Jameson, John Franklin. "Montauk and the Common Lands of Easthampton." *Magazine of American History* 9(April 1883): 225–39.

———. "The Origin and Development of the Municipal Government of New York City." *Magazine of American History* 8(May 1882, September 1882): 315–30; 598–611.

Jones, Clyve, Michael Chapman, and Pamela Carr Woods. "The Characteristics of the Literature Used by Historians." *Journal of Librarianship* 4(July 1972): 137–56.

José, Fr., Bishop of Tuy [Lopez Ortiz, José]. [Foreword]. *Hispania Sacra* 1(1948): 5–10.

Joseph, Thomas. "Introductory: The Spirit of the *Catholic Historical Review*." *CHR* 1(April 1915): 5–12.

"The Journal of Industrial Archaeology." *Journal of Industrial Archaeology* 1(May 1964): 1–2.

Judson, Harry Pratt. "Is Our Republic a Failure?" *American Journal of Sociology* 1(July 1895): 28–40.

Karpovich, Michael. Review of *Russia*, by Sir Bernard Pares. *Russian Review* 1(November 1941): 106–7.

Keepers of the Past. Edited by Clifford L. Lord. Chapel Hill, N.C.: University of North Carolina Press, 1965.

Kent, Christopher. "Higher Journalism and the Mid-Victorian Clerisy." *VS* 13(December 1969): 181–98.

Keylor, William R. *Academy and Community*. Cambridge, Mass.: Harvard University Press, 1975.

Kieniewicz, Stefan. "Czasopiśmiennictwo Historyczne." *Kwartalnik Historyczny* 84(1977): 385–90. Abstract in *Historical Abstracts* 25, 25A–45: 4.

Kisch, Guido. "Historia Judaica, 1938–1961: An Historical Account and Reminiscences of the Retiring Editor." *Historia Judaica* 23(April–October 1961): 3–14.

Knowles, David. *Great Historical Enterprises*. London: Thomas Nelson, 1963.

Konow, Sten. "Introduction." *Indian Historical Quarterly* 1(1925): 1–4.

Kosul'nikov, A. P. "Razrabotvaneto na Problemita na istorikopartiinata nauka v spisanie 'Voprosy istorii KPSS.'" *Isvestva* na Inst. po Istoriya na BKP 30(1974): 7–26. Abstract in *Historical Abstracts* 23, 23A–54: 4.

Kramm, H. *Bibliographie historischer Zeitschriften, 1939–1951*. Marburg: Verlag Akademischen Buchhandlung Otto Rasch, 1952.

LaFeber, Walter. "Roosevelt, Churchill, and Indochina: 1942–45." *AHR* 80(December 1975): 1277–95.

Lancaster, F. W. "Evaluation of Published Indexes and Abstract Journals: Criteria and Possible Procedures." *Medical Library Association Bulletin* 59(July 1971): 479–94.

Lancaster, F. Wilfrid, and Constantine J. Gillespie. "Design and Evaluation of Information Systems." *Annual Review of Information Science and Technology* 5(1970): 33–70.

Larkins, William W. "Introduction." *Journal* of the American Aviation Historical Society 1(Spring 1956): 2–3.

Larson, Magali Sarfatti. *The Rise of Professionalism: A Sociological Analysis.* Berkeley, Los Angeles, London: University of California Press, 1977.

Leneshinskii, P. "Ot Istparta." *Proletarskaia revoliutsiia* 1(1921): 3–9.

Lhotsky, Alphons. "Geschichtsforschung und Geschichtsschreibung in Österreich." *HZ* 189(Dezember 1959): 379–448.

Linder, LeRoy Harold. *The Rise of Current Complete National Bibliography.* New York: Scarecrow Press, 1959.

Lindsey, Duncan. "Distinction, Achievement, and Editorial Board Membership." *American Psychologist* 31(November 1976): 799–804. "Rejoinder." 32(July 1977): 578–86.

Lodahl, Janice Beyer, and Gerald Gordon. "The Structure of Scientific Fields and the Functioning of University Graduate Departments." *American Sociological Review* 37(February 1972): 57–72.

Logan, Frenise. "Appraisal of Forty-one Years of the Journal of Negro History." *JNH* 44(January 1959): 26–33.

Logan, R. "Evolution of the First Twenty Volumes of the Journal of Negro History." *JNH* 20(October 1935): 397–405.

Loosjes, Thomas P. *On Documentation of Scientific Literature.* London: Butterworths, 1973.

"Louis Eisenmann et la Revue historique." *RH* 179(avril 1937): 249–50.

Lucas, John. "Editorial Note." *Renaissance and Modern Studies* 21(1977): 3.

McAnally, Arthur Monroe. "Characteristics of Materials Used in Research in United States History." Ph.D. diss., University of Chicago, 1951.

Macdonald, Gerald D. "American History." *Library Trends* 15(April 1967): 718–29.

Machlup, Fritz. *The Production and Distribution of Knowledge in the United States.* Princeton, N.J.: Princeton University Press, 1972.

Machlup, Fritz, and Kenneth Leeson. *Information through the Printed Word.* Vol. 2: *Journals.* New York: Praeger, 1978.

McMaster, J. B. "The Struggle for the West." *Lippincott's Magazine* 49(June 1892): 758–71.

McMaster, John Bach. "The Abolition of Slavery in the United States." *Chautauquan* 15(April 1892): 24–29.

———. "The North in the War." *Chautauquan* 15(May 1892): 152–57.

———. "The Political Depravity of the Fathers." *Atlantic Monthly,* May 1895, pp. 626–33.

McWilliams, Wilson. "The Private World of Political Science Journals." *Change* 6(September 1974): 53–55.

Maeroff, Gene I. "Faculty Life Is Changed by Plight of the Colleges." *New York Times,* March 8, 1982, p. A15.

Maes, Camillus P. "Flemish Franciscan Missionaries in North America." *CHR* 1(1915): 13–16.

Mann, Thomas. *Betrachtungen eines Unpolitischen.* [Frankfurt am Main]: Fischer, 1956.

Mannheim, Karl. *Ideology and Utopia: An Introduction to the Sociology of Knowledge.* New York and London: Harcourt, Brace, Jovanovich, n.d.

Manzer, Bruce M. *The Abstract Journal, 1790–1920.* Metuchen, N.J., and London: Scarecrow Press, 1977.

Marriott, J. A. R. "History and Politics." *Quarterly Review* 266(January 1936): 23–40.

Marten, C. H. K. *On the Teaching of History and Other Addresses.* Oxford: Basil Blackwell, 1938.

Martin, Michel. "Histoire et actualité: La Revue historique pendant la première guerre mondiale." *RH* 255(avril–juin 1976): 433–68.

Martyn, John. "Citation Analyses." *Journal of Documentation* 31(December 1975): 290–97.

"The Master of the Mediterranean." *Time,* May 23, 1977, pp. 77–78.

"Max Lehman." In *Die Geschichtswissenschaft der Gegenwart,* edited by Sigfrid Steinberg, pp. 207–32. Leipzig: Felix Meiner, 1925.

Mazour, Anatole G. *Modern Russian Historiography.* Rev. ed. Westport, Conn.: Greenwood Press, 1975.

Meany, George. [Message]. *Labor History* 1(1960): 2.

Meinecke, Friedrich. *Ausgewählter Briefe.* Edited by Ludwig Dehio and Peter Classen. Stuttgart: K. F. Koehler, 1962.

———. *Erlebtes, 1862–1919.* Stuttgart: K. F. Koehler, 1964.

"Memorandum on the Russian Situation." *SEER* 8(December 1930): 497–503.

Menz, Gerhard. *Die Zeitschrift: Ihre Entwicklung und Ihre Lebensbedingungen.* Stuttgart: C. E. Poeschel, 1928.

Methods of Teaching History. Edited by G. Stanley Hall. Heath's Pedagogical Library, 12. Boston: D. C. Heath, 1902.

Mirsky, D. S. "Periods of Russian Literature." *SEER* 9(March 1931): 682–94.

Mitchell, B. R. *Abstract of British Historical Statistics.* Cambridge: University Press, 1962.

Mohl, Raymond A. "Editorial." *Journal of Urban History* 1(1974): 3–5.

Monod, G. "Bulletin historique: France." *RH,* various numbers, 1876–1912.

———. "Introduction: Du progrès des études historiques en France depuis le xvie siecle." *RH* 1(janvier–juin 1876): 5–38.

Monod, G., and G. Fagniez. "Avant-propos." *RH* 1(janvier–juin 1876): 1–4.

Morley, Charles. *A Guide to Research in Russian History.* Syracuse, N.Y.: Syracuse University Press, 1951.

Mothersill, Mary. "Comment on Aiken Talk." In Columbia University, Seminar on General and Continuing Education in the Humanities, *Seminar Reports,* May 15, 1974, p. 4.

The New Columbia Encyclopedia. Edited by William Harris and Judith S. Levy. New York and London: Columbia University Press, 1975.

"A New Journal." *Journal of European Studies* 1(1971): 1.

"News and Comments." *MVHR* 1(June 1914): 157–58.

"News from the *AHR.*" *AHA Newsletter* 17(December 1979): 3.

Niemi, Albert W., Jr. "Journal Publication Performance of Economic History Programs, 1960–1969 and 1970–1974." *Journal of Economic History* 35(September 1975): 635–41.

Nikitin, S. A. *Istochnikovedenie istorii SSSR XIX V. (do nachala 90-kh godov).* T.

II. Moskva: Gosudarstvennoe sotsial'no-ekonomicheskoe isdatal'stvo, 1940.

"NISP: Noisy Signal in Psychology." *Trans-Action* 7(May 1970): 10.

Nitschke, August. "German Politics and Medieval History." *Journal of Contemporary History* 3(April 1968): 75–92.

Noyes, G. R. "B. P.: II." *SEER* 28(November 1949): 32–35.

"Ob izdanii c l-go ianvaria 1870 goda ezhemesiachnago istoricheskago sbornika 'Russkaia Starina.'" *Russkaia starina* 1(1870, 3rd ed.): 1–4.

"Ob izdanii c l-go ianvaria 1880 goda ezhemesiachnago istorikoliteraturnago zhurnala 'Istoricheskii viestnik.'" *Istoricheskii viestnik* 1(1880): unnumbered.

Odložilik, Otakar. "Clio in Chains: Czech Historiography in 1939–1940." *Slavonic Review* 20, Am. ser. 1(1941): 330–37.

"On Publication Policy." *Review* 1(Winter–Spring 1978): inside cover.

The Organization of Knowledge in Modern America, 1860–1920. Edited by Alexandra Oleson and John Voss. Baltimore and London: Johns Hopkins University Press, 1979.

Osburn, Charles B. "The Place of the Journal in the Scholarly Communications System." *Library Resources and Technical Services* 28(October–December 1984): 315–24.

"Ot Istparta." *Letopis'revoliutsii* 1(1922): 5–6.

"Ot Petrogradskogo biuro Komissii po istorii oktiabr'skoi revoliutsii i rossiiskoi kommunisticheskoi partii." *Krasnaia letopis'* 1(1922): 5–7.

"Ot redaktsii." *Istoriia SSSR* 1(1957): 3–6.

"Ot redaktsii." *Krasnyi arkhiv* 1(1922): i–ii.

"Ot redaktsii." *Sovremennyi vostok* 1(1957): 1.

"Ot redaktsii." *Vizantiiskii vremennik* 1(1947): 3–7.

Palais, Elliot S. "The Significance of Subject Dispersion for the Indexing of Political Science Periodicals." *Journal of Academic Librarianship* 2(May 1976): 72–76.

Palmer, Richard R. "The American Historical Association in 1970." *AHR* 76(February 1971): 1–15.

Paneyko, Basil. "Galicia and the Polish-Ukrainian Problem." *SEER* 9(March 1931): 567–87.

Pares, Bernard. *A Wandering Student: The Story of a Purpose.* [Syracuse, N.Y.]: Syracuse University Press in cooperation with Howell, Soskin, 1948.

Paul, Huibert. "Serials Librarian and the Journals Publisher." *Scholarly Publishing* 3(January 1972): 175–83.

Peckham, Morse. "The Function of History in 19th-Century European Culture." *Survey* 17(Summer 1971): 31–36.

Perkins, Dexter. "Europe, Spanish America, and the Monroe Doctrine." *AHR* 27(January 1922): 207–18.

_____. *Yield of the Years.* Boston: Little Brown, 1969.

Peterson, Theodore. "Magazine Publishing in the Seventies." *Information:* Part 2, no. 5(1973): 34–38.

Pfeffer, Jeffrey, Anthony Leong, and Katherine Strehl. "Paradigm Development and Particularism in Three Scientific Disciplines." *Social Forces* 55(June 1977): 938–51.

Pfister, Christian. "Gabriel Monod." *RH* 110(1912): i–xxiv.

Pflanze, Otto. [Letter to the Editor]. "Comment and Controversy." *AHA Newsletter* 17(December 1979): 5.

————. "New Editor Talks about *AHR*." *AHA Newsletter* 14(December 1976): 1–2.

Pinkney, David H. "The Dilemma of the American Historian of Modern France." *French Historical Studies* 1(1958): 11–25.

Platzhoff, Walter. "Das erste Auftreten Russlands und der russischen Gefahr in der europäischen Politik." *HZ* 115(1916): 64–77.

Pokrovskii, M. N. "Zadachi Obshchestva istorikov-marksistov." *Istorik-marksist* 1(1926): 3–10.

Pool, William C. "Eugene C. Barker." *Texana* 1(Winter 1963): 43.

Posey, Walter B. "The Southern Historical Association: Its Founding and First Year." *JSH* 43(February 1977): 59–72.

Potter, David M. "An Appraisal of Fifteen Years of the Journal of Southern History, 1935–1949." *JSH* 16(February 1950): 25–32.

Poulton, Helen J. *The Historian's Handbook.* Norman, Okla.: University of Oklahoma Press, 1972.

"Predislovie ko 1-my izdaniiu." *Arkhiv russkoi revoliutsii* 1(1922, 3rd ed.): 3–4.

"Preface." *Traditio: Studies in Ancient and Mediaeval History, Thought, and Religion* 1(1943): v.

"Preface." *Transactions* of the Royal Historical Society 1(1875, 2nd ed.).

"Prefatory Note." *EHR* 1(January 1886): 1–6.

"Prefatory Note." *Sudetenland* 1(1958–59): 8–13.

"Prefatory Note." *VS* 1(September 1957): 3.

"Presentation." *Etudes tsiganes* 1(1955): 2.

"Production Crisis: It Grows Worse." *Publishers Weekly* 190(September 5, 1966): 74–76.

"Programm." *Historisches Jahrbuch* 1(1880): 3–4.

Pundeff, Marin, comp. and ed. *History in the U.S.S.R.: Selected Readings.* Stanford, Calif.: Published for the Hoover Institution on War, Revolution, and Peace by the Chandler Publishing Co., 1967.

"Quarter of a Century." *Journal of American History* 25(1931): 23–26.

Quidde, L. "Zur Einführung." *DZG* 1(1889): 1–9.

Radet, Georges. [Avant-propos]. *Revue des études anciennes* 1(1889): 1–6.

Rand, Edward Kennard. "Editor's Preface." *Speculum* 1(January 1926): 3–4.

R[andall], J[ohn] H[erman], Jr. "Foreword." *Studies in the Renaissance* 1(1954): 9.

Revel, Jacques. "The *Annales:* Continuities and Discontinuities." *Review* 1(Winter–Spring 1978): 9–18.

Review of *Die Ausbildung der Priestherrschaft und die Inquisition,* by Franz Heyer. *Westminster Review* 109, n.s. 53(April 1878): 540.

Review of *A History of England in the Eighteenth Century,* vols. 1 and 2, by William H. Lecky. *Quarterly Review* 145(April 1878): 498–534.

Review of *Die Osmanen und die Spanische Monarchie,* by Leopold von Ranke. *Westminster Review* 109, n.s. 53(April 1878): 541.

Review of *The Personal Government of Charles I,* by Samuel R. Gardiner. *Westminster Review* 109, n.s. 53(January 1878): 276.

"Reviewing in the *AHR.*" *AHR* 75(December 1970): 1889–91.

Rich, George A. "Our Primary Purpose." *Business History Review* 1(1926): 1.

Ricklefs, Roger. "Publish or Perish? Professors Discover Perishing is Simpler." *Wall Street Journal,* May 25, 1979, pp. 1, 24.

Ricklinger, Walter. "Heinrich von Sybel und die Historische Zeitschrift." Ph.D. diss., Universität München, 1936.

Robertson, J. G. *A History of German Literature.* Edinburgh and London: William Blackwood, 1970.

Rockinger, Ludwig. *Die Pflege der Geschichte durch die Wittelsbacher.* Munich: Verlage der K. Akademie, n.d.

Rogers, David. "Francis Dominic Allison, 1892–1966: A Tribute." *Recusant History* 9(January 1967): 3–4.

Roose, Kenneth. "Observations on Interdisciplinary Work in the Social Sciences." In *Interdisciplinary Relationships in the Social Sciences,* edited by Muzafer Sherif and Carolyn W. Sherif, pp. 323–27. Chicago: Aldine Publications, 1969.

Rose, W. J. "B.P.: III." *SEER* 28(November 1949): 36–38.

Rosenthal, Robert. "The Bibliographical Activities of the American Historical Association, 1884–1941." Master's thesis, University of Chicago, 1955. Microfilm copy.

Russkaia periodicheskaia pechat' (1702–1894). Pod. red. A. G. Dement'eva, A. V. Zapadova, M. S. Cherpakhova. Moskva: Gox. izd-vo polit. lit., 1959.

Sachse, William L. "Echoes from Chicago." *AHR* 47(April 1942): 459–87.

Schieder, Theodor. "Die deutsche Geschichtswissenschaft im Spiegel der Historischen Zeitschrift." *HZ* 189(Dezember 1959): 1–104.

Schlesinger, Arthur M. *In Retrospect: The History of a Historian.* New York: Harcourt, Brace and World, 1963.

Scholarly Communication: The Report of the National Enquiry. Baltimore and London: Johns Hopkins University Press, 1979.

Schuyler, Robert Livingston. "The Recall of the Legions: A Phase of Decentralization of the British Empire." *AHR* 26(October 1920): 18–36.

Seely, Barbara J. "Indexing Depth and Effectiveness." *Drexel Library Quarterly* 8(April 1972): 201–8.

Sellers, James L. "The Semicentennial of the Mississippi Valley Historical Association." *MVHR* 44(December 1957): 494–518.

Seton-Watson, R. W. "Bernard Pares." *SEER* 28(November 1949): 28–31.

———. *Masaryk in England.* Cambridge: University Press, 1943.

Shera, Jesse Hauk. *Historians, Books, and Libraries.* Cleveland: The Press of Western Reserve University, 1953.

Shearer, Augustus. "American Historical Periodicals." In American Historical Association, *Annual Report . . . for the Year 1916*, pp. 469–84. Washington, D.C.: 1919.

Sheehy, Eugene P., comp. *Guide to Reference Books*. 9th ed. Chicago: American Library Association, 1976.

Shteppa, Konstantin F. *Russian Historians and the Soviet State*. New Brunswick, N.J.: Rutgers University Press, 1962.

Sieburg, Heinz Otto. *Deutschland und Frankreich in der Geschictsschreibung des 19. Jahrhunderts*. Vol. 2: *1848–1871*. Veröffentlichungen des Instituts für europäischen Geschichte, Mainz, Band 17. Wiesbaden: Steiner Verlag, 1958.

Simcox, William Henry. "Alfred's Year of Battles." *EHR* 1(April 1886): 218–34.

Simonds, A. P. *Karl Mannheim's Sociology of Knowledge*. Oxford: Clarendon Press, 1978.

Simpson, Lesley Byrd. "Thirty Years of the Hispanic American Historical Review." *HAHR* 29(May 1949): 188–204.

Sinaceur, Mohammed Allal. "What Is Interdisciplinarity?" *International Social Sciences Journal* 29(1977): 571–79.

Sinor, Denis. "Editorial Note." *Journal of Asian History* 1(1967): 1.

Skinner, Quentin. Review of *Crisis in Europe, 1560–1660*, edited by Trevor Aston. *EHR* 81(October 1966): 791–95.

"The Slavonic Review." *Slavonic Review* 1(June 1922): 1.

Sloane, William M. "History and Democracy." *AHR* 1(October 1895): 1–23.

———. "The Renascence of Education." *Presbyterian Review* 6(July 1885): 446–66.

"La société d'étude du XVIIe siècle." *Dix-septième siècle* 1(1949): 1–2.

"La société d'histoire diplomatique." *Revue d'histoire diplomatique* 1(1887): 5–9.

von Srbik, Heinrich. *Geist und Geschichte vom deutsche Humanismus bis zur Gegenwart*. 2 vols. Munich: F. Bruckmann; Salzburg: Otto Müller, 1950–1951.

[Statement]. *East Central Europe* 1(1974): inside front cover.

[Statement]. *Franziskanische Studien* 1(1914): inside front cover.

[Statement]. *Magazine of American History* 30(July–August 1930): inside front cover.

[Statement]. *University of Birmingham Historical Journal* 2(1948): inside front cover.

"A Statement by the Editors." *Eighteenth-century Life* 1(September 1974): 1.

Steindorff, Erich. *Bibliographische Übersicht über Georg Waitz' Werke*. Göttingen: Dieterich'sche Verlags-Buchhandlung, 1886.

Stephens, H. Morse. Review of *Bengal M.S. Records*, by Sir William Wilson Hunter. *Academy*, July 14, 1894, pp. 23–24.

———. Review of *The French Revolution*, by B. M. Gardiner. *Academy*, January 13, 1883, pp. 21–22.

———. Review of *The Growth of British Policy*, by Sir John Seeley, and *The*

History of the Foreign Policy of Great Britain, by Montagu Burrows. *Nation,* April 30, 1896, pp. 346–47.

———. Review of *Jean Joseph Mounier, sa vie politique et ses écrits,* by L. de Lanzac de Labordie. *EHR* 3(April 1888): 390–92.

———. Review of *La jeunesse du Grand Frédéric* and *Le Grand Frédéric avant l'avènement,* by Ernest Lavisse. *Academy,* October 6, 1894, pp. 250–55.

———. Review of *Les Mirabeau,* by Louis de Lomenie, *Das Leben Mirabeaus,* by Alfred Stein, and *Vie de Mirabeau,* by A. Mezières. *EHR* 7(July 1892): 587–93.

———. Review of *Recueil des instructions données aux ambassadeurs et ministres de France. Academy,* March 21, 1885, p. 200.

———. Review of *Selections from the Letters and Correspondence of Sir James Bland Burges,* edited by James Hutton. *Academy,* December 22, 1883, pp. 415–16.

———. Review of *Viscount Hardinge,* by Charles, Viscount Hardinge. *Academy,* January 3, 1885, pp. 4–5.

———. Review of *Waterloo Letters,* edited by H. T. Siborne. *Academy,* February 20, 1892, pp. 174–76.

Stern, Fritz, ed. *The Varieties of History.* Cleveland and New York: World, 1956.

Stieg, Margaret F. "The Emergence of the *English Historical Review.*" *Library Quarterly* 46(April 1976): 119–36.

———. "The Information of [*sic*] Needs of Historians." *College and Research Libraries* 42(November 1981): 549–60.

———. "Refereeing and the Editorial Process: The *AHR* and R. K. Webb." *Scholarly Publishing* 14(January 1983): 99–122.

Strachan-Davidson, J. L. "The Growth of Plebeian Privilege at Rome." *EHR* 1(April 1886): 209–17.

Stromberg, Roland N. "History and Present Problems." *Diogenes* 66(Summer 1969): 1–14.

Surrency, Erwin C. "Introduction." *American Journal of Legal History* 1(1957): 2–4.

Svanidze, A. S. "Nashi zadachi." *Vestnik drevnei istorii* 1(1937): 5–13.

Swora, Tamara, and James L. Morrison. "Interdisciplinarity and Higher Education." *Journal of General Education* 26(April 1974): 45–52.

von Sybel, Heinrich. *Vorträge und Abhandlungen.* Introduction by C. Varrentrapp. Munich and Leipzig: R. Oldenbourg, 1897.

———. "Vorwort." *HZ* 1(1859): ii–v.

T., F. N. Review of *Constitutional Studies, State and Federal,* by James Schouler. *AHR* 3(January 1898): 379–82.

Task Group on the Economics of Primary Publication. *Report.* Washington, D.C.: National Academy of Sciences, 1970.

Thaden, Edward C. "Encounters with Soviet Historians." *Historian* 20(November 1957): 80–95.

Thirsk, Joan. "Prof. H. P. R. Finberg." *Agricultural History Review* 23(1975): 96.

Thompson, Elizabeth H. *A. L. A. Glossary of Library Terms*. Chicago: American Library Association, 1943.

Thompson, James Westfall. *A History of Historical Writing*. Vol. 2: *The Eighteenth and Nineteenth Centuries*. New York: Macmillan, 1942; reprint ed., Gloucester, Mass.: Peter Smith, 1967.

Thomson, David. "Must History Stay Nationalist?" *Encounter* 30(June 1968): 22–28.

Trevor-Roper, H. R. "Fernand Braudel, The *Annales*, and the Mediterranean." *Journal of Modern History* 44(December 1972): 468–79.

Tyler, Moses Coit. "The Declaration of Independence in the Light of Modern Criticism." *North American Review* 163(July 1896): 1–16.

Ulrich's International Periodicals Directory, 17th ed., 1977–1978. New York and London: R. R. Bowker, 1977.

————. *18th ed., 1979–1980*. New York and London: R. R. Bowker, 1979.

Unesco Statistical Yearbook, 1969. Paris: United Nations Educational, Scientific, and Cultural Organization, 1970.

————, *1980*. Paris: United Nations Educational, Scientific, and Cultural Organization, 1980.

Vardy, Stephen Bela. *Modern Hungarian Historiography*. East European Monographs, 17. Boulder, Colo.: *East European Quarterly*, distributed by Columbia University Press, 1976.

Vernière, Paul. "Presentation." *Dix-huitième siècle* 1(1969): 5–6.

Vicinus, Martha. "Retrospectives." *VS* 20(Supplement 1977): 9–12.

Vollmar, Edward. *The Catholic Church in America: An Historical Bibliography*. New York: Scarecrow, 1963.

Von Müller, Karl A. "Vorwort." *HZ* 162(1940): 229–30.

Von Richthofen, Bolko, Freiherr von. "Die Völkergeschichte der Vorzeit Ostdeutschlands und seiner Nachbarstaaten im ausländischen Licht." *HZ* 154(1936): 453–90.

"Vorwort." *ZSWG* 1(1893): i–ii.

Wallace, W. S. "Pierre Georges Roy and the B. R. H." *Canadian Historical Review* 25(March 1944): 29–32.

Walton, Clyde C. "Introduction." *Civil War History* 1(March 1955): 5.

Wanderer, Jules J. "Academic Origins of Contributors to the ASR, 1955–1965." *American Sociologist* 1(November 1966): 241–43.

Webb, Walter Prescott. "The Historical Seminar: Its Outer Shell and Its Inner Spirit." *MVHR* 52(June 1955): 1–23.

The Wellesley Index to Victorian Periodicals, 1824–1900. Edited by Walter E. Houghton. Toronto: University of Toronto Press, 1966–1972.

Welter, Rush. *Problems of Scholarly Publication in the Humanities and Social Sciences*. New York: American Council of Learned Societies, 1959.

Werner, Karl Ferdinand. *Das NS-Geschichtsbild und die deutsche Geschichtswissenschaft*. Stuttgart: W. Kohlhammer, 1969.

West, Michael. "Evaluating Periodicals in English Studies: Tell It in *Gath* If Ye Must, Young Men, But Publish It Not in *Askelon*." *College English* 41(April 1980): 903–24.

Whiteing, Richard. "Prussianized History." *English Review* 20(May 1915): 156–67.

Whittemore, Reed. "Black Studies in Glass Houses." Review of *Amistad I*, edited by John A. Williams and Charles F. Harris. *New Republic*, May 9, 1970, pp. 25–27.

Widmann, Hans. *Tübingen als Verlagsstadt*. Contuberium. Beiträge zur Geschichte der Eberhard-Karls-Universität Tübingen, Band 1. Tübingen: J. C. B. Mohr (Paul Siebeck), 1971.

Winston, Michael. "The Emergence of Professional Historical Studies in Austria: An Institutional Study of the Modernization of a Discipline." Ph.D. diss., University of California, Berkeley, 1974.

Wolff, Michael. "Retrospectives." *VS* 20(Supplement 1977): 6–9.

Wolff, Wirt M. "Publication Problems in Psychology and an Explicit Evaluation Schema for Manuscripts." *American Psychologist* 28(March 1973): 257–61.

Wolfson, Philip J. "Friedrich Meinecke, 1862–1954." *Journal of the History of Ideas* 17(October 1956): 511–25.

Wood, David N., and Cathryn A. Bower. "The Use of Social Science Periodical Literature." *Journal of Documentation* 25(June 1969): 108–22.

Woods, Bill M. "Bibliographic Control of Serial Publications." In *Serial Publications in Large Libraries*, edited by Walter C. Allen, pp. 161–74. Urbana, Ill.: University of Illinois Graduate School of Library Science, 1970.

Woolf, Stuart. "The New Historical Journals." *TLS*, May 2, 1980, p. 503.

Wright, Esmond. "History: The New and the Newer." *Sewanee Review* 49(October 1941): 479–91.

Yoels, W. C. "Destiny or Dynasty: Doctoral Origins and Appointment Patterns of Editors of the American Sociological Review." *American Sociologist* 6(May 1971): 134–39.

Yoels, William C. "The Structure of Scientific Fields and the Allocation of Editorships on Scientific Journals: Some Observations on the Politics of Knowledge." *Sociological Quarterly* 15(Spring 1974): 264–76.

"Zadachi Arkhiva." *Arkhiv russkoi revoliutsii* 1(1922, 3rd ed.): 5–8.

"Zadachi sovetskoi istoricheskoi nauki v oblasti izucheniia srednikh vekov." *Srednie veka* 1(1942): 3–6.

"Zadachi zhurnala 'Voprosy istorii.'" *VI* 1(1945): 3–5.

Zangemeister, Karl. *Theodor Mommsen als Schriftsteller*. Berlin: Weidmannsche Buchhandlung, 1905.

Zuckerman, Harriet, and Robert K. Merton. "Patterns of Evaluation in Science: Institutionalization, Structure, and Function of the Referee System." *Minerva* 9(1971): 66–101.

INDEX

Abraham Lincoln Quarterly, 113
Academy of Sciences (U.S.S.R.), Division of Historical Sciences, 174
Academy of Sciences (U.S.S.R.), Institute of History, 174
Acheson, Dean, 147
Acton, Sir John Emerich Edward Dalberg, Baron, 42, 47, 71; "The Massacre of St. Bartholomew," 43
Adams, George Burton, 44, 47, 73, 75, 84, 88
Adams, Herbert Baxter, 44
Administration, 191
Administrative problems: *Catholic Historical Review,* 118; *Zeitschrift für Sozial- und Wirtschaftsgeschichte,* 117
Advertising, 191
Advisory board: *Victorian Studies,* 141
African Economic History Review, 83, 84, 109, 116
African Historical Studies, 83–84
African history, 83–84
Albania, 81
Alexander Kohut Memorial Foundation, 120
All-Union Society of Former Political Prisoners and Exiles, 169
Allgemeine Zeitschrift für Geschichte, 23
Allison, Francis, 120
Alvord, Clarence, 74–75, 84–100 passim; editorial style, 96
Amateur interest, 105, 122; *Catholic Historical Review,* 114–15
Ambix: The Journal of the Society for the Study of Alchemy and Early Chemistry, 103
America: History and Life, 186
American Catholic Historical Association, 118
American historians: lack of theoretical interest, 45; perception of role of historical scholarship, 46; periodicals in which could publish before *AHR,* 44
American Historical Association, 44, 48,

51, 70 , 179; controversy over relationship to *AHR,* 73–76, 99
American Historical Review, 7, 83, 84, 89, 93, 108, 112, 114, 116, 123, 158, 182, 191, 195, 226 (n. 11); audience, 63–64; availability of articles, 55; book reviews, 58–60; circulation, 77–78; contribution to scholarly communication, 81; contributors, 50–51; controversy over relationship with AHA, 99; criteria for acceptance of articles, 56–57; decreasing percentage of articles available published, 55; documents section, 61–62; editor's role, 55; editorial board, 72–73; editorial board, resentment toward, 73–76; editorial policy, 51–53; establishment, 7, 40–46; finances, 76–80, 77; founders, 47–48, 73; frequency of publication, 63; impact on profession, 80–81; importance of acceptance of articles in, 58; interest in European history, 49; leading American scholarly historical periodical, 70; legal ownership of, 78; news section, 61–62; payment of contributors, 79–80; physical size, 63; political bias, 152–54; political orientation, 66; political purpose, 40; prestige, 58; price, 121; purpose, 7, 40; reaction by historians, 80–81; referees, 56; relationship to American Historical Association, 73; relationship to Indiana University, 79; role, 63, 80–81; scholarly orientation, 66; scope of articles, 49
American Journal of Ancient History, 104
American Journal of Sociology, 44
American Literature, 131
Amistad, 128
Andover Review, 44
Andrews, Charles M., 110, 215 (n. 24)
Anglo-American historians: political bias, 151–52
Annales, 66–70, 125–26, 147–48, 191, 195

About the Author

Margaret F. Stieg teaches in the Graduate School of Library Service, The University of Alabama. She received her B.A. from Harvard University, her M.S. in Library Service from Columbia University, and her M.A. and Ph.D. from the University of California, Berkeley.